THE DEFENCE OF TRUTH

For
Linda, Jon and Noll

R. D. BEDFORD

THE DEFENCE
OF TRUTH

Herbert of Cherbury
and the seventeenth century

MANCHESTER
UNIVERSITY PRESS

Published by
Manchester University Press
Oxford Road
Manchester M13 9PL

U.K. ISBN 0 7190 0740 2

British Library cataloguing in publication data

Bedford, R. D.
 The defence of truth.
 1. Herbert, Edward, *Baron Herbert*, b. 1583
 I. Title
 192   B1201.H34

 ISBN 0–7190–0740–2

Computerised Phototypesetting by
G.C. Typeset Ltd., Bolton, Greater Manchester

Printed in Great Britain by
A. Wheaton & Co. Ltd., Exeter

CONTENTS

ACKNOWLEDGEMENTS

The wisdom and stimulation offered by the late Tom Henn of St Catharine's College, Cambridge, who first guided me into the seventeenth century and encouraged me to pursue my studies further, represents that sort of incalculable debt which a host of others who knew him can also acknowledge. I have naturally incurred many debts, both academic and practical, during the dozen years or so since I first began reading Herbert. Special thanks are recorded to the staff of the University Library, Cambridge; to the editors of Manchester University Press for undertaking this book with such unfailing co-operation and good advice; to the Trustees of the estate of Mrs V. E. Carré and to Bristol University for permission to quote from Meyrick H. Carré's translation of Herbert's *De veritate*; and to the British Academy for their generous assistance towards the costs of production.

My thanks are also due to Melba Chapman and Mary Milton at Exeter for tireless typing and copying, and to my wife Linda for both encouragement over many years and for a constantly refreshing Montaignian scepticism. Though much may not have been done without this help, what inadequacies remain are of course my own.

Exeter, 1979

ABBREVIATIONS

Certain works to which frequent reference is made have been abbreviated as follows:

D.V.	Lord Herbert's *De Veritate Prout Distinguitur Revelatione, a Verisimili, a Possibili, et a Falso, editio tertia,* London, 1645. This is the best edition and the last published in Herbert's lifetime. There is a facsimile edited by Günter Gawlick (with Introduction and Bibliography), Stuttgart–Bad Cannstatt, 1966.
Carré	Meyrick H. Carré, *De Veritate, Translated with Introduction,* University of Bristol, 1937. This is a translation of the London 1645 edition.
Rossi	Mario M. Rossi, *La Vita, le opere, i tempi di Edoardo Herbert di Chirbury,* 3 vols. Florence, 1947.
Fordyce and Knox	C. J. Fordyce and T. M. Knox, 'The books bequeathed to Jesus College Library, Oxford, by Lord Herbert of Cherbury', in *Proceedings and Papers of the Oxford Bibliographical Society,* 5, 1936–9, Part II, pp. 53f.

I
HERBERT'S CAREER AND WRITINGS

> What brought Hercules his everlasting renown? Isn't he famous because he wandered through the world, freeing peoples from tyrannies, errors, dangers, and distresses? He put all the brigands to death, and all the monsters, all the poisonous serpents, and harmful creatures. Why don't we follow his example, and do what he did in all the countries we pass through? . . . Come now, shall we go?
>
> Rabelais, *Gargantua and Pantagruel*, V

Among the first words uttered by the infant Edward Herbert was, he tells us, the question, 'How came I into this world?' The reaction of his audience seems to have been immediate: 'but for this, as I was laughed at by the nurse, and by some other women that were then present, so I was wondered at by others, who said, they never heard a child but myself ask that question'.[1] This first recorded response was destined to be repeated: the laughter from some—like Walpole, Gray and Lady Waldegrave in the eighteenth century who, having discovered the MS of Herbert's autobiography and reading it aloud 'could not get on for laughing and screaming'—and the wonder from others, who have seen in Herbert a kind of adult prodigy, an unexpected and eccentric figure going his own distinctive way in an age of which he is, as it were, both a flower and a thorn in the side.

Herbert was born at Eyton on the Severn in 1582, of a famous family which had held the Welsh Marches for over two hundred years. He was the eldest son of Richard Herbert of Montgomery Castle and Magdalen, daughter of Sir Richard Newport. His younger brothers, of whom there were six, were to include George Herbert, the priest and poet, and Sir Henry Herbert, Master of the Revels at the court of James I. He entered University College, Oxford, in 1595 and remained there until 1600. During this time his father died and his mother obtained wardship of her eldest son; by her arrangement he was married to a cousin some years older than himself, Mary, daughter of Sir William Herbert of St Julian's. She died in 1634, having borne him two sons, Richard and Edward, and two daughters, one of whom died in infancy. In the early years of this marriage, Herbert's mother lived with them in a house they had taken in Oxford, while Herbert pursued his studies. In 1600 the household, now a growing family, moved to London, though Herbert continued his academic studies, learning Italian, French and Spanish, and mastering the lute, on which he became very expert. He was one of the many new knights (there were some sixty others) invested 'upon carpet consideration' by James I on his accession in 1603. He was also Member of Parliament for Merioneth, and in 1604–5 appointed Sheriff of Montgomery. The chivalrous order of Knight of the Bath seems to have fired something in his imagination for he took his knightly vows with astonishing seriousness: 'they take an oath never to sit in place where injustice should be done, and they shall right it to the uttermost of their power; and particularly ladies and gentlewomen that shall be wronged in their honour, if they demand assistance, and many other points, not unlike the romances of knight errantry'.[2] In his autobiography he describes the dashing figure he cut at his investiture, and goes on to relate subsequent encounters in which this stamp of honour proved itself in the defence of distressed ladies (whether they demanded assistance or not), in retrieving stolen ribbons on a sword's point, and in barking out challenges to knaves and brigands because, as he says, 'I thought myself obliged thereunto by the oath'.

His hankering now for a less quiet life and the urge to sow some wild oats (the old Queen Elizabeth, he tells us, once touched him on the cheek and said it was a pity he had married so young), led him to obtain a licence to travel abroad. Leaving his wife and children in the country, he set out for France in 1608, with Aurelian Townshend as his companion. While in France he was introduced to and became the intimate of the Montmorency family, visiting the Duke de Montmorency, Grand Constable of France, at his castle at Merlou. When the Duke moved to Chantilly he left Herbert at Merlou with the freedom of the estate and the stables, which doubtless benefited Herbert's accomplishments in horseriding, the use of arms, and in singing and playing the lute. He was rapidly turning himself into the complete *cortegiano*, the courtier–soldier, the heir of Sir Philip Sidney, and he was received with great courtesy by both Henry IV and his divorced Queen. After some eight months at Merlou and Chantilly, he returned to Paris, and lodged in the house of 'that incomparable scholar Isaac Casaubon'. The experience of an intimate acquaintance with the 'Politiques' of Merlou and with the humanist Casaubon in a France striken with religious dissension was to have, as we shall see, a lasting effect on Herbert's general outlook and disposition.

Returning to England early in 1609, he presented himself to James at court, and continued his studies while living with his family. In 1610 he fought—like that earlier exemplum of the complete gentleman, Sir Philip Sidney—in the Low Countries, assisting the Prince of Orange in the siege of Juliers, but also rather straining his claims by issuing challenges on nice points of honour and, as his own picture of himself at least conveys, behaving with irrelevant bravado and posturing heroism. The admiration of the ladies at court, who had, he is sure, heard of his exploits abroad, involved Edward Herbert in a number of verbose and illegal duels, few of which actually drew blood, though one of his affairs of honour and the heart (in which he protested his complete innocence) led to an attempt by a jealous husband to assassinate him. In 1614 he served again with the Prince of Orange against the Spanish in the Netherlands; after a spell of action, he left the army and travelled south to Cologne, visiting the Prince and Princess Palatine at Heidelberg, and continuing to Ulm, Augsburg, Venice, Florence and Rome. On arriving in Rome, he tells us he called upon the master of the English College, evidently with the intention of testing the ground in this centre of the Catholic faith. He was assured that 'men who gave no affronts to the Roman Catholic religion, received none', and in reply Herbert says: 'I thought fit to tell him that I conceived the points agreed upon on both sides are greater bonds of amity betwixt us, than that the points disagreed on could break them; that for my part I loved everybody that was of a pious and virtuous life, and thought errors on what side soever, more worthy pity than hate'.[3]

On his way back from Rome he attended lectures, particularly those of the Aristotelian Cremonini, at the University of Padua, visited Milan and Turin, and was commissioned, in an atmosphere of masked balls, 'dancing and fair ladies' ('it was now in the time of Carnival'), by the Duke of Savoy to lead four thousand Protestants from Languedoc into Piedmont to fight in the Duke's service against Spain. Having made the gates of Lyons, Herbert was interrogated and brought before the governor to confront the new edict that no soldiers were to be raised in France, on pain of death. Since he had not actually raised any soldiers, Herbert felt confident enough. A brisk argument with the governor led to a short imprisonment, from which Herbert was released through the good offices of an old friend, Sir Edward Sackville (afterwards Earl of Dorset), and of the new Duke de Montmorency.

By way of Geneva and Heidelberg, and after a short stay with the Prince of Orange, he returned once more to England. This was the beginning of his illhealth, a quartan ague, which on good days allowed him to study but which brought him, he says 'at last to be so lean and yellow, that scarce any man did know me'. This afflicted him for some eighteen months. In 1619, however, the King nominated him as his Ambassador to France. He took the opportunity to visit Merlou again, 'that sweet place and country', and also, since relations between the two countries were friendly, to work on his philosophical treatise, *De veritate* (which in his autobiography he calls without elaboration 'my book'), interspersed with baiting the Spanish ambassador, courtly socialising, and 'some follies, which I afterwards repented, and do still repent of', though he seems to have held his wife's refusal to accompany him to France partly to blame. In a character full of a boisterous ego and possessed of (in his own words) a 'hasty and choleric' disposition, it is not surprising that the responsibilities of public office did not completely subdue his adventurousness or his social rashness. An encounter with an equally choleric and hasty French Duke, de Luynes, the French king's favourite, during which Herbert says he threatened his old duelling stance, led to his swift recall by James in July, 1621. Luckily the Duke died soon after of some other misfortune, and Herbert was back in Paris in 1622. A few months later he had almost completed *De veritate* and had been warmly urged to print it by Hugo Grotius and Daniel Tilenus, to whom he had submitted it. Any further doubts about its publication were removed by a sign, 'a loud though gentle noise . . . from the heavens', in answer to a prayer for encouragement, and the book, finished in June 1623, was printed in Paris in 1624, at Herbert's own expense.

It is at this point in its author's history that the autobiography breaks off. After five years of faithful, financially costly and also shrewd diplomatic service, Herbert was finally recalled in April 1624. The letter of recall was curt and uninformative, and it perhaps left Herbert (though evidently not many of his modern critics) puzzled at the fall of his star. He was in fact a victim of the devious political strategems and tortuous diplomacy of James, whose ambassador's outspoken and far-sighted advice on the question of his sovereign's plans for matrimonial alliances in Europe had obviously proved an embarrassment. Herbert had run the risk of falling into disfavour in order to alert James to the dishonesty of Spain. Herbert's 'unstable' character is usually brought to the dock to explain his recall. J. H. Handford, for example, amplifies Lee's view:

Lord Herbert's personal weaknesses are well illustrated by the story, incompletely told by Lee, of his ambassadorial career. He entered upon his office under happy auspices and possessed of qualifications which might well have been expected to insure success. The blunders which so soon made him *persona non grata* in France were due to his quarrelsomeness and to his inability to control his tongue. The needless ruffling of the Spanish ambassador, the bickerings with Luynes, the smart talk about the coming downfall of the French nobility, were bound to have reverberations.[4]

According to Handford (and if the Duke of Buckingham is to be believed) Herbert was saved in 1621 only because of the King's inability to pay his arrears of salary.[5] It is 'characteristic' of Herbert, Handford suggests, that when he received his final orders in 1624 he failed to recognise the necessity or justice of his dismissal.

There are other possible interpretations of Herbert's behaviour and of the course of events. Mario M. Rossi, though in some ways unsympathetic towards Herbert's personality, relates Herbert's diplomatic career in great detail (near four hundred pages), with acute historical insight, and with great credit to Herbert. The fault, Rossi argues, was not Herbert's; it was above all the King's. In the Luynes affair, for instance, Herbert was very firmly in the right. 'Luynes', Rossi points out, 'had violated international law and etiquette alike.'[6] Of Herbert's protection of James's better interests Rossi claims: 'Herbert was a better diplomat and certainly a more upright and judicious man than any with whom he had to deal in this case—and in many others.'[7] The picture that emerges is one of a man of ideals, principles and vision, lacking perhaps in social finesse but forced to operate in a world where his values are derided and his principles dismissed.

Sir Edward Herbert was packed off back to Montgomery Castle out of harm's way, disgraced by clarity of vision and a characteristic failure of tact. Having foreseen the failure of James's policy, he had, from his retirement, ample opportunity of watching his predictions duly come about. Meanwhile his salary had not been paid nor his expenses met. The Irish peerage of Castle Island was conferred in

December, 1624—a dismissive rubber stamp—and no financial reimbursement or recognition was forthcoming. When Charles succeeded, Herbert was raised to the English peerage as Lord Herbert of Cherbury in 1629, but no arrears were paid and no further public employment was found for him. In an attempt to engage the King's favour, Herbert wrote in 1630 a defence of Buckingham's recent disastrous expedition to the Isle of Rhé, and in 1632, furnished with rooms in Whitehall and the assistance of an able friend and scholar, Thomas Master of New College, Herbert worked on his eulogistic *Life of Henry VIII*. From his vantage point in the royal palace he sought to attract the King's attention now and again with practical schemes for naval equipment, gun-carriages and an ambitious floating bathing establishment to be installed on the Thames. None of these, nor the historical labours, gained him any further recognition or recompense.

In 1639, during the first Bishop's War, Herbert made the long trip north to Alnwick to join the King's forces in what turned out to be an abortive expedition. With typical detachment, he wrote a poem, 'The Idea, Made of *Alnwick* in his Expedition to *Scotland* with the Army, 1639', which is an abstract and serious contemplation on love as an avenue to knowledge, liberty, unity and eternity, and which has always seemed a very singular production at such a moment and in such surroundings. But Herbert might well have looked on those grotesque stone figures on Alnwick Castle, gazing north to frighten the enemy, and, noting his own situation there, have framed his 'idea' accordingly:

> All Beauties vulgar eyes on earth do see,
> At best but some imperfect Copies be,
> Of those the Heavens did at first decree.
>
> For though th'Idea's of each sev'ral kind,
> Conceiv'd above by the Eternal Mind,
> Are such, as none can error in them find,
>
> Since from his thoughts and presence he doth bear,
> And shut out all deformity so farr,
> That the least beauty near him is a Starr,
>
> As Nature yet from far th'Idea's views,
> And doth besides but vile materials chuse,
> We in her works observe no small abuse:

Some of her figures therefore, foil'd and blurr'd,
Shew as if Heaven had no way concurr'd
In shapes so disproportion'd and absurd.

Which being again vex'd with some hate and spite,
That doth in them vengeance and rage excite,
Seem to be tortur'd and deformed quite.[8]

In 1640, however, Herbert again went with his fellow peers to the King's standard in the north. Perhaps recalling his own military exploits in the past against Spanish aggression and sensitive to the affront now being offered to Charles and the kingdom by the Scots, who had invaded the northern counties, Herbert advised the King to refuse payment of £40,000 demanded by the enemy, and to drive them back over the border. His advice was rejected, and the very temporary treaty of Ripon was signed. 'No prince', Herbert had told the King, 'had ever bought a treaty of his subjects at so dear a rate.' As it turned out, Herbert was all too right, though not altogether in the way he had anticipated. He withdrew again to Montgomery, and it was the last he saw of Charles.

In the decisive Parliament of 1642 Herbert found himself unwillingly involved in the Civil War, and sought to back out by promising to vote for the Commons' resolution that the King broke his oath if he made war only if he could assure himself that the King made war 'without cause'. The Commons committed him to the Tower to reflect on this ambiguity, but he was released after a few days. Things must have seemed, for Herbert, to be falling apart; there was no longer any centre to hold his world together. Most of the friends and fellow courtier–soldiers of his younger days had died; his wife had been buried at Montgomery eight years before; his own health broke down; and by 1640 all his brothers were dead except Sir Henry, to whom he wrote touchingly in 1643: 'And here I must remember that of all of us there remains but I and you to brother it.' His own experience of Stuart coldness left him unenthusiastic about the urgent claims of the Crown; the quarrels of religious or political parties had never managed to engage him at any deeper level than the chance of military prowess and the excitement of a siege or two. But now the war games were in earnest, and upon his very doorstep. In this situation Herbert, according to Sir Sidney Lee, made his personal comfort 'the chief plank in his political platform'. At any rate, he withdrew to Montgomery in neutral isolation, declining

Royalist invitations, while his son Richard raised a troop of horse for Prince Rupert at Shrewsbury and his son Edward fought for the King. Observing all this, Herbert wrote to his brother Henry in 1643: 'I find myself grown older in this one year than in fifty-nine years before.'

Such peaceful withdrawal as Herbert desired was clearly impossible, especially while he resided in the strategically crucial Montgomery Castle. Having rebuffed Rupert with the assurance that he was quite capable of defending himself and his property without help from a Royalist garrison, Herbert found the Parliamentarian forces at his walls. In 1644, and especially anxious for his library, he made terms with Sir Thomas Middleton the Parliamentary commander, and admitted a Parliamentarian garrison into his castle. No sooner was this done than Montgomery was besieged by the King's forces, including Herbert's neighbours, and for a moment it looked as though it might be taken. It was quickly and expertly relieved, and Herbert was left dependent on the goodwill of Parliament. He journeyed to London, petitioned Parliament for relief, and was granted a pension of £20 per week. In his London house in Queen Street, near St Giles's, he pursued his philosophical and literary studies, publishing the revised version of *De veritate* together with *Religio laici* and *De causis errorum* in 1645; he continued his work on *De religione gentilium*, which was published after his death, and he corresponded with foreign scholars. In September 1647 he made a last trip to Paris to visit Gassendi. On 1 August 1648 he made his will, generously providing for his sons and particularly his grandson, Edward, Richard's son. His MSS and English books were to be conveyed from London to Montgomery; his Latin and Greek books (the original catalogue of which consisted of twenty closely written folios) were bequeathed to Jesus College, Oxford, where many of them now remain.[9]

Herbert died on 20 August 1648 and was buried in the church of St-Giles-in-the-Field. The inscription on his tombstone, probably written by himself, records alone of all his achievements, that he was *auctoris libri, cui titulus est de Veritate.*

Lord Herbert is usually regarded as a curious and eccentric figure, a man standing uncertainly in the first half of the seventeenth century and asserting the chivalric and military ideals of an earlier age, while at the same time laying down rather more than the rudiments of an apparently equally untimely body of thought which was to wait, for its fullest expression, until later times. And Herbert certainly is a curious figure and, because of his many paradoxes, a curiously demanding one. The simple enumeration of his chief works reflects something of this paradoxical quality, the peculiarly Renaissance paradoxes of the 'complete man', soldier, poet, humanist, biographer, philosopher, historian, musician and metaphysician: they comprise that racy, disconcertingly serio-comic and deeply nostalgic autobiography which first saw print in Horace Walpole's Strawberry Hill edition of 1764 (of which—and it is perhaps a rather sad reflection—Walpole was able to write: 'The thing most in fashion is my edition of Lord Herbert's Life: people are mad after it . . .'); a small collection of *Occasional Verses*, highly wrought if sometimes fatally obscure, Platonic in their tone, and usually characterised as 'metaphysical'; an anthology of music for lute, including some compositions of his own; a history of the reign of King Henry VIII that was for many generations the standard account; and a few solid volumes of metaphysics and religious philosophy, in tortuous Latin, the chief of which are *Religio laici* the posthumously published *De religione gentilium*, and the foundation stone of all his thought on philosophical and religious matters, *De veritate*.

On the autobiography itself, so often the stumbling block to an appreciation of Herbert's real qualities, Rossi has been able to shed a good deal of light. He puts it beyond doubt that Herbert genuinely wrote it for his own amusement and solely for the eyes of his heirs and descendents, above all for his favourite grandson, Edward. It was conceived as a family history, an intimate and not a public self–advertisement, a memorial of an old-fashioned, ebullient and fascinating grandfather. Rossi seeks to persuade us that 'this personal intimacy explains the absolute sincerity, the absence of shame, which caused the autobiography to be judged light and frivolous when it was presented to the public'.[10] Herbert tells us himself that he intended something rather different for the public: a general account of his diplomatic service based on copies of all his dispatches which he had 'in a great trunk' at his London house. Rossi writes it for him, drawing documents from that same 'great trunk' now at Powis Castle. It is not impossible that Herbert did actually write such an account for the public. In a letter of Horace Walpole's (of which Rossi seemed unaware) to the Rev. William

Cole (22 August 1778, fourteen years after the publication of the autobiography) it is related that a Mr Jonathan Scott claimed to possess 'a MS of Lord Herbert's account of the court of France' and had sought Walpole's aid in publishing it. Scott unfortunately died within the month and nothing is known of the MS which may, conceivably, yet turn up.

Such a diverse body of writing, taken together with the knowledge that Herbert was a keen horseman and a conoisseur of swordsmanship, a bibliophile, an amateur botanist, a collector of medical textbooks, saw military service in the Low Countries, was James I's ambassador in France, was M.P. and Sheriff, and responsible for running a castle and its estates, besides his literary and philosophical endeavours, suggests at once the ambition towards the complete gentleman and Elizabethan man of noble parts, well versed in the 'mysteries of manners, armes, and arts'—though perhaps without the self knowledge and humility of the true 'gentil knight'. Such versatility, and its atendant paradoxes, shows itself everywhere in Herbert. When Horace Walpole, in a famous epigram, said that 'the history of Don Quixote was the Life of Plato', he was indicating that contrast, which has puzzled so many readers of Lord Herbert, between the cavalier knight and the other man, the serious, deeply committed and often profound thinker who walks in the shadow of Quixote. Ben Jonson, a lifelong acquaintance, praised Herbert precisely as the ideal Renaissance *uomo universale*:

> If men get fame for some one vertue: Then,
> What man art thou, that art so many men,
> All-vertuous Herbert! on whose every part
> *Truth* might spend all her voyce, *Fame* all her art.
> Whether thy learning they would take, or wit
> Or valour, or thy judgement seasoning it,
> Thy standing upright to thy selfe, thy ends
> Like straight; thy pietie to God, and friends:
> Their latter praise would still the greatest bee,
> And yet, they, all together, less than thee.[11]

And John Donne addressed to him at the siege of Juliers a complex poem on the nature of man which concluded with the lines:

> As brave is true, is that profession than
> Which you do use to make; that you know man.
> This makes it credible; you have dwelt upon
> All worthy bookes, and now are such a one.

> Actions are authors, and of those in you
> Your friends find every day a mart of new.[12]

Such tributes themselves suggest a number of puzzles. Jonson's reference to Truth (written in 1616) may be a deft anticipation of Herbert's major philosophical concern, but what of his praise of Herbert's 'pietie to God', so much contested by later contemporaries? Or of his praise of Herbert's 'judgement'—that very feature which seems so conspicuously lacking in the autobiography? Donne's remarks on Herbert's learning and experience find little reflection in their subject's own account of his actions at Juliers, which suggest rather the opposite, the rashness of a man only absurdly courageous. Contrasts of this sort abound. Behind the buffoon in the autobiography lurks the shrewd diplomat, while behind the philosopher sharpening his categories lurks the duellist sharpening his sword. The conflicts suggested by Walpole's aphorism are not perhaps as absolute as they appear. Herbert, hungry for distinction and the applause of others, took his chivalric vows as seriously in their way as he took the defence of distressed Truth. There is a peculiar psychological consistency in his aggression, though the scant regard for truth in the autobiography may make its relation to *De veritate* a particularly piquant one. Like his duels and his rescues of ladies, *De veritate* is an undertaking imbued with a 'fureur de se distinguer'. It is—granted its seriousness and its achievement—an equally quixotic challenge, a 'choleric and hasty' defence of Truth, displaying something of the cavalier and amateur spirit which Herbert, as an old man writing his memoirs, liked to think so typical of his active youth.

In it, Herbert takes up unprofessional and apparently quixotic arms against a multitude of hardened, efficient combatants—among them the Scholastic and Aristotelian philosophers, the Sceptics and Pyrrhonians, the Calvinists, and the combined forces of 'the Church' in all its manifestations—and comes out of the encounter with a surprising number of points made and points taken, so much so that it is quite possible to think of Lord Herbert as in the mainstream of English religious thought in the seventeenth century when in fact he was one of those pioneers who were helping to divert the current. *De veritate* is in a sense a work of overweening pride and ambition; it is also a significant contribution to metaphysics, if only ultimately in the questions it sets itself; and it is of seminal influence in determining and not merely reflecting the thought of an age. This is the other Lord Herbert, the philosopher and religious thinker: 'the Bacon of metaphysics and epistemology', in Douglas Bush's phrases, who 'stood as it were between Cicero and Kant'. The treatise seeks to lay down grounds of religious belief beyond the coercions of partisanship, seeks to support those grounds with a species of rationalism unique in contemporary English thought, and attempts to grapple with problems of epistemology that most environing contestants appear unaware of. It is an unsystematic, patchy and (to use a phrase of Leibniz) 'hyperbolic' work. As Herbert himself says at the opening of the book, 'I have had less opportunity for the pursuit of letters than for any other occupation. I have been employed in military life in various parts; five years I have been Ambassador in France; I have been immersed in public and personal business; and in consequence there must not be expected of me in this subject a completely satisfactory discussion.' Yet it is lit with flashes of originality and genuine insight, and has been seen to contain at moments remarkable premonitions of Descartes, of the Cambridge Platonists, of Spinoza, Leibniz, Kant, of Reid and his followers, of the Philosophy of Idealism.[13] Predictably, its ambiguities are manifold. One of its initial and most striking paradoxes is that it qualifies rigorously the claims of revelation as an authority and yet justifies its very existence by a claim of divine revelation. In it is declared a man who believes passionately in the unity of truth and yet is a pluralist in epistemology; who displays simultaneous resistance to a purely material interpretation of nature and support of empirical study; a rational theologian who undermines the claims of reasons; a firm individualist who rests in the doctrine of common consent; a Platonic Aristotelian; a sceptical dogmatist—a man of acute and yet, for the most part, intelligible paradoxes.

If Herbert of Cherbury provides the biographer and interpreter of his works with a number of enigmas, provoking judgements on a man whose 'life was one of compromise', or on a man who was 'not one of the most admirable characters of the age', or even on a man of 'cynical indifference'[14], it is probably as well to remember that a similar kind of energetic ambiguity is just as apparent in Bacon's career and work, or in Sir Walter Raleigh's, or Cromwell's, or Marvell's, or even (and not only to those for whom Satan is Milton and God is Charles I) in John Milton himself. Without the existence of what has always appeared a strangely libellous and misjudged piece of self-revelation, many of these problems in Herbert's case might not arise. Of his ambition in the autobiography, Paul Delany writes with more sympathy than most: 'In his autobiography, Herbert is attempting to bring to life an intrinsically noble ideal, that of the Renaissance gentlemen. He fails, and the blame can be laid partly on his own weakness; but the unresponsiveness of the society in which he lived must be taken into account.'[15] Herbert's sense of honour—'not', as he says himself, 'unlike the romances of knight errantry'—may have been accessible to a Sir Philip Sidney moving in the landscapes of *Arcadia* or *The Faerie Queene*, but Herbert was gesturing to the England of James I and of the Duke of Buckingham, and then to the England of Prayer-book politics, Westminster Assemblies, Laud and Pym, Charles and Cromwell. Even as an autobiography, it is not without its successes: it added a new dimension to the anecdotal *res gestae* form, it is still read with relish, and even the most insensitive vanity, as the example of Benvenuto Cellini reminds us, need not, and has not extinguished it.

After some years of acquaintance with Herbert's writings, both the 'serious' works and the autobiography, the impression that admittedly only gradually emerges is of a man of singular integrity, honesty and toughness of mind. Such an impression seems of course a very odd one, especially to readers familiar only with the autobiography, where precisely opposite qualities appear on display. The integrity, honesty and toughness of mind are not directed towards himself. Once he looks inward, his vanity, or his insecurity, takes over and he seems to go to pieces. But his gaze on the world around him may remain curiously clear, shrewd and uncompromising, despite his appearance of being unable to appreciate the changes going on in the society around him. Just as he could relate inconsequential and self-important nonsense about his time in Paris as ambassador, and give only a glance at the fact that, for one thing, he had just written *De veritate*, and for another that he was handling James's affairs with skill and far-sighted diplomacy, so too he seems capable of persuading his readers that on the one hand he is a garrulous braggart and on the other a deeply concerned moral thinker. The pungency of Herbert's views on, for example, the Calvinism dominant in his day, his refusal to accept what he was expected to accept without asking too many awkward questions, his asking of those questions, and his despair (a despair that is neither patronising nor apocalyptic) at the religious and

ecclesiastical crises and counter-crises of his age, affirm his strength
of mind. But these may be called negative responses, reactions to
stimuli. Herbert is above all constructive. He does not merely sound
off at the Calvinist system, but offers another point of view. He not
only asks the awkward questions, but attempts answers to them too,
and not answers which will throw the whole debate back into the
familiar cockpit of controversy, but designed rather to make all the
contestants take breath. His despair is no throwing up of the hands,
nor a cynical indifference, but begets an eirenic spirit aimed at
reducing the causes of that despair and with the ambition of ending
faction and strife. As for those religious, ecclesiastical and sectarian
motives bound up with the Civil War, Herbert must have found
them as inevitable as they were baffling to him. The familiar picture
of him in the years before his death in 1648 as the failed aristocrat,
the man who was unable to live with the times and unable to find a
satisfying role in life, embittered by courtly indifference and a
recluse in his castle in Montgomery, may give credence to what is
usually called his 'weak-kneed capitulation to the Parliamentary
forces'. It is worth dwelling for a moment on this point. It is of course
not unknown for a man's politics to interfere with his critical sense:
Johnson found Milton's politics abhorrent and *Lycidas* 'disgusting',
while T. S. Eliot judged Milton 'unsatisfactory' as a man and 'a bad
influence' as a poet. Sir Sidney Lee's account of Herbert, and his
continuation of his Life, are punctuated with expressions of barely
concealed revulsion at the attitude of a man who could respond as
Herbert did: clearly no Civil War could be won, nor Empire built,
on such pusillanimity.

   The evidence, in the form of documents in the Historical MSS
Report, the Commons' Journal, memoirs of the Civil War in Wales,
and an occasional letter or two, has usually suggested a view of 'the
treacherous Lord Herbert' who had betrayed his fellows for a
handful of silver (and also a library), and who must surely have had
difficulty, granting 'even his portenteous self-composure' (Sidney
Lee), in reconciling the difference between his own entirely
satisfactory conditions in the surrended Castle and those of his sons,
grandson and brother who had loyally opposed the
Parliamentarians, suffered fines and sequestration of property, and
refused to qualify for Parliamentary pensions. Lee wonders how
Herbert could have 'wholly freed himself of an inward suspicion that
he had renounced from sordid motives the chivalrous ideals of his

youth'. The surrender of Montgomery Castle, the key to Wales, let in the Parliamentarian hordes and brought confusion and dismay to Herbert's Royalist neighbours. Some points might be made here. The first is that a real war, and a civil war at that, can hardly have failed to modify the 'chivalrous ideals' of Herbert's youth. From the point of view of a man of Herbert's cast of mind (a mind, in such a situation, not so unlike the mind of the Marvell of the *Horatian Ode*, aware of purely human ambition and weakness—Herbert had mercilessly anatomised self-interest in religious matters—detached from violent partisanship, perpetually on the brink of a withdrawn speculativeness, but open too to the inevitable workings of providence), self-preservation in the face of a kind of absurdity was hardly a treachery. Only those with passionate allegiances, ambitions, over-riding political, religious or personal motives, would logically be capable of treachery. Herbert had an almost eccentric and, to his neighbours at least, incomprehensible absence of such motives. He had previously taken no part in the Civil War. Long-standing family ties had drawn him inevitably at first to the Royalist side, and he attended the Assembly at Oxford which Charles called a Parliament. But he preserved a neutral position, and refused to take sides. As Sidney Lee rightly says, he aimed at 'a pacific independence'. Lee then follows this with the kind of observation that perhaps reflects not on Lord Herbert but on those very assumptions and attitudes that Herbert, in both the ecclesiastical sphere and in this present catastrophe of Civil War, sought to resist: 'He cared no longer for his country but only for himself'. One might reasonably offer as Herbert's opinion that if fewer men cared for their country (or their Church) in this fashion, then all would be the richer for it. While others were raising troops of horse or foot and rallying to diverse standards, Herbert wrote to his brother Sir Henry about his parks, his failing health, and the disruptions to normal, peaceable life caused by the war. Sidney Lee, and most other onlookers, cannot forgive him for this: 'he confessed to no sentiment except one of resentment at the interference with his comfort'. This appalling lack of commitment seems to some quite indefensible. Herbert *ought* to have known which side he was on; he *ought* to have been committed. Commitment to the ideals offered either by the Royalists or the Parliamentarians would not in Herbert's case make very consistent sense. The picture of him joining in the celebration of Divine Right or, had he survived to witness it, of the martyred

Christ-King, or on the other hand of indulging in either Presbyterian
or Miltonic zeal for the coming Puritan revolution, would be equally
grotesque. His motives, had he actively fought for the King, as Lee
and others would have him, could in that event be equally described
as 'sordid', betraying principle for the sake of class and property.
The war had forced him into a false position, and one of desperate
isolation. The pique and weariness with which this 'weak-kneed'
aristocrat is supposed to have surrendered his castle may be a
species, almost unrecognisable in this arena of trumpeted
convictions and bugle calls, of exceptional strength and integrity.

The Herbert family, for generations at the heart of the monarchist
and hierarchical world, courtiers and servants of the King, was not
of course the only one to be divided by the war, and such divisions
were symptoms of the changing social structures. Family breaches
were one of the most poignantly tragic fruits of the conflict. The
Sydneys, the family of the Earl of Leicester, may be taken as one of
many examples. Leicester joined the King at York in 1642, found,
like Herbert, the demands made by Charles's cause unacceptable
and, also like Herbert, withdrew into retirement. Meanwhile, his
brother-in-law, the Earl of Northumberland, sided with Parliament;
his son-in-law, Lord Spencer, with the King. Leicester's owns sons,
Viscount Lisle and Algernon Sydney, took up arms for Parliament.
Similar divisions took place in the families of the Earls of Warwick,
of Kingston and of Dover. The Countess of Denbigh's letters bear
witness to the anguish of a husband fighting in Prince Rupert's
regiment and a son among the Parliamentarian forces. Examples
could be easily multiplied.[16] Among the gentry and the lower classes
the same story may be told, as for instance in the families of the
Fanes and of the Miltons. It should not therefore be supposed that
such splits were uncharacteristic of the times or that Lord Herbert
was alone in his 'betrayal'.

J. H. Handford endorses Lee's general view: 'when the expansive
days of his youth were over neither the high tradition of his race, nor
the rich resources of his own mind were sufficient to enable him to
accept defeat'. Herbert would probably have regarded the issue as
one not amenable to such terms as 'defeat' or 'victory'. Handford
points out that he was 'the one Herbert who failed to do his full
chivalric duty by the royal cause ... His days of gallantry in the
court or in the field were long since past'. They were indeed long
since past, and that is perhaps the point. Such days of gallantry,

even at the time when Herbert had most flamboyantly flexed his courtly or military muscles, were becoming a thing of the past, and the passing of further years had done nothing to reverse this process. Lord Herbert may well have been the only Herbert 'who failed to do his . . . duty' in the manner required, but it hardly helps Handford's argument that Lord Herbert's son Richard (whose royalist troops had been garrisoned in Montgomery just before the Parliamentarian attack) had married in 1627 Lady Mary Egerton, daughter of John Egerton, first Earl of Bridgwater. Like Lord Herbert, Bridgewater too had betrayed 'the high tradition of his race' and supported, or acquiesced in, the new Commonwealth, and was sometimes in attendance in the House of Lords—on one occasion to represent Lord Herbert's request for payment of his pension.[17]

While his sympathy for the Parliamentarians was something less than passionate, Herbert can hardly have been unaware either of the jostling for favours and of the corruption within the cause he was expected to support. The King created, and sold, peerages by the dozen. The Parliamentarian Colonel Hutchinson was offered £10,000 and the earldom of Nottingham if he would betray the county to the Royalists. So much for the chivalry of Herbert's youth. The much quoted letter which Lord Herbert wrote when Rupert requested his presence at Shrewsbury, and in which he excused himself on the grounds that he had 'newly entered into a course of physic', may be an unintentionally insolent procrastination but it may too be Herbert's pointed way of expressing his distate for the whole business. He may not either have been unaware of the activities of Charles Gerrard, the brutal Royalist commander, who was killing and torturing his way through west Wales in a cruel and ferocious fashion.[18] By comparison, and apart from the special ordinance against Irishmen and Papists taken among the Royalists, the conduct of the Parliamentarian officers in Wales and in England was almost entirely humane and above reproach. Such considerations, notwithstanding the consequent vulnerability of his Royalist neighbours, may well have weighed with the pacific and independent Herbert.

In other words, it is not impossible to surmise, beneath the class treachery and the failure to fulfil his neighbours' expectations, that the eccentric Lord had besides his open self-regard and the preservation of those lovingly collected books ('I ever', he once claimed, like another Montaigne, 'loved my book and a private life'), a less easily perceived motive towards promoting too the 'general good' (a phrase that echoes through *De veritate*), in so far as the chaotic circumstances might allow. It is in any case an interesting fact, behind which might be a story if it could be unearthed, that the old Lord Herbert's favourite grandson, Edward, Royalist son of the Royalist Richard Herbert and the beneficiary of all the first Lord's estates in Wales, married the daughter of Sir Thomas Middleton, the Parliamentary Major General to whom Lord Herbert surrendered Montgomery Castle. Herbert's political eccentricity (granted, that is, that he was a Herbert) is in a sense the logical political outcome of his speculations and his stance on religious questions, and particularly on the nature of authority. Although most of Herbert's religious opinions might make the Puritan mind recoil, as most of theirs did his, there is a kind of logic in Herbert's final submission to a movement which, theoretically at least, sought to uphold the rights of the laity and of private judgement.[19]

In Herbert's most solid achievements themselves, the philosophical and religious writings, ambiguity and enigma are, not surprisingly, present too. Just as Herbert could cheerfully reveal himself to posterity as a popinjay and yet elicit the warmest praise and friendship from Donne and Ben Jonson, men not easily deceived, so he could stand as that odd sort of ecclesiastical iconoclast who, according to John Aubrey, had prayers said twice daily in his house. In his early military exploits he could describe himself as a braggart and a clown who was nevertheless the intimate of the powerful and noble family of the Montmorencys, not noted for their toleration of fools. His later reputation reflects the enigma. The man who strove to establish, against sceptics and atheists, the immortality of the soul, found himself labelled atheist and betrayer of mankind. The man who served his country in France loyally and honestly, and with an impressive sense of style, found himself, after half a lifetime of royal indifference, known as 'the treacherous Lord Herbert'. There is however further ambiguity, indicating the most fundamental and demanding paradox of all lying over and above Lord Herbert's particular personality and idiosyncrasies, and which resides rather in the relation between an individual's thought, or the concerted thought of a number of individuals, and the intricate process of social, religious and cultural change. For, from an historical point of view, Herbert's philosophy of religion led inexorably to the Deism of the eighteenth century—reflected in the repeated description of him as 'the father of English Deism'—to which, in perhaps the most significant respects, that philosophy is itself antithetical.

Many of the paradoxes in his thought are only apparent, or are explicable in terms of certain seventheeth-century attitudes and assumptions shared by many besides Lord Herbert. Others are more intransigent, being the products of confused thinking, of unrecognised internal contradictions proper to Herbert himself. The most interesting are those which require, for both their identification and their explanation, an enquiry into the many cross-currents of thought of the sixteenth and earlier seventeenth centuries which constitute Herbert's inheritance; and also—with a shift of perspective—an investigation of the course of an idea deriving from such currents through subsequent repetitions, distortions, or denials of it under pressure of problems which may be entirely remote from those pressures which generated that idea and formed its source. From such an investigation might emerge a comment both on the use to which Lord Herbert was put by late seventeeth- and eighteenth-century deists and freethinkers, and on the customary, received view of Herbert's position. For example, it is one thing to state that Lord Herbert held the same views as the later deists, and another to say that he represents an earlier phase in a development which in one of its later phases was to produce the views of the deists. In the latter sense, Herbert was a forerunner of the deists; in the former sense, I shall seek to argue, he was not.

However, the laying down of the scope and limits of an exploration of Herbert's intellectual inheritance is hazardous. One source of the ambiguities and inconsistencies of Herbert's thought lies in his own natural eclecticism, a wide and free-ranging mind which gathers in all kinds of heterogenous ideas and philosophical positions and culls from them what seems most immediately useful. Herbert, in true Renaissance fashion, strains after the *magnum opus*, and *summa*, but unlike most of his contemporaries, cites, for reasons which we may suspect have something to do with his desire to appear original, few authorities either by name or footnote. The resulting synthesis, composed of many varied strands and compounded views, is difficult to unravel. In any event such an unravelling might tell us very little that we did not know before: that Herbert is standing on other men's shoulders, and that many sources contribute to, though they do not necessarily explain, the fabric of his work. Moreover, some of the most important elements in his thought are also the common patrimony of his age. For example, the all-pervasive influence of Christian Platonism, which forms a kind of ground bass to Herbert's speculations, is, because it is everywhere, difficult to locate significantly anywhere. The same pervasive 'background' lies behind, for instance, Robert Greville, Lord Brooke, or Sir Thomas Browne, or Marvell, or Henry Vaughan, or Traherne, or the Cambridge Platonists, as well as Herbert. The problem is much the same when one views the 'background' of Christian humanism, or of diffused Renaissance Stoicism; it is difficult to treat significantly in a man's work what is in the very air he breathes. As Herschel Baker observed, the man shaped by the ethical ideals of a Platonically leavened Stoicism came to be something like a normative figure for the Renaissance.[20] Herbert is in many respects such a figure, before whom the apparently meaningful categories of Platonism, Stoicism, or Aristotelianism tend to blur and confuse. His intellectual inheritance is the amalgam of many historical processes. A kernel of Platonic doctrines along with Aristotle's reinterpretations, admixed with Pythagorean mathematics, Stoic ethics, Plotinian and Christian mysticism, Hermetism, Patristic theology and cosmology, Florentine humanism and Neoplatonism, a number of occult symbolisms, several types of logical theory and method, and a turbulent current of religious reformation: these are some of the elements which make up seventeenth-century Platonism and which are reflected in various degrees in Lord Herbert.

Platonism is only the most outstanding example. Similar problems arise with other aspects of Herbert's thought and involve the postures of Aristotelianism, or of scholasticism, or of scepticism. In the face, therefore, of a complex and polymorphous European tradition, I have attempted not to map out this vast territory or to return at all points to sources, but only to trace a number of ideas within a context selected and shaped towards questions relevant to Herbert himself. For instance, in demonstrating the specific relation between Herbert's 'analogical' metaphysics and 'intuitive' epistemology and the emergence of his celebrated common religious notions, it is shown that the examination of a wider European context lends support to the view that there is a definite interaction between the analogical and unifying philosophy of Hermetism and Renaissance Platonism and the growth of 'natural theology' as an eirenic to the warfare and persecution of sectarian religion—a development strikingly crystallised in Herbert's own position and writings.

It is comparatively simple, on the other hand, to pursue the subsequent career of Herbert's suggestions. References by later writers to his work are fairly numerous, and responses to him range among the coolly unperturbed, the vigorously partisan, and the ferociously dismissive. He has been called many things, this 'metaphysick Lord'; Gassendi called him 'England's treasure' risen to succeed Lord Bacon; Charles Blount, an undiscriminating disciple and propagandist, called him Mercury and Mars, 'the Commander and Oracle of his time'; to Walpole he was Plato and Don Quixote, to Sir Leslie Stephen he was Bodadil–Kant, while to several of his nearer contemporaries he was seen as one of the century's three arch-betrayers, in the illustrious company of Hobbes and Spinoza: learned and treacherous, atheist and religious, indifferentist and heretic, destroyer and liberator. He has too been held accountable for many things, most notably of course in that enduring title as 'father of English Deism'. How much such varied responses tell us of Lord Herbert and his own ambiguities, and how much they tell us of their authors, is a fascinating study; as too is the light they shed upon the rapidly shifting intellectual and religious environment as the seventeenth century progresses.

Despite this fascination, Herbert can hardly be regarded as a fashionable figure in modern accounts of the philosophical and religious history of the seventeenth century. Considering his acknowledged place in the history of deism, comparatively little has been written about him, at least in English. Meyrick H. Carré provided an excellent and indispensable translation of *De veritate* in 1937, together with an illuminating introduction, but the book is a fairly scarce 'limited edition' printing. Sidney Lee, at the turn of the century, introduced, edited and continued in his own hand Herbert's autobiography, supplying many useful if incomplete notes and appendices, but revealing (like so many English men of letters at that period) so much of the spirit of the 'imperial ideal' that the unsympathetic Herbert himself emerged as a kind of *persona non grata*. Herbert's *Religio laici* appeared, with a spirited translation and a lucid and suggestive introduction, in 1944, edited by Harold R. Hutcheson,[21] and was a valuable addition to the Herbert canon since Herbert's most important works had, before Carré and

Hutcheson, been available only in the original murky Latin or, in the case of *De veritate*, in a seventeenth-century French translation. A revival of serious interest is indicated by the recent facsimile reprints of Herbert's writings, produced in Stuttgart and edited by Günter Gawlick. The most magisterial and comprehensive account of Herbert's life, career and writings is Mario M. Rossi's three-volume study, written in exile from the Fascist domination of Italy, printed in Florence in 1947 as part of a series of monographs, and which requires of its potential reader both a good copyright library and a reading knowledge of Italian.

Rossi's work is of enormous importance to anyone interested in Herbert, or indeed in currents of thought in the seventeenth century, and is so extraordinary in itself as to require some comment. Its scope and thoroughness are astonishing. In part of the preface written in 1935, Rossi said that no one had ever written a life of Herbert and that no one had ever studied his philosophy. It might have seemed (with contributions from Leslie Stephen, Sidney Lee, Charles de Rémusat, Carl Güttler, C. H. Herford, Edmund Blunden, J. M. Robertson, Heinrich Scholz, W. R. Sorley, A. Carlini, Louis Bredvold, Wolfram Steinbeck, and Basil Willey) a self-important exaggeration. But after Rossi's accomplishment, it is seen to be the simple truth. Rossi provides the last word on most issues of biography and bibliography, apart from the very few facts or items which escaped his omnivorous attention. It is, inevitably, not without its biases and prejudices on questions of emphasis and interpretation, particularly of Herbert's religious thought. Rossi frankly confesses to a personal aversion to any kind of religious rationalism, to every form of Pelagianism, and to every confusion of theology and philosophy, and this on occasions leaves his relation with his subject distinctly problematical. On the one hand, certain qualities in Herbert receive the richest praise. After a minutely documented account of the ambassadorship in France, Rossi moves into an impassioned contrast between the upright and idealistic Herbert and Richlieu, the latter representing the shrewd exploiter, the pure opportunist politician for whom Catholic and Protestant were only political forces and for whom religious and ideal problems were swallowed up in base political motives. Thinking of his own situation (he refused to take the Fascist oath and disqualified himself from a chair in philosophy), Rossi offers a deeply felt panegyric to Herbert: 'In a period so like our own, of servile favourites and of ignoble office-seeking, Herbert appears as an independent spirit, animated by that masculine faith in justice and right which is the profound soul of England, the England of the Puritans and of Cromwell' (II, p. 375). On the other hand, Herbert's general religious stance, his contribution to the emergence of natural religion and of deism, his Pelagianism, and his criticisms of 'revelation', are so far removed from Rossi's own sense of truly religious values that Herbert's lack of religious sensibility is also compared with the 1940s: '. . . when we have reached deism, there is no longer any interest in religious polemic because there is no longer any interest in religion . . . We end in atheologism, in the sunset of the religious sense, in the night of God in which we now vegetate.' Rossi looks for a return to a purer religion, that which 'from Kierkegaard to Barth is a new Calvinism, the Calvinism of pure Revelation, which is in reality a fleeing from polemic, that is from religious naturalism' (I, pp. 592f.).

Over against a Cardinal without religious scruples, a lay philosopher, a freethinker and a deist represented somehow the sound, ideal and honest Europe of the preceding age, a man Rossi both warms to and retreats from. The paradox implicit in Rossi's work —it is only rather cryptically expressed in a footnote that he is in fact enquiring into 'the passage from religious to political motives' and that he seeks to 'show and demonstrate this immense (and disastrous) historic shift of Europe' (II, p. 385 note)—is that Herbert was a forerunner of this shift from religious to political motives and contributed to it, while at the same time as a man of action and ideals he did what he could to resist it. Thus Herbert becomes for Rossi a kind of symbolic figure, a watershed in European culture, on whose unwitting accomplishments in philosophy and diplomacy three large volumes are scarcely sufficient (Rossi also wrote on Herbert and Herbertian questions elsewhere).

In this present study I have neither the ability nor the ambition for such a comprehensive view of Herbert. It was Rossi's hope that he could put into the hands of future students all that could be known of Herbert; and, if he did not quite do that, few ambitions have been so nearly fulfilled. Although some of the conclusions here may depart at points from Rossi's, particularly on Herbert's Platonic or Neoplatonic affiliations, his eirenic aims and his religious sensibility, Rossi's work is always there as a challenge to one's views and disagreements, most often providing the very data that can give them shape.

Notes to Chapter I

1 *The Autobiography of Edward, Lord Herbert of Cherbury*, ed. Sidney Lee, London, 1886, p. 30. (A new edition of the autobiography, ed. by J. M. Shuttleworth, has recently appeared, Oxford, 1976.).
2 *Autobiography*, ed. Lee. p. 84.
3 *Autobiography*, pp. 154–5.
4 J. Handford, 'Lord Herbert of Cherbury and his son', *Huntington Library Quarterly*, 5, 1941–2, pp. 317–32.
5 See Historical MSS Commission, *Tenth Report*, app. 1. pp. 121–2: 'His Majesty oweth him £7000 and without paying him first that which is due to him his Majesty cannot in honour recall him'.
6 Mario M. Rossi, *La vita, le opere, i tempi di Edoardo Herbert di Chirbury*, 3 vols. Florence, 1947, II, p. 239.
7 Rossi, II, p. 258.
8 *The Poems of Edward Lord Herbert of Cherbury*, ed. G. C. Moore Smith, Oxford, 1923, p. 75. On the top of the Gatehouse, the barbican, the Abbot's tower and on the Keep itself are a number of armed figures in various warlike attitudes, looking as if they had just taken up guard duties. The present figures were put up during the restoration of Alnwick Castle in 1750, but almost certainly take the place of earlier ones. See Ward Lock's *Guide to the Northumberland Coast*.
9 See C. J. Fordyce and T. M. Knox, 'The books bequeathed to Jesus College Library, Oxford, By Lord Herbert of Cherbury', *Proceedings and Papers of the Oxford Bibliographical Society*, 5, 1936–9, part II, pp. 53f.
10 Rossi, III, p. 166.
11 Ben Jonson, *Poems*, ed. B. H. Newdigate, Oxford, 1936, p. 38.
12 Donne, *Poetical Works*, ed. H. J. C. Grierson, Oxford, 1912, vol. I. p. 195.
13 See Rossi, and also the comments of M. H. Carré in the introduction to his translation of *De veritate*, Bristol, 1937, p. 44, and Charles de Rémusat, *Lord Herbert de Cherbury, sa vie et ses oeuvres, ou les origines de la philosophie du sens commun et de la théologie naturelle en Angleterre*, Paris, 1874.
14 These remarks are from, respectively, Margaret Bottrall, *Every Man a Phoenix*, London, 1958, p. 81; Douglas Bush, *English Literature in the Earlier Seventeenth Century, 1600–1660*, 2nd ed., Oxford, 1962, p. 160 n.; and Sidney Lee, *Autobiography*, p. xxxii.
15 Paul Delany, *British Autobiography in the Seventeenth Century*, London, 1969, p. 127.
16 See Paul H. Hardacre, *The Royalist during the Puritan Revolution*, The Hague, 1956, pp. 10f.
17 See Handford, *loc. cit.*
18 J. R. Phillips, *Memoirs of the Civil War in Wales and the Marches*, London, 1874, vol. I, pp. 253–4.
19 In his will (printed in Lee) Herbert wrote: 'And whereas I have begun a manifest of my actions in these late troubles but am prevented in the review thereof, I do hereby leave it to a person whom I shall by word instruct to finish the same and to publish it to the world by my direction and as having

the express charge laid upon him by me for doing it.' No unfinished copy of any such 'manifest' has been discovered. See Rossi, III, p. 513. Interesting comment, composed mainly of contemporary documentary evidence, on the surrender of Montgomery Castle may be found in two anonymous articles in the *Montgomery Collections* for 1888 (vol. 22). The circumstances of the surrender would seem to absolve Herbert from any 'treachery'.

20 Herschel Baker, 'Sixteenth-century ethics and the development of neo-stoicism', in *The Dignity of Man*, Cambridge, Mass., 1947, chap. 18.

21 Harold R. Hutcheson, *Lord Herbert of Cherbury's De Religione Laici. With a critical discussion of his life and philosophy, and a comprehensive bibliography of his works*, New Haven, Conn. 1944 (Yale Studies in English, vol. 98). It should be pointed out that the bibliography is not in fact comprehensive, for it omits the important collection of Herbert MSS in the National Library of Wales.

II
THE PROBLEM OF CERTAINTY

> Sure he that made us with such large discourse,
> Looking before and after, gave us not
> That capability and godlike reason
> To fust in us unus'd . . .

Hamlet, IV, iv

Imbeciles and sceptics

As the first proposition of his treatise *De veritate* Herbert baldly states: 'Truth exists'. It is an opening lacking neither confidence nor panache. 'The sole purpose of this proposition', he explains, 'is to assert the existence of truth against imbeciles and sceptics' (*contra insanos & Scepticos*).[1]

At the very outset, then, we are presented with a number of questions. The first concerns the word 'truth' itself: *De veritate* is clearly going to be a defence of truth though it is not yet clear what Herbert means by 'truth'. The word is both resonant and imprecise, and Herbert is well aware of this. The usual procedure, after such an assertion, would be to say something like: 'And *this* is what the truth is . . .' But it is precisely the problems caused by this procedure that Herbert is seeking to avoid. It is part of his distinction that he saw that little good could come of merely asserting one's view of what is 'true', and that what was required was an attempt to answer the much more difficult question of what we mean when we speak of truth. His approach, despite the bold opening of *De veritate*, is not simply one of assertion. In an age when voices on all sides were loudly informing each other of the 'truth', each according to his own criteria, prejudices, allegiances or vested interests, Herbert sought to carry the discussion into the far less frequented field of basic epistemological enquiry. And this forms a large part of his task in *De veritate*.

His overall ambition in the work may be initially summarised from its full title: 'Concerning Truth, and its distinction from revelation, probability, possibility, and falsehood'. In other words, it is an investigation of modes of knowing and their conditions. Herbert does not primarily mean by 'truth' some absolute, objective entity, and his treatise does not seek to establish truth's existence in that sense; rather, he is concerned with the conditions that attach to the notion of 'truth', and concerned above all (and it is a concern characteristic of arguments upholding the existence of truth under pressure from fundamental sceptical objections) with establishing the possibility of certain knowledge which may correctly be described as 'true' knowledge. Herbert should not perhaps be held too rigorously to the occasional metaphorical flourish which depicts Truth as an Andromeda to be released from her bonds; and even less should he be thought to anticipate, or share in, that kind of militant Miltonic vision which sees 'armed justice in defence of beleaguered Truth' when it is precisely the adoption of some objective 'Truth' to one's partisan interests that Herbert is resisting. The chief content of the concept as Herbert uses it is best rendered in the word 'certainty'. *De veritate* is a defence of certainty, and an argument seeking to prove through epistemological investigation that genuine and certain knowledge is possible.

If Herbert's most original concern is with fixing the nature and limits of truth, and with the examination of the possibility of certainty and the conditions for its existence, such an enquiry is bound to run up against the problems posed by specifically religious truth. Despite a prefatory disclaimer that he is interested only in 'truths of understanding, not truths of Faith' and that 'any points bearing on the mysteries of Faith which the reader may find scattered through the book must be accepted as arising naturally out of the course of the argument',[2] his design could fairly be said to include the identification of religious truth with the principles of universal reason. Although he sees his task as a problem of epistemology and not of theology, it is of course from this initial strategy of assimilation that the towers of rational theology inevitably rise up.

Further questions arise out of Herbert's accusation *contra insanos & Scepticos*. Who are these imbeciles and sceptics? Since 'imbecile' is Herbert's customary description of scholastics, we may recognise echoes of the fashionable anti-scholasticism of the late sixteenth century. The treatise participates too, *contra Scepticos*, in the great controversy surrounding the Pyrrhonian crisis of sceptical doubt. In his declaration that 'the whole aim of the work is the common nature of the search for truth which exists in every normal human being'[3] the word 'normal' is a cautionary one intended to exclude not only the literally abnormal but also the 'imbeciles and sceptics'. Nevertheless, Herbert could not simply disregard scholastic and sceptical arguments. If the identification of religious truth with the principles of universal reason was to be achieved—indeed if the whole of his investigation into the operations of the human mind and its perceptions was to stand up at all—it was necessary to establish first of all that such universal reason did exist, that it was the same in all men at all times (unless they were not normal), and that both its own workings and the world upon which it worked were intelligible to men. Those who deny truth's existence (in the sense of denying the existence of internal rational principles which assure us of certainty) are, Herbert says, the scholastic philosophers in so far as they deny truth's intelligibility without divine aid, and the sceptics, who deny it absolutely. And his programme of demonstration is conditioned by the pressure exerted by these two approaches.

The treatise is dedicated 'to every sane and unprejudiced reader', expressing the two necessary conditions of disinterested enquiry: sound faculties and an open mind. 'Those who enter the shrine of truth', Herbert warns, 'must leave their trinkets, in other words their opinions, at the entrance, or, one might say, in the cloakroom.'[4] The dangers of prejudice are manifest everywhere: 'now this party, now that, loudly proclaims the truth of its own doctrines, and calls the rest plagiarists, liars, and impostors'.[5] Herbert deals shortly with the 'imbeciles', impugning the motives of the 'ancient schools' who appear, he says, more concerned with exposing one another than with seeking truth. The scholastic contribution to debates about the nature of truth, and their continued influence, are not of course to be dismissed in an aphorism, and Herbert has implicitly to recognise throughout his work the fact of their existence. He then turns, in the Preface, to confront the neo-scholastics of 'our latter age' who

may plume themselves upon their brilliance as much as they will, yet, as long as they discard reason and enslave themselves to the theories of others, they appear to have entirely lost their spirit at the moment they have gained their freedom ... They seem to bind themselves hand and foot to the orthodox views, and do not release a finger except to display their own subtlety.[6]

The narrow Aristotelian curricula which Herbert himself followed at an Oxford still labouring under the injunction of 1585 that bachelors and undergraduates must confine themselves in logic to Aristotle 'and those that defend him', is clearly in mind here and lends to the term 'reason', which they are said to have discarded, the particular sense of individual discrimination and intellectual enterprise. It is worth noting, incidentally, a strong vein of polemic in Herbert which, though some of it may be mere abuse, is not altogether ignoble: its drive may be in part the egotist's ambition to appear original and indebted to no one, but it is also venially tempered by a desire to penetrate mere opinion and 'orthodoxy' to its source. The imbecile as a type of mind is, in the famous 'character' satirised by Herbert's contemporary, Sir Thomas Overbury, the 'Mere Scholar or Intelligible Ass' who is only 'the index of a man';[7] or the man who, to use Herbert's distinctive terminology, refuses to 'look into his own faculties' and who may be seen burying his head in a heap of authoritarian citations and preferring to 'stop his ears, shut his eyes, and strip himself of all humanity'.[8]

But why should such a man also refuse to agree that truth exists? The disposition to uphold authority, tradition and orthodoxy in matters of natural philosophy, or of religion, and the discomfort caused by the effort to accommodate the new evidences of reason or instinct or pragmatic observation, presents a familiar 'Renaissance' dilemma of the kind vividly portrayed by that celebrated foreign visitor to the Oxford of the late sixteenth century, Giordano Bruno. In his *De l'infinito universo e mondi* (1584) (of which Herbert owned a copy)[9] Bruno inserts a fiery exchange, rendered in his raciest manner, between Fracastoro (an historical figure who died in 1553, an influential humanist and philosopher of the new breed) and Burchio, the usual academic scholar or intelligible ass who may be a satirical portrait of the arrogant English Franciscan, Thomas Bourchier, who was a product of the Oxford that so incensed Bruno.[10] Burchio, clearly exasperated by the wilful independence of the 'new philosophy', interrupts with great passion to defend Aristotle's works which, he says, have cost

countless hours of application to generations of commentators, men who have paraphrased and glossed, written compendia and summaries, scholia and translations, reducing them to questionnaires and theorems. These are the works that have formed our *doctores profundi, subtiles, aurati, magni, inexpugnabiles, irrefragabiles*, our angelics, our seraphics, our cherubics, our divines!

If Aristotle is held an ass and Aquinas a fool, what a fine chaos the world will be in. Fracastoro answers the charge in words which capture the very spirit of Renaissance enquiry and which are everywhere underwritten by Lord Herbert: 'As I said at the outset, in my eyes they are the heroes of the earth. I refuse, however, to believe everything they say unquestioningly, much less admit theories of theirs which, as you have heard if you have any ears at all, are flatly contradictory to the truth.' To which Burchio inevitably retorts, 'Well, who is going to decide what truth is?' The answer is that it is the 'prerogative of every careful and wideawake intelligence, of everybody who is as judicious and free from obstinancy as he can be'. But Burchio, thoroughly upset, departs hurling insults. Burchio's confusion, ridiculed though it is, was of course the confusion of many minds unable to surrender old and trusted beliefs and unwilling to understand or accept new theories which appeared to be turning the familiar world upside down. Indeed, Burchio turns on Fracastoro, calling him (as Bruno himself was called) 'a sophistical assailant of good letters, a disturber of established order, a perverter of truth'. And in the midst of this confusion many men, wishing to appear judicious and free from obstinancy, found a convenient refuge in a sceptical shrug of the shoulders. Who, indeed, can decide what truth is?

Herbert is emphatically not one of the shoulder-shruggers. Equally, however, he is aware that, for practical purposes, the generality of men seem bound by the decisions about the nature of truth made, on their behalf as it were, by others, and predominantly of course by the Church. The scholastic contention that reality exceeds the capacity of human knowledge without divine aid because, however much it may have to be interpreted it is ultimately divinely revealed, is one which Herbert labours to resist. Though he freely acknowledges truth's divine origin he cannot free himself from the suspicion that what in any particular case is divinely revealed may too often mean only what the priesthood asserts. Decisions, Herbert implies, are constantly being made about what truth is, despite the formal caveats of both super-naturalism on the one hand and philosophical scepticism on the other. *De veritate* is an attempted redefinition of the limits of human knowledge which, as Herbert pursues it, pushes further and further back the point at which 'revelation' may be allowed to take over as our sole remaining guarantee of certainty.

Scholasticism

Throughout *De veritate* the schoolmen receive the benefit of Herbert's contempt and sarcasm. The butt of his ponderous epigrams is invariably the 'Peripatetic philosophers', and his most studied incredulity is reserved for Aquinas. Although the scholastic world did not know even the names of Pyrrho and Sextus Empiricus, the early Greek sceptics who were to be thrown into prominence by the motions of the Renaissance, it was not without its own forms of scepticism and antirationalism. And at the root of scholastic antirationalism lay the complex problem of universals. Although it was a scholastic axiom that reality exceeded man's grasp without God's aid, and that the natural human intelligence was restricted to the understanding of sense perceptions (which were not regarded as likely to deceive), it was nevertheless agreed that abstraction was 'the law of the intellect' and the abstract concept the perfect and definitive type of our knowledge. The 'universal' was such an abstract concept. Yet the tension between the truth of the universal on the one hand and the individual, the particular, on the other, suggested a philosophical choice which Aquinas described as follows:

The Platonic philosophers held that bodiless universal forms and ideas were the cause both of the being and of the being known of particular things, and they sought the pure and essential soul, the cause and idea of all that is in particular souls. The physical philosophers, on the other hand, felt no hankering for universal substances and kept to facts. From these two conflicting opinions rises the issue whether we should investigate soul as such or keep to this or that soul, of horses, men, and the heavenly bodies.[11]

Aquinas explained how Aristotle arrived at a compromise between the two, a position of 'moderate realism' adopted by Aquinas himself which asserts that the universal exists and is of importance but that it exists only in the particular. Aquinas's own form of baptised Aristotelianism was roundly criticised by Duns Scotus and especially by William of Ockham. Scotus's metaphysics, like Aquinas's, perpetuate a compromise between a thorough-going 'Platonic' realism and a thoroughgoing nominalism, although Aquinas's terms and arguments are attacked in the process. But already even in the thirteenth century there was an opposition party, chiefly within the Franciscan Order, moving towards the rigorously nominalist position that the *only* reality is in the individual. The chief spokesman of this view was to be William of Ockham, who flatly denied the existence of universals. The universal cannot be a thing, a *res*, a reality, since—despite the realists—the same thing cannot exist simultaneously in several things: the intellect cannot make the mobile immobile, the perishable the eternal, nor the singular universal. In his commentary on *The Sentences of Peter Lombard* he argues by reviewing the traditional notions which conclude that 'universality is held to be really present in the singular objects themselves'—an opinion which, he claims, 'is simply false and absurd'. The analysis of a thing into essence and existence, substance and attribute, is merely a conceptual elaboration which cannot be incorporated into the structure of the thing itself. 'To conclude, I say that there is no such thing as a universal, intrinsically present in the things to which it is common. No universal, except that is such by voluntary agreement, is existent in any way outside of the soul, but everything that be predicated of many things is by its nature in the mind, either psychologically or logically.'[12] Universals are thus merely names or terms, either mental, spoken or written.

Ockham consequently arrived at an epistemological distrust of intellect and reason. Our abstract concepts are, in his view, a kind of make-believe, or at best a form of mental exercise. In matters of faith he rejects the validity of rational theology and advocates a fideistic approach to religion. If we apply reason to the realm of faith we are in constant danger, his view suggests, of involving ourselves in a whole series of mental fabrications immediately we speak of universals such as 'the Church', or 'mankind' whose being, according to the nominalists, is simply their being understood. The universal 'Church' has no meaningful existence apart from individual churches as they exist in space and time; nor has the universal or 'form' of 'man' any reality apart from individual men.

Although Ockham's radical nominalism was proposed primarily as a defence of faith, his epistemology inevitably raised theological difficulties: what, for instance, of the Pauline doctrine that 'as in Adam all men sinned, so in Christ were all men made alive again', when without a universal of 'man' and a universal of 'Church'—the vicar of Christ on earth—the whole structure appeared to be threatened? And what of its implications for doctrines of the eucharist? Despite a personal devotion to faith, Ockham's analysis laid instead the foundations of religious scepticism, an attitude which began to condemn as *contrary* to reason those aspects of Christian faith which Ockham himself had declared only *inaccessible* to reason.

Equally vulnerable, under the keen eye of nominalism, was a universal concept of 'truth', over and above individual, particular truths. 'Truth' could be divided into 'truth of reason' and 'truth of faith', and it could further be splintered into an infinity of relative truths appropriate to different modes of cognition and experience. The apparently relative nature of truth was one of the most acute problems that harrassed both scholastic and Renaissance thinkers. Averroes, a twelfth-century physician and judge, was perhaps the first to introduce the 'double truth' into European thought. The theory arose out of his interpretation of Aristotle, and for the Italian Aristotelians of the rising universities Averroes became the chief guide and commentator. But Averroes's commentary was based on Arabic texts (he knew no Greek), liberally supplemented by the observations of Neoplatonic Hellenistic commentators who had infused a good deal of cosmic mysticism and pantheism into the original Aristotle—with the result that Averroes's Aristotle came to some embarrassing conclusions, maintaining for instance that Creation is not fixed at a point in time but is eternal, by emanations; that matter is eternal, as is also 'that mysterious Intellect of which Aristotle speaks'. For man there is no prospect of personal immortality, only an anonymous absorption into the single Intellect of mankind, and hence no heaven and hell, and no last judgement.[13]

The schoolmen, from Aquinas on, handled Averroes with great caution; but Renaissance Aristotelians did not scruple if Aristotle appeared to divert from the true faith. This version of Aristotle, 'without benefit of clergy', has come to be known as Latin Averroism. One of the Latin Averroists, Siger of Brabant, recognising that there was a good deal of difference between the conclusions of reason and philosophy (that is, Averroes's Aristotle) and the conclusions of faith, offered the opinion that faith was of course true but Aristotle was much more interesting. It was a small step from this to say that faith was true in its own way, and philosophy true in its own way. The cohabitation of Averroism and Ockhamism gave birth to an attitude which could blur the distinctions between what, in questions of faith, is beyond reason's power to grasp and what is contrary to reason. In anti-clerical Venice and Padua Averroes's Aristotle flourished throughout the

fifteenth century; in the universities the denial of Creation and of
personal immortality, with all their theological consequences, were
taught and apparently accepted by many Venetian gentlemen,
though usually under the protection afforded by the 'double truth'.
By the sixteenth century the 'double truth' had become a
fashionable commonplace, a way, both convenient and witty, of
disposing of difficulties. While serious thinkers might maintain only
that an article of faith may not be demonstrable on the basis of mere
reason, and that its opposite may seem to be supported by strong
probable arguments, less cautious theorists were not averse to
talking as if something were true in theology and its exact opposite
true in philosophy. For men who held nominalist or empirical
positions and who yet professed Christianity the 'double truth' came
to be regarded a necessary evil. 'Who', asked the early seventeenth-
century Jesuit François Veron, repeating a familiar question, 'would
believe in the resurrection if faith is to be regulated by philosophical
axioms?'[14] One way out of the difficulty was to try to prevent the two
kinds of truth from contaminating each other. If the certitude of
religion is of one kind and the certitude of reason of another, then
religious experience, bereft of reason, is allowed only the support of
faith. Aware of the injury being offered to Christian philosophy by
such a division, the Church had condemned the error of 'fideism' as
early as 1348.

Fideism asserts that there are in fact no rational motives for
assenting to divine revelation, only the act of blind obedience and
faith. Such a view has always been a negative and a minority view,
and in historical accounts has usually been contrasted with the
dominant majority view which, in the tradition Aquinas and
Richard Hooker, has generally prevailed in the Catholic and
anglican churches. According to what has been called 'Christian
rationalism' a form of natural religion, discoverable by unaided
human reason, is possible but is insufficient and inadequate without
the illumination of revealed religion. Nevertheless, the inevitable
drift of both Latin Averroism and of nominalism towards a species of
rational scepticism in matters of religion, leaving the claims of faith
altogether outside the province of intellectual enquiry and the
processes of reason, became a strong antirationalist current
developing its own distinctive eddies in the sixteenth and early
seventeenth centuries and which Herbert saw it as his duty to
challenge.

Scepticism

For other men the sceptical shrug of the shoulders in the face of the 'double truth' or of collisions between reason and revelation was much more than a merely convenient refuge. Scepticism became a sophisticated and systematic method for coming to terms with the confusions of an age and of making at least qualified sense of the intellect's predicament. For both the reactionary scholar–scholastic and the sober defender of epistemological certainty the villain of the piece was to be Montaigne—or rather, the Montaigne of the genial and urbanely destructive *Apologie de Raimond Sebond* and of the famous motto 'Que sais-je?'. Montaigne's *Apologie*, written in the years 1575–6 in his chateau in Gascony, was incidentally provoked by his reading of a work by a Spanish 'natural theologian', Raymond Sebond. The relationship of the *Apologie* to Sebond's work is tenuous to say the least (it is in fact an 'apologetic' which demolishes natural theology), though a single quotation from Sebond's early brand of 'natural religion' will give some indication of the kind of assertion Montaigne found interesting. Speaking of natural knowledge, Sebond buoyantly claims:

It makes a man cheerful, modest, kind and obedient, and causes him to hate all vices and sins and so love virtue; it puffs not up nor makes proud its possessor. Moreover it proves by arguments which none can gainsay, for it proves by means of what is most certain to every man by experience, that is by all the creatures and by the natural qualities of man himself and by man himself, and by what man knows most assuredly of himself by experience, and above all by the inner experience which every man has of himself; and so this science seeks no other witness than a man's own self.[15]

Montaigne, though he does not believe a word of it as far as a natural theology is concerned, responds in his own way to the criterion of selfhood and of one's own inner and individual experience. But much more important than Sebond to the *Apologie* are the attitudes and arguments of the ancient Greek sceptics; the *Apologie* is a testimony both to their revival and their influence and became their most persuasive advertisement in the later sixteenth century.

Because the *Apologie* is Montaigne's longest and most substantial work it has often been taken as the sum of his most serious thought. Montaigne's earlier essays are full of a Stoicism decorated with quotation and misquotation from Plutarch, Seneca and Montaigne's early hero, Cato the Younger. In them he advocates self-mastery and self-control as the marks of the typical Stoic response. But then he moved into a much more speculative and sceptical frame of mind, as exemplified in the *Apologie*. It is also less typical of his final ideas, though they do grow naturally out of the stance of the *Apologie*. His final work tends towards a more 'epicurean' posture, a *naturam sequere* inclination, and especially advocating the discovery and pursuit of our own particular, idiosyncratic, individual nature—the very opposite of the Stoical ideal of self-control and discipline of his earlier years. Instead there is that characteristic quirkiness of self-absorption and self-fascination which has always made Montaigne so engaging to read.

Montaigne evidently began to find the claims of Stoical humanism inadequate, presumptuous and even comical in their assertions of the truth about this or the truth about that. His discontent with dogmatic statements coincided with the publication, in Latin, of the works of the Greek sceptic, Sextus Empiricus, and particularly Sextus's *Hypotyposes* or *Outlines of Pyrrhonism*. These, and Sextus's *Adversus mathematicos*, were published by Henri Estienne in 1562 and quickly ran through a large number of editions. While the *Outlines*—a text unknown to the Middle Ages and which represented the sole surviving literature of the Pyrrhonian movement—enjoyed popularity, the works of the classical sceptics Diogenes Laertius and Cicero received increased attention and were ransacked, in the wake of Sextus, by all manner of thinkers and theorists, plundered for their novel riches in materials and methods for dealing with the particular problems of the late sixteenth and earlier seventeenth centuries. On his discovery of Sextus's *Outlines* Montaigne ordered a medal to be struck in celebration of the event; and the rafter beams of the study in which he wrote the *Apologie* were carved with maxims and epigrams from Sextus.

One is bound to speculate on the reasons for this great revival of interest in the early Greek sceptical philosophers, who flourished roughly from the fourth century B.C. to about 200 A.D. and of whom Sextus Empiricus himself is, apart from a few fragmentary writings, the only surviving spokesman. Why did its teachings appeal so much to certain kinds of mind in the context of the Reformation? And what would Montaigne have found so exciting about this philosophy? Montaigne's *Apologie* is by no means the only instance of revived scepticism, though to most readers in the period it is the best known example. Cornelius Agrippa von Nettesheim, an early exponent of sceptical arguments who died in 1535, was known in England through a very popular translation of his *De incertitudine et vanitate scientiarum* by James Sanford, printed in 1569. Sebastian Castellio of Basle's *De arte dubitandi* (1563), Francisco Sanchez's *Quod nihil scitur* (1581), Sir Walter Raleigh's *The Skeptick*, and Montaigne's successor Pierre Charron's *De la sagesse* (1601), translated by Samson Lennard in 1608, together with the plethora of pro-sceptical and anti-sceptical polemics which warred back and forth until interrupted by Descartes's formidable answer to Pyrrhonism in the *Discours* (1637), provide ample evidence of the currency and the impact of sceptical arguments.[16] It has even been claimed, though no doubt it is a claim to be taken with a sceptical pinch of salt, that in the seventeenth century 'every reader of any pretensions to cultivation knew Montaigne and Charron intimately, and almost every scholar had read Sextus Empiricus'.[17]

Historians have sometimes argued that the fourth century B.C. signalled the breakdown of Athenian and Alexandrian culture and civilisation. Alexander the Great, pupil of Aristotle, himself successor of Plato to the Platonic Academy, died in 323 B.C., at which the time the founder of scepticism, Pyrrho of Elis, began teaching his sceptical philosophy. It has been suggested that into the vacuum left by this cultural breakdown various 'practical' philosophies — for example, Stoicism and Epicureanism — offering both metaphysical structures and ethical guidance rushed in and enjoyed popularity, and that it was largely as a defence against the claims and counter-claims made by the various philosophies that scepticism (which is not so much a *philosophy* but rather an *attitude*) began to strap on its armour. A recent commentator has suggested that it is not too fanciful to find resemblances between this situation and the situation in sixteenth-century Europe.[18] The contestants in one arena might be the Platonists, the Aristotelians, the Stoics, the Epicureans; in the other arena they might be the Calvinists, the Lutherans, the Roman Catholics.

A concrete example might make the point (*mutatis mutandis*) in another way. One of the Greek sceptics, Aenesidemus (fl. somewhere between the death of Pyrrho in 270 B.C. and the death of Sextus in 210 A.D.) made an important and interesting contribution to enquiry by a criticism of the notion of Indicative Signs. What was meant here was that the sign by which we recognise something is supposed to indicate the essential or real nature of the object signified: for instance, a sense impression can be said to indicate the inner nature of the object causing the impression. But Aenesidemus pointed out that there are all sorts of conflicting claims about what is indicated by the sign, and that we do not really have any certainty. Plato made certain claims about what the 'reality' was that sense impressions indicated; Aristotle made other claims; the Epicureans and Stoics had made still other claims about what the underlying reality indicated by our experiences is. Our inability to settle all these claims showed that we have no criterion for deciding the issue. What we should do, Aenesidemus suggests, is suspend judgement on such indicative signs and get on with the real business of living by talking about the 'reasonable' and the 'probable', and by talking about experience, not what that experience signifies or does not signify. Such a 'sceptical' response does not imply (as the word now in common usage often implies) a systematic negation or an aloof indifference; but it does stress the 'eudaemonistic' stance of sceptical thought, its emphasis on practical wisdom and on happiness in the conduct of life.

If a similar sort of debate is transferred to the sixteenth century, one might imagine the Marburg Colloquy of 1529 between the Lutherans and the Zwinglians on the eucharist, or a Catholic, a Calvinist and a Lutheran disputing over transubstantiation, or the 'rule of faith'. The Reformation dilemma of faith and of religious allegiance involves the question of certitude, and the conflicts of both reformers and of Catholics revolve specifically round the problem of the criterion of truth. R. H. Popkin observes: 'To be able to recognise the true faith, one needed a criterion. But how was one to recognise the true criterion? The innovators and the defenders of the old were both faced with the same problem. They usually met it by attacking their opponents' criterion.'[19] Thus Luther attacked the authority of the Church; the Catholics attacked the criterion of conscience and pointed to the difficulty of establishing any true meaning of Scripture without the Church's guidance. Both sides warned of the intellectual, moral and religious catastrophe that would follow from adopting the other's criterion. And out of this sort of disputation arose the impulse to shrug the shoulders and to suspend judgement, to turn from unverifiable dogma or assertions that were unresolveable because of the absence of any common criterion for judging them, and to follow the lead of common sense and practical experience. The more momentous the issues and the more vigorous the proselytising, the more attractive the sceptical refuge. Sextus had characteristically summed up the Pyrrhonist position, and it needed little imagination to apply the advice to a later age: 'It is sufficient, I think, to live by experience, and without subscribing to beliefs, according to common practices and preconceptions, suspending judgement with respect to those statements that issue from dogmatic subtlety and are furthest removed from the usage of ordinary life.'[20]

There were ancient sceptics who were not in the true sense of the term *skeptikoi*, 'enquirers' or 'investigators', but who held the view, alien to scepticism, that 'nothing can be known'. The problems of such a statement are obvious. The question arises whether the man who says that thinks he can know that he cannot know anything. Or again, the statement 'no statement is true' is self-defeating. Such assertions were made by those who are usually called Academic Sceptics (members of the Sceptical Academy), but who were rejected out of hand by Pyrrho. The Academics asserted that no knowledge was possible; the Pyrrhonians claimed that we were unable to determine whether any knowledge was possible or not because of insufficient data. The Pyrrhonians consequently, and logically, regarded the Academics not as sceptics at all but as dogmatists. In the Renaissance the term 'sceptic' is generally used as equivalent to 'Pyrrhonian'. What the Pyrrhonians emphasised was suspension of judgement. Rather than make judgements, the sceptic seeks to avoid that gesture altogether. Well, not quite altogether. The judgements he necessarily makes (unless he is a vegetable) are grounded in common sense, in the reasonable or probable, which can be used as the basis for his own actions, passions and practical judgements. Rather than make dogmatic assertions or give assent to metaphysical structures, the sceptic would (as both Sextus and Montaigne indicate) try to cultivate a sort of emotional and perceptual sensitivity. As this sensitivity increased so disquiet and doubt (which troubles only when the need for an answer is admitted) and the yearning for objective, total certainty and truth diminish. As Sextus again put it in the *Outlines* (IV): 'Scepticism is the ability to place in antithesis, in any manner whatever, appearances and judgements, and thus — because of the equality of force in the objects and arguments opposed — to come first of all to a suspension of judgement and then to mental tranquillity.' What Sextus offers is a set of maxims or sayings (but not principles or general rules), and it was with some of these that Montaigne had decorated his tower study. Sextus puts forward strategies of this sort: 'arguments and counter-arguments balance each other'; 'to every argument an equal argument is opposed'; 'I do not assert that honey is sweet, but I grant that it appears so', and so on. Donne's *Satyre III* contains, in the Reformation context, a perfect example of a Pyrrhonian motif:

> O, will it boot thee then
> To say a Philip, or a Gregory,
> A Harry, or a Martin taught thee this?
> Is not this excuse for mere contraries,
> Equally strong? cannot both sides say so?

A moment's reflection will indicate how much more appealing sceptical arguments would be to the Catholic than to the Protestant. To have painfully endured, for example, Bunyan's record of his search for his version of certainty is to see how Pyrrhonism would hardly have met the case. The Protestant is not, in the nature of his protest, allowed the luxury of mental tranquillity *except* in the conviction of utter certainty. As Luther put it, if you do not know whether you are saved or not, you are not, and the only recourse is 'to get on your knees, man, and pray'. But to the Catholic mind the sceptical way can be readily invoked as an aid to faith. The Church has in its inherited and divinely sanctioned wisdom all the answers, and there is no need to bother one's head about it all. Tranquillity of mind can come by taking it on trust. This is very similar to the recommendations of Pyrrho, who seems to have taught that since the ambition to find certain knowledge is vain and pointless, the only way to achieve peace of mind is by admitting its futility. He held that since no moral standard (or in the sixteenth-century case, religious standard) can be established by reason the wise man who has his own long-term interests at heart will conform to the laws and conventions he finds around him. So the sceptic is most often a conservative in social and political matters, and the advice 'when in Rome' would appeal to him as very reasonable. If one adds to this the confirming advice of those frequent scriptural warnings issued by Solomon, the wisest of men, (in Proverbs especially), by the author of Ecclesiastes ('vanity, saith the preacher, all is vanity'), by St Paul, and by the Church Fathers against the vanity of wordly knowledge, together with the strong currents of nominalism, mysticism and anti-Aristotelianism in the sixteenth century, a formidable response of distrust of reason as the organ of religious knowledge is apparent.

Of course, Protestantism too had its own in-built antirationalism. With the typical 'puritan' experience of conversion, like that of Saul on the road to Damascus, came a certainty, an unshakeable assurance of God's grace and of salvation. 'The just,' Luther had said, 'shall live by faith'. The implied alternative in Luther's axiom is of course 'and not by works', but it equally militates against that other possible alternative, 'and not by reason'. A tendency to disregard thought and reasoning, and a distinction between God's free grace and all our attempts to storm the kingdom of heaven by intellectual force, is apparent in the Protestant position. But along with this anti-intellectualism, this 'fideism' which is perhaps always a basic component of any truly religious response, there is in Protestantism—as there is in Catholicism—the paradox of the systematisation of beliefs and the structures of dogmatic theology. The just may be saved by faith, even by faith alone, but what they are then invited to master are the *Institutes of the Christian Religion*, the propositions of the Synod of Dort, or the metaphysics of the *Ecclesiastical Polity*, not to mention the reading and analysis of the scriptual texts themselves.

Sceptical arguments in the 'rule of faith' controversy were, however, most often a defence of the Catholic Church—or where they were not, a defence, beyond the particularities of churches, of 'natural religion'. Erasmus, for instance, has a similar voice to that of Montaigne—or rather, Montaigne echoes Erasmus: bursting with 'common sense', perpetually deflating presumption and pretension, and recommending a non-theological, non-dogmatic piety which rests without inappropriate intellectual contortions in the ancient wisdom of the Church. This is the drift of his *Praise of Folly* (1509), just as it is the message of his sceptical defence of faith in his reply to Luther, *De libero arbitrio* (1524). The sceptic in this situation is not, it should be noted, an unbeliever. Both Erasmus and Montaigne were true sons of the Church, though in Erasmus's case somewhat precariously. What the sceptical attitude seeks to maintain is that necessary and sufficient reasons neither have been nor could be discovered to prove that any particular dogma must be true and cannot possibly be false. If he is asked to accept unreservedly some proposition as true, the sceptic cannot in one sense (and granting the variability in the use of the term) 'believe'. If, on the other hand, beliefs are understood in terms of action and behaviour which may in principle be dissociated from commitment to the truth of propositions, the sceptic can be a believer. The sceptic avoids the categories 'true' and 'false', and may still accept beliefs, like any one else, on the grounds of faith. As Montaigne warned: 'Hath God obliged himself not to exceed the bounds of our knowledge?'[21]

In the *Apologie* Montaigne argues for a Christianity which cultivates ignorance in order to believe by faith alone. He cites a favourite text of the *nouveaux Pyrrhoniens*, St Paul's quotation from the Old Testament, 'It is written, I will destroy the wisdom of the wise and will bring to nothing the understanding of the prudent . . . Hath not God made foolish the wisdom of this world?' (I Corinthians, I. 19, 20). The *Apologie* is Montaigne's fullest expression of his reasons for a sceptical approach and its driving force, similar to that of Sextus, is the desire to confound dogmatism and the type of mind that announces its full possession of final, public Truth. Montaigne's manner, reinforcing his point, is explicitly that of a man speaking *in propria persona*, personal, relative, and according to his lights.

To a religion nurtured on faith alone is allied a philosophy of sceptical doubt on the rational level. Using many of the methods furnished by Sextus, Montaigne undermines our pretensions to perfect knowledge and adopts the frequent sceptical strategy of reducing man to what he has in common with animals in order to demonstrate human stupidity and even human inferiority to the beasts. 'Nature' is no longer the laws of nature rationally discoverable by men alone, but the common passions and forces that drive both animals and men. He is pointing his finger at man, the 'naked ape': 'When I am playing with my Cat, who knowes whether she have more sport in dallying with me, than I have in gaming with her? We entertaine one another with mutuall apish trickes. If I have my houre to begin or to refuse, so hath she hers.'[22] He describes nests of swallows, spider's webs, the domestic economy of bees—all of them effects of orderliness and planning and instinctive judgement. Our own problem is that we yearn for everything but what we are equipped by the gifts of nature to achieve.

And if it be so, that he alone, above all other Creatures, hath this liberty of imagination, and this licence of thoughts, which represent unto him, both what is, and what is not and what him pleaseth, falsehood and truth; it is an advantage bought at a very high rate, and whereof he hath little reason to glorie: For thence springs the chiefest source of all the mischiefs that oppresse him, as sinne, sicknesse, irresolution, trouble and despaire.[23]

Montaigne points too to the relativity of all systems of morality and ethics, which vary from country to country, time to time, and even from man to man. He wonders how we can possibly tell which of the vast number of theories put forward to govern our social life is true. He does not find in Nature (as most Renaissance men had found) some common knowledge of some uniform law situated in man's common, natural intelligence, but infinite diversity both in Nature and in men's judgements: 'We see an infinite difference and varietie in this world';[24] 'And never were there two opinions in the world alike, no more than two haires, or two graines. *Diversity is the most universall quality.*'[25] But what, then, of those unassailable monuments, the law of Nature, the 'natural' human reason, the objective, permanent structures of justice and law in men, the state, and in Nature, the echoing proof of the *consensus gentium*? Fables and inventions, Montaigne replies, 'to allow the lawes some certaintie'. 'Lawes', he explains, 'take their authoritie from possession and custom': 'this law thou aleagest is but a municipall law, and thou knowest not what the universal is'.[26]

On the scientific front he accelerates the growing discontent with Aristotelian modes of enquiry by posing a series of problems about the reliability of sense experience. The basis for any knowledge of externals we might have lies in sense experience; but the soul's arbitrary treatment of sense impressions tricks and confuses us; as a possible criterion of knowledge it leads only to a vicious circle or infinite regress until, realising that our knowledge has ultimately no reliable foundation, our only course is, like the ancient Pyrrhonists, to suspend judgement. Montaigne, like his contemporary Francisco Sanchez, whose work was specifically directed against Aristotelianism, attacks the Aristotelian stance which accepts as fundamental that our senses and our rational processes are not subject to doubt. '*Nothing comes to us*', Montaigne contends, '*but falsified and altered by our senses*', and he backs up his argument (as he often does) with some sceptical lines from his favourite Lucretius. Our inability to determine any rational criteria, our inability to know anything but appearances, our lack of any knowledge of first principles, leave us islanded on the rock of faith in the midst of 'doubt's boundless sea'. Donne, it may be recalled, was to pursue a similar kind of questioning in his *Second Anniversarie*:

What hope have wee to know our selves, when wee
Know not the least things which for our use be?
We see in Authors, too stiffe to recant,
A hundred controversies of an Ant;
And yet one watches, starves, freeses and sweats,
To know but Catechismes and Alphabets,
Of unconcerning things, matters of fact;
How others on our Stage their parts did Act;
What Caesar did, yea, what Cicero said.
Why grasse is greene, or why our blood is red,
Are mysteries which none have reached unto . . .

Montaigne indicates in fact our total lack of any certain evidence
of the existence or nature of the real world: 'there is no constant
existence, neither of our being, nor of objects': 'Thou seest but the
order and policie of this little little Cell wherein thou art placed: The
question is, whether thou seest it: His divinity hath an infinit
jurisdiction far beyond that: This peece is nothing in respect of the
whole.'

The impulse behind the *Apologie* is, as has been suggested, a
criticism of dogmatic rational philosophy and theology, a resistance
to, above all, the moral consequences of presuming to have
possession of 'the Truth'. Its target is, in a way, the whole circus of
Reformation disputation. But its scepticism, although apparently
devastating, is not comprehensive; it is mitigated by the very
ambition to reinstate common sense and good judgement and
reasonableness. The scepticism derives from an awareness of
complexity, of persistent variety and diversity. Yet it is a means to an
end. When Montaigne frankly speaks of the importance of reason in
distinguishing between conflicting human pronouncements, it can
only mean that 'reason is helpless—except where it helps; that
Montaigne is a Pyrrhonist—except where he is not'.[27] Montaigne is
certainly not consistent, and is sometimes remarkably un-
Pyrrhonian. Dogmatic opinions and judgements slip out, even in the
very celebration of the sceptic disposition:

This representeth man bare and naked, acknowledging his natural
weaknesse, apt to receive from above some strange power, disfurnished of all
humane knowledge, and so much the more fitte to harbour divine
understanding, disannulling his judgement, that so he may give more place
unto faith: Neither misbeleeving nor establishing any doctrine or opinion
repugnant unto common lawes and observances, humble, obedient,
disciplinable and studious; a sworne enemy to Heresie, and by consequence

exempting himselfe from all vaine and irreligious opinions, invented and brought up by false Sects.[28]

How, we may wonder, do phrases like 'enemy to Heresie' and 'false Sects' marry with this praise of Pyrrhonism? It is obviously a very unsceptical judgement and its tone of confidence is quite inconsistent. I think the answer must be that Montaigne has no taste for revolutions and reformations and that the Pyrrhonism is a tactical weapon to be abandoned if anarchy begins to threaten.

Similarly, although the *Apologie* demonstrates our inability to achieve perfect knowledge and to isolate truth and falsehood, it certainly does not deny that the imperfect (in absolute terms) and conditional sort of knowledge that we can and do possess may be useful. And it is the *use* to which knowledge may be put, rather than its 'truth' or 'universality', which matters most to Montaigne. The instrument of this knowledge is sense and judgement, 'sens pour sa provision', and its chief faculty is the ability to sidestep dogmatic or irreconcileable issues and take hold on what is 'évidemment', what is obviously so. Montaigne is not interested in 'the answer', but in self-knowledge and peace of mind. Through scepticism we are made aware of both our powers and our limitations. The attempt at 'the truth' about God, or goodness, or law, or conscience, or religion, is foolhardy, for one is always up against the relativity of custom, tradition, environment and individuality. If one wishes to discover such a thing as universal reason, then the faculty one must employ is the empirical and not the speculative faculty, for such reason, Montaigne argues, can only be approached experientially, not intellectually. His attack on, for example, the conventional idea of 'natural law' is part of his more general rejection of the 'metaphysical universe' of the Renaissance theologian and philosopher and betrays his fundamental distrust of 'metaphysics' and *a priori* systems of thought. He is led to seek 'truth' in the only place he can find it—in his own judgement and experience:

It is an absolute perfection, and as it were divine for a man to know how to enjoy his being loyally. We seek for other conditions because we understand not the use of ours: and go out of our selves, forsomuch as we know not what abiding there is. *Wee may long enough get upon stilts, for be wee upon them, yet must we goe with our owne legges. And sit we upon the highest throne of the World, yet sit we upon our owne taile.*[29]

On the particular question of the possibility of 'sceptical belief' Montaigne, as we have seen, seems to have the best of all possible worlds, advocating a sceptical *isosothemia*, a use of reason to prepare the ground for faith, and yet in the last resort willing, if reluctantly, to hold to an accusation of falsehood against the disturbers of order. The directions Montaigne's arguments and influence take are on the one hand towards 'fideism, a deliberate anti-rationalism consistent with doctrines of human depravity and of corrupted reason and faculties; and on the other hand towards epicureanism, a 'libertine' approach of 'eat, drink and be merry', 'follow nature', indulge yourself and refrain from asking too many questions. The key to the matter might lie in what is understood by 'reason' and by 'rational', and all sorts of arguments open up about the status of reason in man and its viability in helping us to work out our own salvation. For along with Pyrrhonism march all the strategies for reinstating the human reason and defining the areas where it works or where it does not work, and of mitigating the effects of a rigorous Pyrrhonism.

Montaigne's contemporary, Sebastian Castellio of Basle, may illustrate some of the difficulties. In his work *De haereticis an sint persequendi* (1554) Castellio had sought to attack the claims of religious certainty. Provoked by the execution of Michael Servetus, who was burnt for heresy by the Calvinist Inquisition in Geneva in 1553, Castellio attempted to undermine, through sceptical arguments, the assurance of certitude. If this could be successfully attacked, the grounds of Calvin's belief might be shaken and the right to burn heretics brought seriously into question. Castellio's primary concern (a concern characteristic of one mode of deploying the weapon of scepticism) was with the nature of religious persecution; his basic plea was for a reduction of necessary dogma on the grounds of uncertainty, and by this means to avoid the necessity of inquisitorial executions. But at the same time Castellio wished to preserve the possibility of human knowledge. He was no intoxicated Pyrrhonian, but a strategic sceptic. His own epistemology, as we have it in his final work, *De arte dubitandi* (written in 1563 but never published *in toto*), is founded on sense experience and reason; he accepts the testimony of the senses (with some minor reservations about optical and other illusions) as valid; and he upholds the dignity of human reasoning. Nevertheless, he argued that in matters of religion not everything is wholly certain or uncertain; at different times and with respect to different questions, doubt, belief, ignorance and knowledge are all justified. Specifically theological problems are to be approached in the same way as one approaches the problems which arise in secular life; the grounds of belief are the same as the grounds upon which one believes any principle, and the kinds of evidence one has and the criteria by which the evidence is evaluated are the same in either case. For Castellio the human capacities of sense and judgement and intelligence were the most satisfactory principles, though he was forced to recognise that they are in fact severely limited in their operations. True to his own argument, he confessed that the quest for absolute certainty would have to be abandoned and a quest for 'reasonableness' substituted.[30]

Castellio's position indicates some points concerning the role of scepticism in religious dispute. Scepticism, as employed by Erasmus or Montaigne, may be used to enhance the claims of faith; as employed by Castellio it may be used as a tool in the attack on the theoretical basis of religious persecution. In either case the possibility of workable 'certainty' must be preserved. For without some criterion of truth or of assurance the choices, in terms of natural philosophy and ethics as well as religion, seemed to lie only between a blind 'fideism' or simple dogmatic assertion, and a total and unremitting doubt. Castellio had, with transparent optimism, pressed the need for a convincing criterion of truth, founded neither upon a circular argument of inner persuasion nor upon an authoritarian fiat: 'It will be necessary to search for a principle according to which the truth will be so manifest, so well recognised by all, that no force in the universe, that no probability, can ever make the alternative possible.'[31] It was precisely this principle for which Lord Herbert was to seek in *De veritate* in which, in a flamboyant if precarious sort of way, he claimed to have found.

De veritate and some responses

In many important respects the arguments of Montaigne represent the enemy against which Lord Herbert contended. At the same time, the relationship between Montaigne's thought and Herbert's (and by relationship here I mean not the direct 'influence' of one upon the other, but the relationship that exists between two men exploring the same problems within fifty years of each other), this relationship is fraught with complication and paradox. But before discussing Herbert's specific contribution to the debate it is helpful to view briefly the modifications which the sceptical approach underwent in the years between the *Apologie* and the appearance of the 'metaphysical' solutions to the problem of Pyrrhonism of Descartes and, later in the century, of Spinoza—the more so since the key figures in this development are the critics and correspondents of both Descartes and Lord Herbert, Pierre Gassendi (1592–1655) and Marin Mersenne (1588–1648).

Gassendi began his philosophic career as an 'orthodox' sceptic influenced by his reading of the new edition of Sextus Empiricus published in 1621, and by the writings of Montaigne and Montaigne's 'pupil' Pierre Charron. His *Exercitationes paradoxicae adversus Aristoteleos* (1624) was the first instalment of a sceptical attack on those who claim knowledge of the nature of things. What they fail to see is that all we actually ever do know, or can know, are appearances. The second, unfinished, book of the *Exercitationes*, published a little later, attacks Aristotelianism generally and points out, once more, that although we can tell how things seem to us we cannot know how they are in themselves. But Gassendi increasingly found the negative and defeatist attitude of thoroughgoing scepticism unsatisfactory. In his *Syntagma philosophicum logica*[32] he develops further a more constructive scepticism suggested by Marin Mersenne.

Mersenne spent much of his time and influence in encouraging all the leading workers in the 'new philosophy', including Galileo, Herbert of Cherbury and Hobbes besides Gassendi and Descartes. It was probably Mersenne who made the French translation of *De veritate* that appeared in 1639 and did so much to further familiarity with Herbert's thinking—though Herbert himself, unlike Mersenne, displays virtually no active interest in the new sciences of physics and mathematics. Mersenne's *La Vérité des sciences, contre les Sceptiques ou Pyrrhoniens* (1625) capitulates to Pyrrhonism and acquiesces in the view that philosophically speaking, there appear to be no possible refutations of the sceptical arguments pointing to the futility of the search for absolute human knowledge. But, Mersenne insists, there is enormous scope for knowledge at a lower level, knowledge of appearances and events, convincing and probable truths about experience. Some things, after all, are not open to doubt: for example, 'the whole is greater than the part', or the statement 'there is a world', or the logical truth that 'it is not possible for the same thing to both have and not have the same property' (though, as Kant was to show, these propositions are of very different kinds). If one is reasonable one will realise that something *is* known. Mersenne did not expect this scientific, mathematical, or logical kind of knowledge to reveal ultimate reality, nor need it be dependent upon some particular metaphysical 'truths' about the nature of the universe. What he advocates, as a more constructive approach to the problem, is a positivistic, pragmatic conception of 'knowledge'.

Such a position is of course very much like Bacon's moderated scepticism. The search for the essence of things, for formal causes of particular substances, is put aside as too difficult. Before they can ever be discovered one must proceed as it were adjectivally. In the *De augmentis scientiarum* Bacon says: 'to enquire the form of lion, of an oak, of gold, nay even of water or air, is a vain pursuit; but to enquire the form of dense, rare, hot, cold, heavy, light, tangible, pneumatic, volatile, fixed, and the like . . . constitutes and defines that part of Metaphysics of which we are now enquiring.'[33] His basic plea, rather like Montaigne's, is that we simply do not know enough to proceed in any other way. The ambition here of men of science like Gassendi, Mersenne and Bacon is (having admitted for logical convenience the radical sceptical argument) towards scientific utility and the investigation, upon principles of observation and common sense, of effects, not first causes.

And Gassendi, encouraged by his own interest in the 'new science', adopted this constructive attitude, a compromise between scepticism and dogmatism. In the *Syntagma logica* he argues that sceptical quibbles about the value and foundation of reasoning are unimportant; the important thing is that we can discover how to reason correctly by experience and verification, so that we can arrive at certain principles which are sufficiently evident for a basis of our inferences. Nevertheless, when Gassendi was confronted with a metaphysical picture of the universe the Pyrrhonian basis of his thought came out sharply as an avowal of complete epistemological scepticism; hence, when he came to consider the views of Descartes, or even the mathematical physicists (whom he took to be Platonists or Pythagoreans), he advocated nothing but scepticism in its full rigour about the world beyond appearances. His earliest work, directed against Aristotle, had concluded with the words *nihil sciri*—the answer to Montaigne's 'Que sais-je?' made explicit. And in Herbert of Cherbury's *De veritate* Gassendi was confronted with just such a metaphysical picture.

By the date of Gassendi's first publication in 1624 (which marked also the first printing of *De veritate*) philosophical answers to the 'nouveau Pyrrhonisme' were beginning to appear in large numbers. Among them were refutations based on the principles of Aristotelian philosophy (principles which Pyrrhonism had already severely atttacked); refutations, like that of Mersenne, which admit the sceptical argument and then seek to mitigate the implications of total scepticism; and refutations such as those of Lord Herbert and subsequently of Descartes which attempt to construct a new system of philosophy to meet the challenge. *De veritate* is, then, an attempt at a final answer to the 'crise pyrrhonienne' through the assertion, made as forcefully as possible, of the validity of human knowledge and the possibility of certainty in matters not merely of scientific fact but on all fronts, including religion. It is an affirmation of the somewhat wistful remark of Montaigne himself in the *Apologie* that 'Truth ought to have a like and universal visage throughout the world'. Herbert assumed that what was needed to rout the sceptics was a definition of truth, a suitable criterion of truth, and a methodology for its discovery; and this object determines the form of his treatise. His contribution is by any standards a brave one—even if its bravery, like its author's duelling propensity, may be several parts rashness and its actual achievement in meeting the sceptics, like the much-vaunted duels, more and more doubtful.

With a customary show of independence of mind Herbert insists that he belongs to neither faction; that is, he agrees neither with those who say we can know everything nor with those who say we can know nothing, but anticipates Mersenne's position by pointing out that 'there are some things which can be known'. He declares that

there has always existed at every period an incongruous and perverse class of professors who expounded with equal zeal and confidence both these doctrines at the same time; that we can know everything, and that we can know nothing. The latter group say that truth lies hidden in a well, that we know one thing only, namely that we know nothing; and utter a hundred idle paradoxes of the same character, with the hope of acquiring a reputation for profundity. The former party, on the other hand, maintain with remarkable daring that the principles of the Universe can be deduced from the principles of thought, in spite of the fact that these refer only to us. They proclaim, with unaccountable disregard for truth, that there is nothing which is not open to their understanding.[34]

Such a declaration is immediately worthy of comment. It bears a

remarkable similarity to Bacon's opening paragraph of the preface
to the *Novum organum*—a similarity resulting no doubt from the
clarity of the issue:

The more ancient of the Greeks (whose writings are lost) took up with better
judgement a position between these two extremes,—between the
presumption of pronouncing on everything, and the despair of
comprehending anything; and though frequently and bitterly complaining
of the difficulties of enquiry and the obscurity of things, and like impatient
horses champing at the bit, they did not the less follow up their object and
engage with Nature; thinking (it seems) this very question,—viz. whether or
not anything can be known,—was to be settled not by arguing, but by
trying. And yet they too, trusting entirely to the force of their
understanding, applied no rule, but made everything turn upon hard
thinking and perpetual working and exercise of the mind.[35]

Bacon's approach to the question 'whether or not anything can be
known' is a pragmatic one, to be settled 'not by arguing but by
trying'; and part of his task was the narrowing down of the area of
investigation to what may be 'tried', to scrutiny of things themselves.
Bacon and Herbert here, in their resistance to both radical
scepticism and epistemological over-optimism—like perhaps that of
the Florentine Neoplatonist Marsilio Ficino, who without hesitation
could answer the question 'whether or not the intellect can attain a
clear understanding of everything which is included under being'
with a resounding 'Certainly it can'[36]—appear to have a good deal in
common. But Herbert's views, on the most fundamental points,
depart radically from Bacon's. Herbert in fact has more in common
than he admits with those who maintain that 'the principles of the
Universe can be deduced from the principles of thought', for he
proceeds to lay down his theory of truth in terms which Bacon would
have been forced to designate a 'mere exercise and talent of
disputation'.

The discussion begins formally with seven propositions regarding
truth: (1) Truth exists, (2) This truth is as eternal or as ancient as
things themselves, (3) This truth is everywhere, (4) This truth
reveals itself, (5) There are as many truths as there are differences of
things, (6) The differences of things are recognised in virtue of our
innate powers or faculties, and (7) There is a truth of all these
truths.[37] These opening axioms maintain that truth is both an
intuition and that it is a relation, and they illustrate at once
Herbert's main belief that a true apprehension is a *conformatio*: truth
is a conditional conformity (and Herbert is following scholastic

usage) between objects and our faculties, and also a direct conformity between our minds and the fundamental notions or ideas. He presents a working definition: a successful relationship with an object, in which the appropriate faculty is directed towards its proper object, according to fitting conditions, is truth. Herbert proceeds thus:

> It is clear . . . that every truth can be analysed into truth of thing, truth of appearance, truth of concept, and truth of intellect. Now the truth of thing is the inherent conformity of the thing itself, or that ground in virtue of which everything remains constant with itself. The truth of appearance consists in the conditional conformity with the thing. The truth of concept is the conditional between our subjective faculties and the thing as it appears. The truth of intellect consists of the right conformity between all the preceding conformities. All truth according to this doctrine consists of conformity. And since all conformity consists of relation, it follows that all instances of truth will be relations, or aptitudes realised in acts, that is in perception.

To this he adds the warning: 'No other way of describing truth is adequate'.[38]

He then distinguishes further these four classes of knowledge and pursues a detailed analysis of the conditions necessary for the perception of each type.[39] *Veritas rei* is defined as the truth of a thing as it is, independent of all conditions; yet Herbert immediately attaches to it a number of conditions: it must be in conformity with our cognitive capacity, it must be of a certain size (we cannot, for example, know atoms), it must possess *differentiae* or distinguishing marks, and it must be related to an inner faculty. *Veritas apparentiae* relates to the sensible images of things—the *species sensibilis* of the Schoolmen. After discussing *veritas conceptus*, which is dependent on unimpaired sense organs, and *veritas intellectus*, which knits together the preceding truths into a composite whole, Herbert specifies the four main divisions of the human faculties. According to the theory that every kind of cognition corresponds to an item in reality, the cognitive forms are called 'faculties', in the sense of a capacity of the mind.

The four faculties are (1) Natural Instinct, and its proper object of concern, eternal blessedness;[40] (2) Internal Senses, the chief among them being 'conscience', including in a manner all the rest, whose proper object is the good—and since eternal blessedness is the ultimate good, their object is identified with that of Natural Instinct;[41] (3) External Senses, that is, the generally recognised five senses;[42] (4) the *discursus*, or the faculty of logical enquiry and reasoning.[43] For every object there is a faculty. When a faculty is in conformity with its object, a *sensus* occurs, and we have apprehended truth. In other words, when a proper object of knowledge is perceived under the proper conditions so that a true appearance can be obtained, we are able, under specifiable conditions, to obtain a true concept of the thing.

But there still remains the problem of the criterion of truth. Having by means of Herbert's rather elaborate system discovered a method of establishing accurate appearances of true concepts, how do we know that they are in fact true, and that we are not profoundly deceived? Herbert's epistemology, in one of its aspects, is based upon a theory which asserts that truth consists in the correspondence of judgements and objects. But if this is so, the criteria of truth are criteria of whether this relation of correspondence actually holds; the terms of the relation cannot themselves provide the criteria. Hence there must be something outside either the faculties of perception (including the logical faculty or *discursus*) or things themselves which will provide the test of truth. As the long-sought criterion for judging the truth of our most reliable information, Herbert offers the theory of Common Notions. He finds the 'something outside' either perception of things or things themselves in the intellect, whose highest faculty of God-given Natural Instinct apprehends truth independently of perception. And in making this claim Herbert steps at once outside the limits of empirical enquiry and into the realm of metaphysics.

His conception of Common Notions is derived chiefly from Cicero and his Stoic authorities. Herbert is of course drawing on a commonplace of Renaissance humanism; whether the specific terms is *vivere secundum naturam*, the Law of Nature, *recta ratio, synderesis*, the Law of Reason, the Light of Nature, conscience, Natural Instinct or Common Notion, the primary significance of the approach is always retained as the belief that there is within man an innate capacity for comprehending truth. Herbert appears blandly to ignore Montaigne's devastating objections, and finds in the theory the principle by which, in Castellio's words, 'the truth will be so manifest, so well recognised by all, that no force in the universe, that no probability, can ever make the alternative possible'. He proceeds to explain how the Common Notions may be distinguished. They are, he says, assumed prior to reflection and experience; they cannot be derived from further principles; whatever imbeciles and sceptics may say to the contrary, they are universally acknowledged; they are certain; they are necessary to our preservation and salvation; and they are in immediate conformity with their objects, that is, they are intuitively grasped.[44] Common Notions are, in terms of his general theory of correspondence, conformities between Natural Instinct in man and its spiritual objects.

Herbert illustrates the application of Common Notions to a particular problem in the structurally unnecessary but historically important outline of the celebrated five common religious notions: that there is a God, that he is to be worshipped, that virtue and piety are the chief parts of worship, that we should repent of our sins, and that there is reward or punishment after this life.[45] These propositions are true because such beliefs have maintained among all men at all times and in all places, regardless of race or creed, however much the beliefs may have been obscured by later distortions and accretions.

Mention must be made of the much-boasted *Zetetica*. When in difficulties about a particular case the reader is told that he can find the solution codified in the Zetetics; equally, when Herbert is in difficulties he makes a gesture towards *nostra Zetetica*. The discursive reason is, Herbert says, the least useful of the faculties; *inter omnes Facultates erroribus maxime obnoxium*.[46] It is superfluous where a Common Notion is available or where the inner or outer *sensus* provide a judgement. It is the source of all error and folly. But it has its uses. It is the faculty employed when we draw conclusions from general principles and distinguish, with the help of the Zetetics, what is true from what is false in logical propositions.

The work concludes with a short but highly provocative discussion of revelation, of the probable, the possible and the false.[47]

If one extracts, as in this brief account, some of the threads from the varied sources and influences that mingle in disorder throughout *De veritate*, it is possible to regard it as yet another of the traditional answers to the sceptical crisis. Herbert shares with the Aristotelians the view that there are proper conditions either for perception or reasoning and that we have faculties, which, when operating properly under these conditions, are able to give us true knowledge. The sceptical sort of evidence discrediting sense and reason is either false or else deals with abnormal conditions and corrupted faculties. But what this Aristotelian kind of reply failed, or refused, to recognise was that the Pyrrhonists were challenging the reliability of our faculties even under the best possible conditions, and were denying the very criteria Aristotle had laid down for deciding when our faculties are functioning properly. Herbert too refuses to recognise this objection. Of course, these shortcomings of *De veritate* were seized on by Gassendi and by Descartes, and both pointed out—though with differing emphases—how far short Herbert had fallen of meeting the sceptical challenge.

Gassendi wrote (but apparently never sent) a letter to Herbert himself, couched in the politest terms.[48] He flatters Herbert by calling him 'England's treasure' who has arisen to succeed Francis Bacon, but goes on to explain firmly how Herbert has failed to refute scepticism. All *De veritate* shows us is more about the conditions under which truth appears to us, not more about truth itself. In a letter to their mutual friend Elias Diodati, to whom Herbert had given a copy of *De veritate* for transmission to Gassendi,[49] he is more blunt. Herbert's scheme appeared to him a maze of confusion which accomplished very little. If the criterion of truth is to be the Common Notions (and the Pyrrhonists had already shown that every fundamental belief had been contested by someone), and if each person is convinced of this criterion by his own natural instinct and interior faculties, how do we account for variety of opinion? Each man will declare the other 'n'est point sain et entier' and each will believe this on the basis of his own truths of intellect. Herbert himself might well have brushed this argument aside by asserting that the controversialists must have been madmen; but Gassendi anticipates this response by asking how does one tell who is mad and who is not without begging the whole question at issue? Gassendi's criticisms are coloured in part by his own strongly Pyrrhonist inclinations. *De veritate* was an indefensible piece of dogmatism. 'La vérité, selon mon jugement, est très cachée aux yeux des hommes et Monsr Herbert me semble estre allé un peu bien viste et avoir en un peu trop bonne opinion de son fait quand il a condamné si deshonnestement les raisonnemens des Sceptiques.'[50]

Descartes was more sympathetic to Herbert's aim of refuting scepticism: *De veritate*, Descartes wrote to Mersenne, deals with 'un suiet auquel i'ay travaillé toute ma vie'; but Herbert 'tient un chemin fort different que celuy que i'ay suivi'.[51] For whereas Herbert was trying to find out what truth is, Descartes never entertained any doubts; truth is 'une notion si transcendentalement claire, qu'il est impossible d'ignorer'. But because of his greater sympathy he was perhaps more acutely aware of Herbert's inadequacies. Descartes argues in this letter that if one did not antecendently know what truth is there would be no possible way of discovering it, for how could one know that what one had discovered was true? If we wished to agree that Herbert's results were true, we would have to employ a criterion of truth in order to recognise that the method of *De veritate* was a method for discovering or measuring truth. You cannot know the nature of truth simply by defining it, for in order to know that the definition is true one would have to know what truth is; and if one already knew, then the whole business was pointless. Montaigne had already sounded the warning to such criterion arguments: 'To judge of the appearances that we receive of subjects, we had need have use of a judicatorie instrument: to verifie this instrument, we should have demonstration; and to approve demonstration, an instrument; thus we are ever turning round . . .'[52] As comment on Herbert's avowed method—that is, where Herbert says: 'In the first place, then, I shall proceed to examine truth itself, and in the second place, assertions which claim to be true, just as scales are tested before goods are weighed out; for unless the scales are accurate, what we measure by them will also fail to be exact'[53]—Descartes remarks that Herbert has many intricate measuring devices but he cannot tell what they are measuring. He notes, however, that although he may not agree with all Herbert's conclusions, 'ie ne laisse pas de l'estimer beaucoup au dessus des esprits ordinaires'.

Descartes himself took the step which Bacon and the empiricists, and Lord Herbert, were unwilling to take. He saw that to attain any real assurance complete doubt must be carried to its logical conclusion. The most radical and devastating sceptical possibilities must be considered, the possibility not only that our sense information is deceptive or illusory, but also that our faculties themselves may be no more than a chaos of error. He inflamed the fever of doubt to the highest pitch. His approach has been described as a progression 'from the partial Pyrrhonism of the dream hypothesis, doubting the reality of our knowledge, to the total Pyrrhonism of the demon hypothesis, doubting the reliability of our rational faculties', until 'we finally discover the *cogito*, a truth so subjectively certain that *we* are incapable of doubting it at all'.[54] Descartes leads us further and further back to what for him is the only and irreducible criterion we possess, ourselves. We are not in a position to claim that we do not exist. Herbert's problem, so

Descartes implies, was that he had no *cogito* as a criterion of truth, and his theory of Common Notions was, as a rebuff of scepticism, less than adequate.

Descartes had read—or had tried to read—the tortuous Latin text of *De veritate*. By the time he had received and studied the French translation of 1639, possibly made by Mersenne and which Descartes admitted he found much easier going, he had recently published the *Discours de la méthode* (1637) and was about to begin writing his *Méditations*, which appeared in 1641.[55] The *Méditations* have an apologetic aim, not unlike Herbert's, and the epistemology of the *Discours*, though more sophisticated and elegant than Herbert's confused structure, is, like Herbert's based on innate ideas of a divine origin. In his dedication of the *Méditations* to the doctors of the Sorbonne Descartes clearly states that the aim of the work is to prove by demonstration the preambles of faith in order to convince unbelievers (though it was of course meant at the same time to lay the ground for his physics).[56] Descartes's apologia, also like Herbert's, stops short of specifying particular Christian doctrines. One motive was undoubtedly his awareness that Catholic theology was a highly specialised province; but another was his lifelong anxiety about being involved in theological disputes. When he first read *De veritate* Descartes was rather uncomfortable, as he confided both to Mersenne and Samuel Hartlib, about the way in which Herbert was prepared to gather up religion with metaphysics and epistemology.[57] But when, in 1639, Mersenne sent him the French translation his judgement, though cautious, was more favourable: 'il a plusieurs maximes qui me semblent si pieuses et si conformes au sens commun, que je souhaite qu'elles puissent estre approuvées par la théologie orthodoxe.'[58] Later, Descartes made Herbert a gift of a first edition of the *Méditations*, and Herbert in his turn began an English translation of the *Discours de la méthode*.[59]

Mersenne's relationship with Herbert is a fascinating one, and will be discussed in more detail later. Mersenne's involvement in the religious and philosophical affairs of the mid seventeenth century was profound and extensive, and his chief role was that of an indefatigable publicist on behalf of new learning and, particularly as he got older, on behalf of religious peace and the cause of religious reunion. In this cause he made considerable use of Herbert's writings. For the moment we are concerned with criticisms of the method and substance of *De veritate*, on which question Mersenne, though he conveyed reports, texts, letters and opinions from one to another, has little that is specific to say. The response of Gassendi indicates how, within its own terms of reference of a scientific materialism Herbert appears as the very opposite of sceptical, whereas to others whose terms of reference are religious orthodoxy he may appear as a thorough-going sceptic. There is obviously a certain ambiguity in the term 'sceptic' depending on the area of doubt, so that the paradox can easily arise of a man, like Herbert, seeking to refute philosophical scepticism and in turn being regarded as himself a sceptic. But doubt about the validity and proper persuasive power of received customs, traditions or 'authoritative' pronouncements is by no means the same thing as doubt about the capacities of human reason and the possibility of achieving certain knowledge. The point is important, since Herbert of Cherbury is usually regarded as in some sense a 'sceptic', by which it is meant that he is critical of tradition and authority, especially in matters of religious organisation. This particular judgement is quite accurate, as long as it does not imply that Herbert has philosophical doubts about the possibility of certainty. Where the Pyrrhonian may be a radical doubter and at the same time an acquiescent, obedient conservative, the proclaimer of certainties may be a cavalier disrupter of order and show a scant and 'sceptical' regard for customs and institutions. Herbert's specific scepticism about the validity of religious authoritarianism, with all its conflicting injunctions, is precisely the point of departure for a theory of knowledge which upholds the power and utility of the human mind.

Montaigne's position, perhaps contrary to appearances, is not in fact so very dissimilar, though its outcome is different. The *Apologie* is a Pyrrhonian manifesto; but it is also deeply rooted in common sense. A recent writer says: 'As a therapeutic public document the *Apologie* is a plea for common sense—a plea for using our heads to save our hides'.[60] The use to which our heads (that is, our instinctive reason and common sense) are to be put is, for Montaigne, towards self-knowledge and contentment. That truth of self-experience is possible is both a mitigation of scepticism and the key to the use Montaigne makes of it, for from scepticism emerges Montaigne's own view of the *proper* power and utility of the mind. The ambition is as it were conservatively eirenic, and Pyrrhonism has an unrivalled facility for revealing the absurdities of conflicting truth-claims. Yet it is quite possible to share in Montaign's eirenic motive without necessarily turning aside to self-study and individualistic withdrawal. Bacon or Herbert or Descartes may be regarded as being equally concerned with reunion and achieving an end to philosophical and religious strife. But Descartes, for all his *cogito ergo sum*, cannot remain in an 'epicurean' posture. From the inward criterion he goes out once more in the armour of rationalism. Montaigne appears content to suspend judgement, to avoid making claims about truth; Descartes, while exhibiting an initial and equally tactical doubt as restless and as penetrating as Montaigne's, speaks not in terms of the suspension of judgement but in terms of adverse judgements, error, falsity. Similarly Herbert, like Descartes, discourses freely on error and goes about finding the truth (though in doing so he involves himself, as will be pointed out, in an inconsistency). If Montaigne's scepticism derives from his appreciation of the complexity of the issues, Herbert's narrower scepticism indicates a kind of simplicity. His criterion is not the *cogito* but the theory of Common Notions and Natural Instinct, and what scepticism he exhibits is like Montaigne's only in so far as it is as vigorously resistant to religious dogmatism and absolutism. And Herbert is particularly interesting in the way he seems to fall between Montaigne's position and Descartes's. The questions Herbert explores are Descartes's: he seeks for method, he speaks of truth and error, he appeals to clarity and unanimity of convinction; but equally his motives are like Montaigne's, seeking a critique of the moral code of a rigoristic dogmatism by means of a sceptical *isosothemia* directed against what Sir Thomas Browne was to call 'the Goliah and Giant of Authority', and resting in a theory of common sense or 'Natural Instinct' which, as we shall explore it further, is remarkably like Montaigne's insistence on 'jugement', the power to preserve our being, and its instrument the 'sens natural'.

Yet Herbert is found wanting both from Montaigne's point of view and from Descartes's. We have already noted the latter's objections. Montaigne's point is that yearnings for 'truth', for metaphysical structures that are stuffed with imaginings, make us forget our proper concern for self-preservation, tranquillity, security, the good life, the 'natural' life. While Herbert has a very great deal to say in *De veritate* about Natural Instinct in man and the universe and about the instinct for self-preservation (which he regards as a kind of ontological datum), he is committed too to those metaphysical structures and imaginings which Montaigne (and Bacon, for different reasons) found so pointless. The duality here is suggestive. Walpole's description of Herbert as Plato and Quixote may come to mind. The speculative, straining *De veritate*, revealing at times the barely concealed impatience and frustration of a philosopher trying to shore up a Universal Science, exists in curious counterpoint with the 'epicurean' autobiography for whose subject, speaking with all the quirkiness of self-absorption, 'truth' is relative only to ego and circumstance.

Notes to Chapter II

1 *D.V.*, p. 8; Carré, p. 83.
2 *D.V.*, p. a3; Carré, p. 71.
3 *Ibid.*
4 'Preface: To the Candid Reader', *D.V.*, p. a3v; Carré, p. 72.
5 *D.V.*, p. 3; Carré, p. 77.
6 *D.V.*, p. a3v; Carré, pp. 72–3.
7 Sir Thomas Overbury, *Miscellaneous Works*, ed. E. F. Rimbault, London, 1886, *Characters*, p. 89.
8 *D.V.*, p. 52; Carré, p. 131.
9 See Fordyce and Knox.
10 Bruno, *De l'infinito universo e mondi*, dial. 3, in Arthur Livingstone's translation in *The Age of Adventure*, ed. Giorgio de Santillana, New York, 1956, pp. 260–8. See also D. W. Singer, *Giordano Bruno, His Life and Thought*, New York, 1950, p. 102.
11 Aquinas, *De anima*, commentary I, lect. i. In *Philosophical Texts*, ed. T. Gilby, Oxford, 1951, p. 195.
12 *Ockham: Studies and Selections*, trans. Stephen Chak, Tornay, Ill., 1938.
13 See *The Renaissance Philosophy of Man*, ed. E. Cassirer, P.O. Kristeller and J. H. Randall, Chicago, Ill., 1948, p. 10.
14 Cited by Louis I. Bredvold, *The Intellectual Milieu of John Dryden*, Ann Arbor, Mich., 1934, repr. 1956, p. 79.
15 Quoted in C. C. J. Webb, *Studies in the History of Natural Theology*, Oxford, 1915, p. 296.
16 See especially R. H. Popkin, *History of Scepticism from Erasmus to Descartes*, Assen, 1960. Popkin's survey has proved very useful in determining Herbert's relation to contemporary sceptical arguments.
17 Louis I. Bredvold, *loc. cit.*, p. 15.
18 See Philip P. Hallie, *Scepticism, Man and God: Selections from the Major Writings of Sextus Empiricus*, Weslyan University Press, Middletown, Conn., 1964, pp. 7–8.
19 R. H. Popkin, *loc. cit.*, p. 4.

20 Sextus, *Outlines of Pyrrhonism*, II, 246, ed. and trans. R. G. Bury, Loeb Classical Library, 1933–49.

21 *Apologie*, in *Essayes*, trans. John Florio, Everyman edition, vol. II, p. 229. For a discussion of scepticism and belief, see Arne Naess, *Scepticism*, London, 1968, pp. 47–8.

22 *Apologie*, p. 142.

23 *Apologie*, p. 151.

24 *Apologie*, p. 231.

25 *Essayes*, 'Of the Resemblance between Children and their Fathers', vol. II, p. 523.

26 *Apologie*, p. 301.

27 Donald M. Frame, *Montaigne's Discovery of Man: The Humanization of a Humanist*, New York, 1955, p. 76.

28 *Apologie*, pp. 208–9.

29 *Essayes*, 'Of Experience', vol. III, p. 386.

30 Castellio's *De haereticis an sint persequendi*, 1554, was published pseudonymously and with a false place name. French translation, *Traité des hérétiques, 1554*, ed. A. Olivet, Geneva, 1913; modern English translation with introduction by R. H. Bainton, *Concerning Heretics*, New York, 1935. *De arte dubitandi et confitendi, ignorandi et sciendi* may be read in *Reale Accademia d'Italia, Studi e Documenti*, VII, ed. D. Cantimori and E. Fiest, Rome, 1937, pp. 307–403. On Castellio's use of 'reason' see especially pp. 363f. The work has been translated as *De l'art de doubter et de croire, d'ignorer et de savoir* by Charles Baudouin, Geneva–Paris, 1953.

31 *De arte dubitandi*, ed. Cantimori and Fiest, p. 357.

32 Gassendi, *Opera omnia*, ed. L. Anisson and J. B. Devenet, 6 vols, Lyons, 1658. *Syntagma* in vols I and II.

33 In *Works*, ed. Spedding, Ellis and Heath, 15 vols, London, 1861, VIII, pp. 505–6. See also *Advancement of Learning*, *Works*, V, p. 220.

34 *D.V.*, p. 2; Carré, p. 76.

35 *Novum organum*, in *Works*, VIII, pp. 59–60.

36 Ficino, 'Five Questions Concerning the Mind', trans. J. L. Burroughs, in *The Renaisssance Philosophy of Man*, loc. cit., p. 199.

37 *D.V.*, pp. 8–13; Carré, pp. 83–9. Cf. a similar list given by Aquinas, *Quaestiones disputatae*, I, art. i.

38 *D.V.*, pp. 12–13; Carré, p. 88.

39 *D.V.*, pp. 13–30; Carré, pp. 90–107.

40 *D.V.*, pp. 37–74; Carré, pp. 115–45.

41 *D.V*, pp. 75–127; Carré, pp. 146–207.

42 *D.V.*, pp. 128–51; Carré, pp. 208–31.

43 *D.V.*, pp. 151–207; Carré, pp. 232–88.

44 *D.V.*, pp. 60–1; Carré, pp. 139–41.

45 *D.V.*, pp. 208–26; Carré, pp. 289–307.

46 *D.V.*, p. 151; Carré, p. 232.

47 *D.V.*, pp. 226–50; Carré, pp. 308–34.

48 Gassendi, '*Ad Librum D. Edoardi Herberti Angli, De Veritate, Epistola*', in *Opera omnia*, III, pp. 411–19.

49 Sidney Lee mistakenly claimed that 'Herbert presented a copy of the *De*

veritate to Charles Diodati, Milton's friend' (*Autobiography*, London, 1886, p. 1v). The intermediary was in fact the diplomat Elias Diodati, a distant cousin of the English family.

50 Gassendi, letter to Diodati, 29 August, 1639. Printed in *Correspondance du P. Marin Mersenne*, ed. C. de Waard, Paris, 1955, IV, p. 337.

51 Descartes, letter to Mersenne, 16 October, 1639. In Descartes, *Oeuvres*, ed. Adam and Tannery, II, 'Correspondance', Paris, 1898, pp. 596–9.

52 *Apologie*, p. 322.

53 *D.V.*, p. 1; Carré, pp. 75–6.

54 R. H. Popkin, *loc. cit.*, p. 194.

55 See Henri Gouhier, *La Pensée religieuse de Descartes*, Paris, 1924, p. 100.

56 See *Meditationes*, Paris, 1641, in Descartes, *Oeuvres, loc. cit.*, VII, Paris, 1904, pp. 1–4.

57 Letter from Descartes to Mersenne, 27 August 1639, in *Correspondance du P. Marin Mersenne*, VIII, pp. 495–6; Descartes to J. W. Eding, for Hartlib, April or May 1638, *ibid.*, VII, pp. 435–6.

58 Letter to Mersenne, 16 October 1639.

59 See Fordyce and Knox, pp. 53f; and Rossi, II, p. 537.

60 Philip P. Hallie, *The Scar of Montaigne: An Essay in Personal Philosophy*, Weslyan University Press, Middletown, Conn., 1966, p. 53.

III
THE STRATEGY OF TRUTH

Reason in it selfe confounded,
Saw Division grow together,
To themselves yet either neither,
Simple were so well compounded.

That it cried, how true a twaine,
Seemeth this concordant one,
Love hath Reason, Reason none,
If what parts, can so remain.

Shakespeare, The Phoenix and the Turtle

Reason and intuition

The arguments with which Descartes confounded scepticism are
'rationalistic' in the sense of falling back upon the very core of being,
of existing, and the evidence, or the expression, of that existence in
thought and self-consciousness. The emphasis is subjective rather
than empirical. The criterion of truth, the evidence of certainty, is
simply that we know something, that we think it. Truth is
dependent, in Descartes's celebrated phrase, upon 'clear and
distinct ideas'. If the rationalist says that the criterion of truth or of
certainty is that we should have a clear and distinct idea, an
intuition that, for example, the sum of five is implied in the addition
of two and three, or that God exists, then it follows that the logical,
weighing-and-measuring faculty is only second best to this intuition.
In the face of this approach the problem of assessing the scales and
balances, and hence the problem of the infinite regress, is rendered
innocuous. Even the empirical Locke was to comment on sceptical
doubt and the criterion problem by pointing out that to demand a
criterion for the criterion would lead to a cul-de-sac which only the
intuitive nature of knowledge can prevent, for, he says dryly,

intuitive knowledge neither requires nor admits any proof, one part of it
more than another. He that will suppose it does, takes away the foundation
of all knowledge and certainty: and he that needs any proof to make him
certain, and give his assent to this proposition, that two are equal to two,
will also have need of proof to make him admit, that what is, is.[1]

The gesture towards 'internal principles' or 'congenite notices' or
'common notions' as proof of a thing's truth is a frequent rationalist

posture on the question of knowledge and how it is acquired—and such a gesture involves a disparagement of the faculty of comparing, analysing, evaluating. When Descartes says, for example, that the idea of God is 'implied' in the human mind in the same manner 'in which the equality of its three angles to two right angles is implied in the idea of a triangle'[2], he is, fundamentally, asserting that it is true because I think so, because I am persuaded by the clarity and distinctness of my idea of it being so, and this persuasion is adequate because my thought is the evidence of my existence. Such knowledge is dependent upon the presence in the mind of ideas, or aptitudes, which are there prior to experience, reflection, and logical thought or demonstration. Where the empiricist says that all knowledge comes from experience and reflection, the rationalist argues that we only understand experience because we have an innate and prior capacity in the mind. The distinction might be put in another way by speaking of two different conceptions of truth—the first, the empirical, which regards truth as a relation, and certainty a matter of correct classification, measurement, experiment, reflection; the second, the rationalistic, regards truth as an intuition adequately present in the mind, though it has of course to be extracted; the validity of this knowledge is dependent upon the prior and finally irreducible status of the human intellect. And Lord Herbert's problem is that he appears to be caught somewhere between the two.

The exact nature of this problem hinges on the word 'reason', that faculty which aids us in the search for certain and reliable knowledge. The word could mean many different things in the sixteenth and early seventeenth centuries, sometimes even different things to the same writer in different situations. It could mean at one extreme 'the Light of Nature' in an almost mystical sense, and at another merely the ability to add up one's laundry bill. The word could be further complicated by adding to it the adjective 'right': 'right reason' is invoked variously as a rational concept, or a mode of knowing; a moral principle, or way of doing; and as a human faculty, or a condition of being.[3] But within its many roles and offices, two distinct modes of its scope and operation can be distinguished, recognisable in the extreme distinction Herbert himself makes when he calls one aspect of 'reason' *discursus*, and the other *instinctus*. Behind this separation of functions lies the authority (though not in Herbert's view the practice) of Aquinas, who speaks of 'lower' and 'higher' reason, the first 'intent on the disposal of temporal things', and the latter 'intent on the consideration and consultation of things eternal'. The 'lower' reason depends upon sense-data for its operation, and works through discursive processes to a limited goal of contingent truth. The *ratio superior* is a faculty which men share—though as a consequence of the Fall in a lesser degree—with angels, in which mode knowledge is accomplished immediately and without any discursive process taking place. Aquinas attributes 'wisdom . . . to the higher reason, science to the lower'.[4] Broadly, it could be argued that the endeavour of empirical science is the exploration of the lower reason, in this sense, and the emphasis of the Platonic strain is upon the 'non-rational', intuitive sense of 'reason' (sometimes called 'understanding') which moves away from sense-data towards the realm of the Ideas and towards God. It is this latter kind of 'intuition', raised above reason and sense, which Herbert frequently expresses in his poetry through the Neoplatonic, Ficinean metaphor of the non-analytic, non-discursive unity of love:

> our love
> Springing at first but in an earthly mould
> Transplanted to our souls, now doth remove
> Earthly effects, what time and distance would.[5]

The external signs of this division (though not necessarily incompatibility) within the idea of 'reason' are at once evident in the outward form of *De veritate*. An important part of its strategy involves the laying down of a *method* of investigation, and Herbert's work is carefully arranged in a series of general propositions, divisions, subdivisions, and logical classifications. The inspiration for this came in part from scholastic method itself (one of Herbert's many paradoxes is the unembarrassed co-existence in his work of scholastic logic and the denunciation of scholastic beliefs), and also from Peter Ramus's celebrated and influential *Dialectique* (1555), which lay down 'in a sort of long chain of gold' the principles of method according to the degree of generality of propositions, with those 'of the utmost generality first' and the 'most particular last'.[6] Herbert was not the first to use an amended scholastic logic to present a new theory of knowledge: Thomas Wilson's *Rule of Reason* (1551) attempted such an epistemological enquiry, and Wilson has a verse on the 'seven liberal artes' which contains the lines,

Logique by art settes furth the truth,
And doth tel us what is vayne,[7]

indicating the importance of logical *method* in distinguishing the nature of both 'truth' and error. Herbert's own concern with logical method is apparent both in the superficial divisions of his work, and particularly in the *Zetetica*, which are tables taken, with little modification, from Ramus and from Raymond Lull's *Quaestiones* and drawn up to furnish ten necessary questions about the subject of enquiry: whether the object exists, what it is, what are its kind, magnitude and relations, and how, where, when, whence, and wherefore it exists.[8] Here there is an obvious indebtedness to Aristotle's *Categories*, notwithstanding Herbert's proud independence of tradition—an indebtedness equally apparent in his later survey appended to the 1645 edition of *De veritate*, *De causis errorum*. The important point is that the Zetetics reveal Herbert in a squarely Aristotelian frame of mind; that is, he is regarding truth, or certainty, as something which can be perceived by the discursive reason through analysis, can be weighed, measured, classified.

But an argument like Herbert's seeking to prove that genuine and certain knowledge is possible is bound to say too why that knowledge so described is in fact true and certain, and it usually does so either by invoking and appealing to some general criterion of truth, or by pointing to the indisputable practical consequences of its assumptions—or of course, as Herbert does, to both at once. In so far as Herbert invokes a general criterion he is in the end committed to the defence of truth as a concept whose existence is guaranteed on metaphysical or systematically logical grounds, though the approach may be made to resemble a species of induction. His overall declaration of independence allows him to hope for the best of both worlds. He responds to the sceptic and nominalist cry for the 'brute fact', striving for a pragmatic approach to 'things as they are' and 'men as they are' (by which of course is meant things and men as they *appear*); he pretends to display no hankering for universal substances and frequently argues as if he is pursuing an empirical proof. He says 'I am not attempting to construct a new philosophy based upon pure theory or upon authority or upon some form of trickery; but at every point I refer the reader to his own faculties.'[9] And yet there are metaphysical assumptions at work which it is impossible to disguise. For example, Herbert seems to hold on the one hand the current view that everything which exists is an individual, a being centred in itself, incommunicable in what constitutes it. He even goes as far as to say at one point that we cannot actually penetrate to the essential nature of things because our faculties are conditioned by analogy. When he explains that 'there is a twofold nature in every object, namely, general and particular', and adds that 'an object therefore has a twofold essence', we are within the traditional definitions in terms of which, and following a nominalist approach, Herbert draws unusually close to a sceptical pragmatism. The answer to the question 'What a thing is' 'is particularly difficult in reference to natural objects, since our faculties being limited by their own analogy cannot penetrate the internal essence of things. Thus we cannot completely understand what a natural object is in itself, whatever its relation to our knowledge may be.'[10] One can imagine Gassendi raising his eyebrows hopefully at this for it was, of course, a position he had reached himself. But on the hand, while accepting that *nihil est praeter individuum*, Herbert does not press his arguments to their empirical conclusion (as Gassendi would wish). He does not go on to say something like 'therefore let us concentrate our attention upon externals, upon appearances'; rather he denies that the matter can be left at that. It does not seem to follow for Herbert that each individual must be utterly distinct and inscrutably separate from all other things which co-exists with it, for the mere fact of co-existence is pregnant with metaphysical and speculative possibilities.

This cast of mind comes out clearly in his discussion of the class of truth he calls *veritas rei*, truth of the thing-in-itself, and it is something Gassendi seized on in order to expose the weakness of metaphysics. *Veritas rei* is sometimes called the only *unconditional* truth, but most often it is a truth conditioned by its conformity to our cognitive capacity and its relation to an inner faculty (an inconsistency which Gassendi of course did not overlook).[11] *Veritas rei* contains *differentiae* or distinguishing marks, rather like the scholastic doctrine of 'difference' and echoing something of the *haecceitas* of Duns Scotus and Ockham's nominalist insistence on particular knowledge. But for Herbert the possession by every individual thing of an inner mark (or *terminus*) by which it is distinguished from every other individual thing is intimately connected with his metaphysical principle of *analogia*:

Every difference ... indicates a principle of individuation which characterises it and serves to distinguish it from others. Accordingly, just as external knowledge of things is derived from acquaintance with external limits, so because of the principles of individuation or interior limit of a thing, every object corresponds to a reciprocal faculty in us. This must be noted at the outset of our doctrine; otherwise the relationship between microcosm and macrocosm cannot be understood.[12]

Or as Herbert again puts it, 'the principles of all the *differentiae* in the world are inscribed in man', and 'the analogous faculties in us respond to every object'. No wonder Herbert was able to 'refer the reader to his own faculties'.

Gassendi replied that Herbert's synthesis showed us, perhaps, more about the conditions under which truth appears to us but nothing whatever about the ultimate *veritas rei*. As a true Pyrrhonian he held that knowledge of absolute truth was essentially impossible, and he explained to Herbert that like the sceptics he himself knew only about such appearances as, for example, the sweet taste of honey. He could explain these appearances adequately in terms of natural, experiential qualities, but he could not discover the ultimate essence of honey, for unfortunately beyond this experiential knowledge we can never, and will never, pass. (Incidentally, the frequency of reference to the example of honey in sceptical discussion is to be explained by a popular sceptical fragment from Timon's *On the Senses*: 'I do not assert that honey really is sweet, / But that it appears sweet I grant'.)[13] Gassendi was unconvinced by those who claim, like Herbert, or for that matter Descartes, to uncover these ultimate verities: 'Concerning what you think to be the truth of the thing, or the intimate nature of honey, this is what I ardently desire to know, and what remains still hidden from me, despite the almost infinite number of books which have been published up to the present with the pretension of communicating to us, what they call, a demonstrative science.'[14] That Herbert intended *De veritate* to have pretensions to being such a 'demonstrative science' is amply illustrated by the confusion of Aristotelian and pseudo-scientific categorising and measuring that he employs to elaborate a basically metaphysical premise. But Gassendi at least was not deceived. Yet it is also clear that both Gassendi and Descartes found something more in Herbert than a mere dogmatist rehearsing already discredited theories: Gassendi perceived and responded to the ambivalence of Herbert's criticisms of empiricism and materialism, and Descartes was moved to recognise an affinity between Herbert and himself—an affinity which, despite Descartes's impatience with the 'measuring devices', is brought about by Herbert's distinctive emendation of the empirical 'reason'.

The longest section of *De veritate* is devoted to a discussion of reason—which Herbert there calls *discursus*. It is, he says, the least reliable and most easily abused of all our faculties. Discursive thought—the faculty of intellection by which we arrive at logical conclusions from given data—is 'undisciplined' and 'apart from the support of the Common Notions it is useless': 'Discursive thought wanders among by-paths, often stumbling in its tracks, and when it seeks support from the yielding confusion of truths it brings to the ground its whole crazy structure of principles.' In a resonant assertion Herbert claims that 'Thus man, though bound by birthright only to the law of Nature, submits himself to a different code'.[15] *Discursus* is so hedged about with conditions that its proper sphere of operation is frequently neglected whilst it is applied indiscriminately in matters where it is no more than misleading. Herbert repeatedly reproves the schoolmen for examining everything in the light of reason alone, and their errors, like all errors in Herbert's view, are due to a confusion of the respective provinces of Natural Instinct, internal and external perception, and discursive reasoning. Herbert is genuinely amazed that Aquinas, having recognised the distinctions, should have failed to observe them and should have employed only the *ratio inferior*.

But what exactly does Herbert mean by *discursus*? He gives a fairly substantial definition: discursive thought considers the existence, essence, quality, etc. of particular objects 'by means of certain Zetetic or heuristic faculties and the Common Notions', and it does this 'either by combining or dividing them, in order to discover the analogy obtaining between things'. It is therefore highly dependent on conditions.[16] And Herbert certainly identifies *discursus* with *ratio*.[17] The question of its meaning is important because of the apparent paradox of Lord Herbert the 'rationalist', the advocate of a theology based upon 'reasonable' beliefs, the avowed enemy of philosophic scepticism and upholder of the value and dignity of human judgements, who is here found expending a great quantity of argument to the discredit of 'reason'.

According to Herbert, when reason is not rightly conformed to its object but is applied in a haphazard fashion, then it recoils upon the user and breeds only confusion. To be 'right', reason must be subordinated to the higher faculties, the Natural Instinct chiefly and its fruits the Common Notions, without which it is useless: 'Reason [*Ratio*] is the process of applying Common Notions as far as it can, and has nothing beyond them to which it can appeal'.[18] Therefore reason, in this sense, is not an ultimate authority, but only the most humble of processes. Herbert adds an elegant explanatory epigram: 'The Reader must observe that discursive thought has as great a tendency to error as free will to sin'.[19] The operations of reason divorced from Natural Instinct would be just like the assertions of the human will divorced from Grace. Milton's Adam, it will be remembered, warns Eve of this danger; for though God made reason 'right', he also made the will free, leaving reason, and hence the very possession of Paradise, in doubt:

> Firm we subsist, yet possible to swerve,
> Since Reason not impossibly may meet
> Some specious object of the Foe suborND,
> And fall into deception unaware.

> (*Paradise Lost*, IX. 359–62)

And the exercise of this kind of reason is a seductive pursuit. With a creak of typically wooden humour Herbert leaves the fools to their folly: 'The Peripatetic School may wander at will in a maze of terms, problems, and probabilities; I have no wish to deprive them of these trifling pleasures'. The schoolmen too (whom Herbert calls simply 'the authorities') guided reason not by Natural Instinct but by *unicum ignorantiae asylum, Auctoritas*, 'Authority, the sole refuge of ignorance'.[20]

Allied to the proper functioning of *discursus*, Herbert proposes a higher and primary reason, or 'Natural Instinct', an inward principle which may be regarded as in one sense anti-rational. It is at least not the kind of close reasoning which could produce the sort of integrated theological system which Aquinas's *Summa* or John Calvin's *Institutes* so magnificently achieved. It is rather the expression, in Herbert's phrases, or our 'birthright', the 'law of Nature' embodied in the 'voice within'. He employs the word 'instinct' in much the same Platonic sense as Sidney, for example, uses the word 'reason', that is, as the highest principle within a man, 'his own divine essence'. It bears resemblances to the radical Protestant 'inner light', and resembles too the 'reason' of the Cambridge Platonists later in the century, for whom equally there are two forms, the lower of which is the discipline of thinking exactly and logically about the things which are real, and the higher of which is the organ of the super-sensuous, not merely a logical but a spiritual faculty. Though Ralph Cudworth, for instance, held that religion could be justified as 'reasonable', he was very far from holding that it was rational in the sense that everything in it could be reduced to logic: there is, he says, 'a natural *prolepsis* or anticipation in the minds of men concerning it [truth]', often 'preventing ratiocination'.[21] For such men every objection to reason in this sense would apply equally to God himself. As Nathaniel Culverwel put it, 'To blaspheme reason is to reproach Heaven itself, and to dishonour the God of reason, to question the beauty of his image'.[22] Similarly Herbert calls his Natural Instinct something 'essentially due to Divine Providence' and its immediate instrument in man. Just as the Cambridge men do not conceive of reason as something which can be derived from the power of thinking alone, so Herbert argues that the real instrument of religious knowledge, and of all knowledge, is not to be found in thought and discursive inference—so that we are presented with the apparent paradox, again, of the exponent of 'rational' religion informing us in utter seriousness that 'the common saying that a man must embrace some beliefs that surpass his understanding is justified'.[23] It is justified because discursive reason, demonstration and logic are of themselves inadequate to the task.

In Herbert's assessment of the human faculties, therefore, *ratio* takes the lowest place, *instinctus naturalis* the highest. In this respect Herbert is, despite his novel terminology, following Plato and is firmly within the rationalist tradition. Once it is recognised that 'reason' in the rationalist sense—that is, the sense in which Descartes, or the Cambridge Platonists or Spinoza use it, as a faculty whose dictates are certain, immediate, infallible and universal—is Natural Instinct and not *ratio* or *discursus*, we find a classification of types of knowledge something very like Spinoza's. As the lowest form of knowledge Spinoza speaks of sense perception or *imaginatio*, which is not true knowledge but is in some sense uncertain and subjective and is, as Plato called it, 'opinion'. The second kind of knowledge is that derived from reasoning or intellection, from which we gain true scientific knowledge consisting, as Spinoza expresses it, of 'adequate ideas' or 'common notions'. But the absolutely true and adequate knowledge is revealed only in *scientia intuitiva*, 'intuitive knowledge', the highest mode of understanding, and of which *imaginatio* and *ratio* are, respectively, distorted and abstract expressions. Intuitive knowledge grasps immediately and without need of demonstration or argument the single, comprehensive system of ideas which reflect the universe as a whole, and this intuitive understanding Spinoza regards as the only adequate and satisfactory means of attaining truth.[24]

Although Herbert's division of the types of knowledge is slightly different from Spinoza's he is remarkably like him in the sharp distinction he makes between 'reason' and 'intuition'. He admits that there are many truths that can be reached only with the help of discursive reason, but truths of this kind—or Common Notions of this kind, for any true idea is, to Herbert, a Common Notion in some sense—he refers to the second rank of ideas. Ideas of the first rank, however, 'can be brought into conformity by their own activity without aid from discursive reason', and are first order Common Notions. These are characterised chiefly by their priority to reflection and experience and by the intuitive nature of our understanding of them. According to Milton's Raphael, who follows Aquinas on the point, this intuition is the primary angelic mode of knowledge. He explains to Adam how

> the Soule
> Reason receives, and reason is her being,
> Discursive, or Intuitive; discourse
> Is oftest yours, the latter most is ours,
> Differing but in degree, of kind the same.
>
> (*Paradise Lost*, V,486–90)

For Herbert it is also the ideal human mode, and he even goes so far as to deny any necessary connection between 'discourse' and 'intuition', stating that 'these faculties are quite distinct'—'in spite', he adds, 'of the contrary opinion of those whose philosophy is wholly based on the futile processes of reason'.[25]

Spinoza's well-known example of the three kinds of knowledge is of the merchant given three numbers through which he must discover a fourth which shall be to the third as the second is to the first. The merchant

does not hesitate to multiply the second and third together and divide the product by the first, either because he has not yet forgotten the things which he heard without any demonstration from his schoolmaster, or because he has seen the truth of the rule with more simple numbers, or because from the 19th Prop. in the 7th book of Euclid he understands the common property of all proportionals.[26]

Herbert's example, equally directed to the establishment of a difference between reasoned inference and immediate intuition, is not of mathematics but of architecture: 'Natural Instinct anticipates reason in perceiving the beauty of the proportions of a house built according to architectural principles; for reason reaches its conclusions by a laborious consideration of the proportions, first severally and then as a whole.'[27] The same difference can be perceived, he says, 'in judging beautiful features, or graceful form, or harmony in music'. The labour of 'reason' is in fact the labour of applying Common Notions. He speaks of mathematics itself—that paradigm of all rational knowledge—in reply to the objection that there is nothing new in his doctrine of Common Notions: 'I answer that by it facts acquire a mathematical certainty. For all proof is derived from their principles.'[28] His Common Notions seem to fulfil the same function as mathematical demonstration in Galileo or Descartes; like the mathematical relationships which ride above the deceptions and fluctuations of sense perceptions and which we can intuit directly, Common Notions approach this condition of absolute reality and are regarded by Herbert as if they possessed the properties of mathematical truths. The truth of Common Notions extends to logical inferences derived from them ('fire struck from a stone is as real as the stone itself'), and to their application to the data of sensation, provided the Notions are applied 'under the proper conditions'.

The intuitive nature of our most important knowledge is dependent of course on the metaphysical assumptions of *De veritate*. Because God himself constitutes the essence of the human mind, the primary knowledge granted by Natural Instinct will be knowledge of God's reality, incapable of distortion, misunderstanding or error. Such knowledge will necessarily lead us finally to 'Eternal Blessedness', or, as Spinoza has it, that blessedness which is 'nothing but the peace of mind which springs from the intuitive knowledge of God'.[29] The use of the word *instinctus* is also significant. Natural Instinct, as we shall investigate it further, has a biological and psychological basis in Herbert's metaphysics, for it is the agent of life's conservation and continued evolution. 'Instinct' and 'intuition' come to mean virtually the same thing. It is interesting to note that Henri Bergson uses an illustration very similar to Herbert's to indicate the ultimate harmony of the universe and the analogy obtaining between all forms of life. Speaking of the force which preserves and directs all creatures, Bergson says 'The Ammophila no doubt discerns very little of that force, just what concerns itself; but at least it discerns it from within, quite otherwise than by a process of knowledge—by an intuition (*lived* rather than *represented*).[30] Herbert speaks of the instinctive 'knowledge' of animals, 'zoophytes' and even plants and elements directing them towards self-preservation: 'All other creatures behave under the spur of necessity or at least uniformly and without deliberation. Man alone has the misfortune, through his tendency to discursive reflection, to be the frequent victim of indecision . . .'[31] And like Herbert, Bergson suggests a teleological vision of life's harmonious processes and allows a common origin of instinct and intuition in a general mind or mental functioning.

The common mind

The notion of a 'general mind' indicates at once Herbert's most basic assumption about the foundations of knowledge: that the expression of this 'mind' is identical in all men. Instead of pointing to diversity and variety the emphasis is upon uniformity and the discovery of the principles of that assumed uniformity. Such an assumption is traditional enough, and its course may be followed from Plato through the Stoics to Cicero and, in the seventeenth and eighteenth centuries, to Herbert, Matthew Tindal or Voltaire. A classic text for the universal and equal capacity of learning in man was Cicero's 'Reason certainly is a common possession of men; there are differences in the amount of acquired knowledge, but an equality in the faculty of learning . . . the rudiments of intelligence [or rudimentary concepts] are implanted in a similar way in all men.'[32] If the capacity for knowledge is identical in all men, then universality of consent is taken to be both the guarantee and the criterion of truth; it may or may not follow, however, that differences of opinion are evidences of error. Although Herbert certainly relies solidly on a form of 'epistemological primitivism', he also integrates it into his total philosophy with a number of contributory metaphysical arguments and often a touch of sophistication. On a purely logical level he is careful (though perhaps not careful enough) to guard against philosophical absurdities in his description of Common Notions; he defines and conditions his theory with some acute argument that has not always been noted by his critics. For example, Herbert does not look on universal consent as applying to particular opinions about this or that. If we were to argue that, in spite of an ancient, constant and universal belief to the contrary, the earth actually moves round the sun, Herbert would answer that many conditions are necessary to the perception of particular truth and when they are lacking truth will be hidden to all men. He saw it as part of his function to try to explain the nature of those conditions. From such an example we are able to perceive the Common Notion, supported certainly this time by universal consent, that two contradictory statements cannot both be true in the same way at the same time—that the sun cannot go round the earth and the earth round the sun at the same time.

On the face of it, there is no reason why the whole of mankind should not have been as wrong on a speculative topic as it has been on some more empirical questions on which, history teaches, it has been mistaken. To guard against this objection Herbert advances a species of 'biological' argument of instinctive assent and of innate and incorruptible faculties of the mind which rests ultimately on a metaphysically supported gesture of faith. He does not tackle the problem of whether the universality of an idea or faculty necessarily established its innateness; he merely recoils from the implications that might follow if it does not. If J. S. Mill were to ask Herbert why an innate or instinctive belief should be regarded as *for that reason* true, Herbert's only recourse would probably be a dumb gesture at the heavens.[33] His insistence on the Common Notions and the finality of universal consent (together, it must be said, with the lack of any finally satisfactory examples of such notions, beyond some ethical do-as-you-would-be-done-by axioms, some logical truisms, and the religious *exampla* of the Five Articles of Religion) tends to unbalance *De veritate* and diminish its philosophical value. Once the theory of Common Notions has been introduced the work is thereafter punctuated with resounding celebrations of these 'sacred principles': 'whatever is believed by universal consent must be true'; 'universal consent . . . will be found to be the final test of truth'; 'holding fast to this universal consent as irrefragable truth'; 'nothing fairer can be imagined than the harmonious array of the Common Notions', and so on. The rhetoric may indicate something of Herbet's persuasiveness, but it renders the disinterestedness and objectivity of his enquiry, to say the least, suspect. Throughout there is a conspicuous lack of self-criticism and discrimination. So strenuous and dogmatic is his support of Common Notions (though his metaphysical presuppositions may mitigate the dogmatism) that one suspects their necessity is demanded by other than strictly 'philosophical' reasons. Herbert wants them up his sleeve for a specific purpose: the defence of religious toleration. It is the alternative and opposite strategy to that of Castellio, for example, whose sceptical stressing of the fundamental *uncertainty* of religious knowledge was equally intended as a means of achieving peace. Herbert chooses to point not to our uncertainties but to what anyone, of whatever particular persuasion, can assent to, and in his view must assent to.

A number of problems now suggest themselves. There is of course an obvious difficulty involved in a theory of primary, independent and universal Common Notions which, as Herbert says, 'it is not legitimate to dispute'—already a contradiction in terms. From this principle of non-contradiction spring further difficulties. One important aspect of such a dogma of Common Notions is that it contraverts the nominalist epistemology which, together with Averroism, was the axe which split the original Thomist harmony of reason and faith. The Elizabethan Anglican apologist Richard Hooker, for example, stands firm in the realist camp, claiming the existence and demonstrating the workings of universal laws and concepts which he justifies by the *vox populi*, intending thereby to establish that *universalia sunt realia*, that there is such a 'thing' or reality as the universal 'man', and the universal 'church', and hence infinite atonement through the 'vicar of Christ' on earth. Rather like Hooker, though for different reasons, Herbert attempts to make universals of his Common Notions. One of the characteristics of Common Notions is their universality, and Herbert says that 'accordingly I take the chief criterion of Natural Instinct to be universal consent': 'In a word, pure Common Notions are universals, distilled as it were from the wisdom of Nature itself; though they may be broken up into particular forms by discursive reason.'[34] In these sentences Herbert passes from one meaning of universality to another, from the universality of their acceptance to the universal nature of the notions themselves, quite apart from the question of their acceptance. Yet such a procedure, though it may be bad philosophy, occurs again and again in this period. Herbert may have been the less conscious of any difficulty since he was not concerned with proving the universality of any particular Church for special ecclesiastical purposes, but only the universality of certain beliefs irrespective of Church or creed. At any rate, in maintaining such a position Herbert is again within an ancient tradition; for the idea of an innate notion of God is found in the pious non-Christians Xenophon and Cicero, was employed in the spread of Christianity among the pagans by Tertullian, St Augustine, Irenaeus, Clement of Alexandria and St Jerome, was philosophically ratified by St Anselm in his famous ontological proof that the reality of God is made necessary by our concept of him (another example perhaps, as Kant was to show, of bad but influential philosophy), and was carefully cherished throughout the Renaissance. Mersenne relates how a Roman missionary, using the proper catechism, 'evoked from the lips of a savage inborn knowledge about the Christian God and the Mosaic Decalogue'.[35]

The implicit argument relating universality and universality of consent would seem to be that if, as Ockham had said, *universalia* are merely *vocalia* or *nomina* and certainly not *realia*, then once the assertion has been made that God's existence was held by all men at all times, the universal is once more established as an objective reality and not a mere name; for it can be demonstrated that men who have never heard the name yet have a knowledge of the reality. And once this platform has been erected the remaining structures of natural theology almost build themselves. The making of what is posited as universally accepted into a universal reality would seem to be dependent on the assertion of the uniformity of men's minds and capacity of reasoning: fundamental agreement is then taken as evidence of truth.

It is characteristic of Herbert's thinking that he cannot dwell for long in the abstract—*De veritate* has the air of being a necessary evil, a strenuous accumulation of abstract argument and demonstration, vital to the cause, necessary to the complete and respectable picture, but impelled by, and finally breaking out in, a strongly ethical and moral purpose—a tendency which led Rossi to wonder whether this is not the sign of a typically English mentality, with its inevitable desire to 'consider truth, especially the truths of faith, as *rectitudines*, as guides to action'.[36] Donne, looking at the matter from the other end, praised a young Herbert for whom 'actions are authors'. But before discussing the application of Herbert's theory of knowledge to ethics and religion it is vital to appreciate the reasons for Herbert's

labours in *De veritate* and the importance of his metaphysical
assumptions. These will be discussed in the next chapter. At this
point it is worth mentioning, however, the famous polemic of Locke
against the theory of innate ideas in his *Essay Concerning Human
Understanding* (1690).

Herbert and Locke

Most students of philosophy and of literature are likely to make
Herbert's acquaintance first of all, if not only, in the pages
apparently devoted to him in Locke's *Essay*, or in Leibniz's *Nouveaux
essais*. Locke's inclusion of Herbert's name is puzzling, for his
examination of Herbert's theory is cursory and in the nature of an
afterthought, and Locke further says that he had worked out his own
ideas before ever reading *De veritate*.[37] R. I. Aaron has argued,
following Leibniz and Voltaire, that the object of Locke's attack is
not Lord Herbert (though Herbert is the only person mentioned by
Locke), nor necessarily even the Cambridge Platonists (some of
whom upheld while others rejected innate ideas), but the
Cartesians.[38] Certainly, as a criticism of Herbert Locke went far
wide of the mark. It was not ideas as such that Herbert claimed to be
innate (and this may explain in part the very few instances Herbert
himself is able to give of innate ideas), but modes of thought, the
very processes of the mind. Faculties, certainly, are innate, and
when brought into conformity by the mutual stimulation of external
and internal objects will inevitably lead a normal man (unless he is
confused *en route* by *discursus*) to certain ideas; as soon as Natural
Instinct begins to operate a man will be compelled, at risk of
perverting his nature, to believe certain things. Curiously enough,
Locke argues as a perfect Herbertian when he himself discusses the
way in which the mind gains insight into truth. The power which the
mind has of apprehending truth is, Locke says, direct, immediate
and, moreover, infallible. This kind of knowledge he calls 'intuition'
and it is 'the clearest and most certain that human frailty is capable
of': 'Certainty depends so wholly on this intuition that in the next
degree of knowledge, which I call demonstrative, this intuition is
necessary in all connexions of the intermediate ideas, without which
we cannot attain knowledge and certainty.'[39] That is to say, Locke
considers reason, in the sense of the act of knowing, to *be* intuition,

and hence an innate faculty. And this is primarily the sense in which Herbert had spoken of Natural Instinct, the faculty on which Common Notions are based. Locke's intuitionism, in this part of the *Essay*, is essentially the intuitionism of Descartes (especially Descartes's *Regulae ad directionem ingenii*), allowed at this crucial point to modify Locke's empiricism.

But the difference between Locke and Herbert—as between Locke and Descartes—is that intuition consists for Locke in the perception of a relation between ideas ultimately derived solely from sensation and reflection; the object of intuition is always something concrete and given. Locke's examples, in describing this intuition in the *Essay*, are that the mind perceives intuitively 'that white is not black, that a circle is not a triangle, that three are more than two, and equal to one and two'.[49] This difference is also apparent in Locke's witty comment on the arguments of the radical sceptics: '. . . for I think nobody can, in earnest, be so sceptical, as to be uncertain of the existence of those things which he sees and feels. At least, he that can doubt so far (whatever he may have with his own thoughts) will never have any controversy with me; since he is never sure I say anything contrary to his opinion.'[41] When Locke asserts, as he frequently does, that 'reason must be our last judge and guide in everything'[42], he is using reason in that discursive and demonstrative sense Herbert had so little patience with, and arguing as an empiricist who denies the existence of anything in the mind prior to experience—on the contrary, the mind at birth is like 'a white paper, void of all characters, without any ideas'. In this sense Locke's position differs fundamentally from that of both Herbert and Descartes.

It is perhaps interesting to note the way in which Herbert's stance on the question of knowledge anticipates, implicitly at least, the criticism of empiricism which David Hume proposed in the eighteenth century. Hume based his argument against certainty of the kind which Locke called demonstrative certainty upon the unreliability of discursive reasoning. In his *Treatise of Human Nature*, in the section 'Of Scepticism with regard to Reason', Hume observed that 'in all the demonstrative sciences the rules are certain and infallible; but when we apply them, our fallible and uncertain faculties are very apt to depart from them and fall into error.'[43] Hume's point is that in every case of reasoning we need to judge whether the judgement concerning the application of the rules is correct, and so on *ad infinitum*. The original reasoning cannot be known to be correct, and uncertainty is thus built into all demonstrative arguments. Herbert does not of course put it in this way, since it is an avenue he is simultaneously exploring; but he does insist that we must be clear that the kind of proof we are demanding and the kind of subject matter we are dealing with are taken into account: 'every point in dispute', he says, 'may be referred to this question: "What faculty is assumed in proving the point at issue?" '[44] Despite the fact that Herbert, with disarming inconsistency, went on to elucidate the operations of *discursus* in his *De causis errorum*, the basic caveat here, having scholastic *discursus* particularly in mind, is that demonstrative argument is useful and necessary but there are areas which it cannot accommodate without being caught in its own toils and confusing truth with error. Some truths, Herbert argues (and it is an important aspect of his thought which needs to be stressed), we are bound to accept not through reason or demonstration but through the agency only of our divinely implanted Natural Instinct.

Some logical problems

There is, then, a tension in Herbert's thought between the empiricist and the metaphysician which is part of the fascination of his philosophical thinking. His philosophy starts from a phenomenology of truth, that is, from a search for the signs and characteristics of truth, 'as distinguished from revelation, probability, possibility, and falsehood'. But on the way he draws in and tries to accommodate many other strategies, so that the result is a patchwork of different ideas about truth which imply different theories of knowledge. Some of the steps Herbert takes towards 'truth' and its conditions imply a Platonic point of view, some derive from the scholastic mental conformity theory, while others imply an intuitive theory of knowledge. Many of these strands are disentangled by Rossi, who finds in Herbert a confusion of phenomenology, gnoseology, psychology and deontology. In Rossi's opinion the central point of the gnoseology—'the principle of correspondence and the multiplication of faculties and of their objects'[45]—was also its central weakness. Yet, as an investigation of Herbert's metaphysical assumptions will help to indicate, it is also his most fruitful and fundamental point.[46] We can see in *De veritate* the way in which Herbert's mind inclines, despite the frequent appearance of the official intellectualism of the Schools, towards an intuitive theory of knowledge of a Stoic and Neoplatonic nature. 'Such a canon of truth stated in this way', Rossi had commented, 'cannot escape inconsistency.'[47] While this is undoubtedly true it is not of course without great interest. Herbert exhibits clearly the unresolved discord between an approach to a 'theory of truth' which finds its most natural expression in comparisons and categories, dividing and compounding appearances with the tools of logical demonstration and analysis, and an approach which finds its most natural expression in a phrase like Descartes's 'une notion si transcendentalement claire': a distinction between truth or certainty as a relation, understood by classification and measurement, and truth as an intuition fully and adequately implicit in the human mind. For example, if fundamental and universal agreement is the evidence of truth, does it follow that fundamental and universal disagreement is evidence of error? If the criterion of truth is its non-contradictableness, how is error possible? On the question of error Rossi shrewdly comments:

Herbert forgets that he is bound to explain error in a way compatible with his explanation of truth, and gives a definition of error which is in accord only with the intellectual theory, whilst his previous references to an intuitive theory (according to which truth is the immediate perception of the mind) should preclude any such definition. The intuitive theory excludes indeed the very possibility of error—at least, the possibility of explaining error on intellectual grounds.[48]

The discord expressed in Herbert's search for truth is one which is a constant in philosophical enquiry and is still in the process of resolution. The very nature of his undertaking in *De veritate* is akin to that of Descartes and, later in the century, to that of Spinoza and indeed of all philosophical approaches which seek formulate, as Herbert does, a *general* method, or criterion, for establishing genuine and certain knowledge; that is, the search, however fumbling and misdirected at times in Herbert, for a method of distinguishing true from false propositions and thus eliminating error and based tacitly on the axiom, as Spinoza expressed it, that 'Truth is the criterion of itself'. Necessarily such a general approach will have to be metaphysical or logical; it will involve either exercises in logic (hence Herbert's categories) or speculative metaphysics, rather than exercises in observation and experiment with particulars. In modern terms, it is the difference between a 'coherence' and a 'correspondence' theory of truth. Where the empiricist will claim that 'truth' consists in some form of correspondence between a belief and a fact, the idealist will argue that a statement or a judgement is 'true' because it coheres with a system of other statements whose elements are related by ties of logical or metaphysical implication and that the more our beliefs hang together in a coherent system the truer they are. And the examination of the possibility of such a general undertaking has led empiricists to argue that the search is senseless in relation to general criteria, and that questions about 'truth' can be applied only in particular, specified instances—which is as much as to say that if we *can* only attend to specific instances, a general method is totally excluded.

Yet Herbert's search represents at the same time one of philosophy's most basic impulses and most cherished ideals: the attainment of some unifying criterion or concept which will set in assigned relationships within itself the whole province of possible knowledge. Such a search itself helps to explain many of the paradoxes of Herbert's thinking. In the words of A. N. Whitehead:

That far off ideal is the motive power of philosophical research; and claims allegiance even as you expel it. The philosophic pluralist is a strict logician; the Hegelian thrives on contradictions by the help of his absolute; the Mohammedan divine bows before the creative will of Allah; and the pragmatist will swallow anything so long as it 'works'.[49]

The course of the examination of the possibility has been long and arduous. Lord Herbert, like any metaphysical thinker after him, puts the question, 'Under what conditions is a proposition (any proposition whatever) true?', and seeks a general solution. That there can be only one answer—'It depends on the proposition'—has been a long time emerging. As Stuart Hampshire laconically observes, 'to have shown this was (strangely) a great achievement of modern logic'.[50]

But our judgement of Herbert does not of course rest upon his ability to match modern standards of logic or analytic philosophy. The conditions under which a proposition is 'true' or 'false' are not, in the Renaissance at least, philosophically or logically isolable in this way. What was understood as constituting 'conditions' is of crucial importance. Despite Herbert's stance of disinterested enquiry into our mental processes, the stimulus to his speculations is at bottom a theological one. His thought revolves around what are essentially theological questions, the fundamental scholastic problems of God, of freedom and of immortality—indeed there is a real sense in which *De veritate* could accurately be described as a defence not so much of truth as of the soul's immortality. And to such questions there are conditions attached which are extra-logical, taking the form, for example, of a diffused and pervasive commitment to an *a priori* theory of nature and hierarchy, where 'conditions' of truth are understood in relation to a general and essentially unquestionable religious and metaphysical background. In a sense, Herbert's appeal to some general criterion of truth is dependent on assumptions which, strictly speaking, prevent from the first an adequate solution.

In seeking to resolve the new problems of individualistic epistemology Herbert naturally tends to display the question in its own empirical terms; his solution of it however is basically through an appeal to the total European past. His basic premise grows out of a synthesis of Stoical philosophy, Ficinean Platonism, a submerged Hermetism, and an appeal to the ancient doctrines of 'faculty', *conformatio*, and 'universal analogy', of macrocosm and microcosm refurbished to meet a new situation. Gassendi, for the sake of a compliment, called Herbert the successor to Bacon; but Herbert's total approach is peculiarly un-Baconian, in the sense that it lays itself wide open to the charge expressed in Bacon's diagnosis of the causes of learning's atrophy. Bacon singles out for attack the traditions of philosophical speculation, chiefly Platonic and Stoic, which have as their basis the belief that man's inner nature and faculties are so constituted that they can apprehend reality—a reality which is seen as being made up of the same essential materials. Bacon seeks to destroy that 'glassy essence' of the mind in which man can gather in and reflect the beams of the essential light. The presupposition of order, the tendency to welcome and affirm analogies and similarities, the very nature of the human imagination itself, are severely criticised. Montaigne's 'now our condition appropriating things unto it selfe, and transforming them to its owne humour: wee know no more how things are in sooth and truth; for: *nothing comes unto us but falsified and altered by our senses*'[51] is turned by Bacon into 'the human understanding is like a false mirror, which, receiving rays irregularly, distorts and discolours the nature of things by mingling its own nature with it'.[52] Man, Bacon says, is predisposed to believe in 'order and regularity'; he plays loose with the evidence and is 'moved and excited by affirmatives' and by unexamined coincidences, 'which strike and enter the mind simultaneously and suddenly, and so fill the imagination'. This imagination then goes on to invent fictions that are similar 'to those few things by which it is surrounded'.[53] If it had been up to man to dispose the stars throughout the universe, Bacon says man would have arranged them 'into some beautiful and elegant order, as we see in the vaulted roofs of palaces . . . so great a difference is there betwixt the spirit of man and the spirit of the universe'.[54] We must bear in mind our weakness here and recognise that 'whatever the mind seizes and dwells upon with peculiar satisfaction is to be held in suspicion'.[55] And Herbert is singularly guilty of this sort of 'peculiar satisfaction'. It is to Herbert's speculative aspect, his metaphysics, that we shall now turn.

Notes to Chapter III

1 Locke, *An Essay Concerning Human Understanding*, London, 1690, IV, 7. 19.

2 Descartes, *Discourse on Method*, IV.

3 See Robert Hoopes, *Right Reason in the English Renaissance*, Cambridge, Mass. 1962, p. 1 and *passim*.

4 Aquinas, *Summa theologica*, I.Q. LXXXIX.A.9. Translated by the English Dominican Fathers, London, 1922.

5 'Parted Souls', in *The Poems of Lord Herbert of Cherbury*, ed. G. C. Moore Smith, Oxford, 1923, p. 17.

6 Ramus, *Dialectique*, Paris, 1555, pp. 120–22.

7 Thomas Wilson, *Rule of Reason*, London, 1551, sig. B2r.

8 D.V., p. 204; Carré, pp. 284–5.

9 *D.V..*, p. 74; Carré, p. 154.

10 *D.V.*, p. 165; Carré, p. 247.

11 Cf. *D.V.* p. 13; Carré, p. 88.

12 *D.V.*, 15; Carré, p. 91.

13 In Hermann Diels, *Poetarum philosophorum fragmenta*, III, No. i. in *Poetarum Graecorum fragmenta*, ed. U. Wilamowitz-Moellendorff, Berlin, 1901, frag. 74. Cf. Sextus, *Outlines of Pyrrhonism*, I, 20.

14 Gassendi, *Epistola*, in *Opera*, 1658, III, pp. 411–19.

15 *D.V.*, p. 152; Carré, p. 233.

16 *D.V.*, *ibid.*

17 See e.g. *D.V.*, p. 153.

18 *D.V.*, p. 42; Carré, p. 120.

19 *D.V.*, p. 154; Carré, p. 235.

20 *D.V.*, p. 160.

21 See J. M. Muirhead, *The Platonic Tradition in Anglo-Saxon Philosophy*, London, repr. 1965, p. 50.

22 Culverwel, *A Discourse of the Light of Nature* (1652), ed. J. Brown, Edinburgh, 1857, p. 17.

23 *D.V.*, p. 42; Carré, p. 120.

24 The classification is found in *Ethics*, part II, trans. W. Hale White, 4th ed., Oxford, 1910, pp. 86–7. In the *Tractatus de intellectus emendatione* Spinoza lists four kinds, subdividing the second class of *ratio*; *Tractatus*, trans. W. Hale White, London, 1895, pp. 9–10.

. 25 *D.V.*, pp. 58–9; Carré, p. 137.

26 Spinoza, *Ethics*, II, prop. XL., schol. 2.

27 *D.V.*, p. 60; Carré, p. 139.

28 *D.V.*, p. 56; Carré, p. 135.

29 Spinoza, *Ethics*, part IV, appendix iv. Trans. W. Hale White, *loc. cit.*, p. 241.

30 Bergson, *Creative Evolution*, trans. A. Mitchell, London, 1911, p. 185. Cf. *D.V.*: the faculty of Natural Instinct 'promotes self-preservation' and 'forestalls at every point the processes of reason' (p. 60; Carré, p. 139).

31 *D.V.*, p. 152; Carré, p. 233.

32 Cicero, *De legibus*, I, x.30 : *Ratio . . . certe est communis, doctrina differens, discendi quidem facultate par . . . inchoate intelligentiae similiter in omnibus imprimuntur*. Quoted in A. O. Lovejoy and G. Boas, *A Documentary History of Primitivism and Related Ideas*, Baltimore, Md., 1935, p. 257. Cf. Cicero, *De re publica*, III, xii: *Est quidem vera lux, recta ratio, naturae congruens, diffusa in omnes, constans, sempiterna*.

33 See J. S. Mill, *Three Essays on Religion*, London, 1874, p. 156.

34 *D.V.*, p. 60; Carré, pp. 139–40.

35 See Xenophon, *Memorabilia*, I, lv.4; Cicero, *De natura deorum*, II, 5; Mersenne, *Quaestiones in Genesim*, Paris, 1623, cols. 261–2. Cited by D. C. Allen, *Doubt's Boundless Sea: Skepticism and Faith in the Renaissance*, Baltimore, Md., 1964, p. 134.

36 Mario M. Rossi, *Alle fonti del deismo e del materialismo moderno*, Florence, 1942, p. 54.

37 See *An early Draft of Locke's Essay, Together with Excerpts from his Journals*, ed. R. I. Aaron and J. Gibb, Oxford, 1936.

38 R. I. Aaron, *John Locke*, 2nd ed., Oxford, 1955, pp. 84–8. Culverwel, for example, specifically argues against 'innate ideas'; see especially *A Discourse of the Light of Nature*, 1652.

39 Locke, *Essay*, IV, 2.1.

40 Locke, *Essay, ibid.*

41 Locke, *Essay*, IV, 11.3.

42 Locke, *Essay*, IV, 19.14.

43 Hume, *Treatise of Human Nature*, book I, part IV, i. Ed. L. A. Selby-Bigge, Oxford, 1951, p. 180.

44 *D.V.*, p. 150; Carré, p. 231.

45 Rossi, I, p. 479.

46 On Rossi's criticism here Max H. Fisch comments: 'So perhaps a critic must judge, but a Whitehead might have found it immensely suggestive, and

a Vico, as I should have thought an Italian historian would remind us, did find it so' (Review of Rossi's *La Vita*, in *Journal of Philosophy*, 46, 1949, pp. 195–203).

47 Rossi, 'The nature of truth and Lord Herbert of Cherbury's Inquiry', *The Personalist*, 21, 1940, pp. 243–56.

48 Rossi, *ibid.*

49 A. N. Whitehead, *Concept of Nature*, Cambridge, repr. 1964, p. 2.

50 Stuart Hampshire, *Spinoza*, London, 1951, p. 91.

51 Montaigne, *Apologie, Essayes*, Everyman ed., vol. II, p. 321.

52 Bacon, *Novum organum*, XLI

53 *Novum organum*, XLV–XLVII.

54 *De augmentis*, V, iv.

55 *Novum organum*, LVIII.

IV

THE PLATONIC METAPHYSIC

Consider the immensitie of the creatures this world produces; our *creatures* are our *thoughts, creatures* that are borne of *Gyants*; that reach from *East* to *West*, from *Earth* to *Heaven*, that doe not onely bestride all the *Sea*, and *Land*, but span the *Sunn* and *Firmament* at once; My thoughts reach all, comprehend all.

Donne, Devotions upon Emergent
Occasions, IV

The Platonic heritage

Everything we can imagine exists in the infinite, and everything beyond this. God is beyond all things, and alone independent of all. He transcends transcendence, and fills, informs, and encompasses the infinite itself in the vastness of His unity. This is proved by the fact that just as we encounter the finite and universal order in the infinite, so in all that is finite can we find some traces of the infinite. Thus everything seems capable of being divided into an infinity of parts, but since it must be in the end resolved into a unity (the ultimate characteristic of the infinite) infinity and unity appear to meet.[1]

These words are not, as one might reasonably think, an extract from Nicolas of Cusa's mystical mathematics, or Pico della Mirandola's Platonic *Heptaplus*, or from Giordano Bruno's paradoxical speculations on the infinite. They are in fact from the hard-headed 'rational' theology of Herbert's *De veritate*. Admittedly, the words occur in the particularly rhapsodic section entitled 'On Possibility', yet far from being a momentary lapse on Herbert's part into old-fashioned Renaissance arcana they are entirely characteristic and imply succinctly the sum of Herbert's philosophy of nature. In them are contained the fundamental tenets of his metaphysics: the Platonic, or rather Plotinian, doctrines of the hierarchy of being and the absolute priority of form over matter; the Hermetic principle of the One and the Many and of the unity of whole and part; and the Neo-platonic postulate of the *coincidentia oppositorum* in which all extremes, the 'infinity of parts', meet in the Infinite, or the Absolute, or God. Such notions are, at points in *De veritate*, crystallised out in a manner indicated by the above quotation; at other times they are implicit in his total procedure. If his doctrine of the nature of truth rests upon the assumption that 'truth is a certain harmony between objects and their analogous faculties', then the process is only intelligible on the supposition of a harmony between the world and man's mind; the bond of union is the human body, fashioned out of the material of the external world and containing the sense-apparatus which lead to the 'inner court' of consciousness. The supposition of such a harmony is basic to *De veritate*, and Herbert inherited it, together with all the complexities of its many manifestations, chiefly from the Renaissance Neoplatonists, however much such conceptions may be disguised in Herbert's writings behind an appearance of fashionable—that is, empirical—ratiocination.

Herbert's particular point of view here draws upon a central tradition of European philosophy, revitalised to meet a new problem. With the rise of nominalism and the revival of scepticism came a new object of philosophic knowledge: the world of experience—which Montaigne and Bacon, in their different ways, sought to lay hold on. The world of experience is Herbert's concern too, but his approach is through a Neoplatonic metaphysic, founded upon analogy; and it is also, incidentally, an alternatively 'fashionable' way of dealing with the issue. It has been argued that in the search for a method by which to study this new philosophical object the Neoplatonic view of the cosmos gained a revived force and its concepts of universal analogies and cosmic affinities proved a basis for a new theory of knowledge which, through analogical reasoning and 'unified imagination', could suggest an approach to this new object—an analogical method best seen in the work of Renaissance speculators like Bruno, Paracelsus, Campanella or Kepler.[2]

The specific sources of Herbert's ideas are a matter for dispute—inevitably so since his mind, like that of many a Renaissance syncretist, does not sift its material and provide the sort of attributions that would make the task of defining those sources simple. Ideas and philosophies are absorbed in a kind of osmotic percolation. Rossi points out the difficulties of separating Platonism from Stoicism, and also Platonism from Aristotelianism 'in the learned, dilettante, mystical world of Renaissance Hellenistic culture.'[3] Rossi does, however, seriously minimise the Platonic elements in Herbert's thought, arguing that 'his expressed philosophy is Neoplatonic only in some particulars' and is rather

Aristotelian and Stoic in its sources.[4] There are clear indications, granting the inconsistencies in Herbert's confusion of an adequation and an intuitive theory of knowing, that his basic epistemology of Natural Instinct reflects the Platonic (or in scholastic terms Augustinian) view of the understanding and its relation to the objects it comprehends, emphasising the innate powers of the mind rather than the Aristotelian view of a 'potential' intellect or *tabula rasa* which is determined by the objects perceived in sensation.

Herbert's Common Notions are found in all normal persons and are, he says, 'constituents of all and are derived from universal wisdom and imprinted on the soul by the dictates of Nature herself'.[5] Through them 'our minds are enabled to come to decisions concerning the events which take place upon the theatre of the world'.[6] Without some such innate processes the universe would be meaningless, for they form the cornerstone of all possibility of knowledge.

These elements or sacred principles are so far from being drawn from experience or observation that, without several of them, or at least one of them, we could have no experience at all nor be capable of observations. For if it had not been written in our soul that we should examine into the nature of things (and we do not derive this command from objects), and if we had not been endowed with Common Notions to that end we should never come to distinguish between things, or to grasp any general nature. Vacant forms and prodigies and fearful images would pass meaninglessly before our minds, unless there existed within us, in the shape of notions imprinted in the mind, that analogous faculty by which we distinguish good from evil.[7]

And he throws out the innocent question which Locke and others were to take up and answer for him: 'From where else could we have received knowledge?' 'Let us have done', he says roundly, 'with the theory that asserts that the mind is a clear sheet, as though we obtained our capacity for dealing with objects from objects themselves.'[8] He claims, moreover, that for every object there is a faculty in the mind, and not merely a faculty corresponding to objects of sense but to every conceivable item of reality. Faculties not only correspond to objects; objects correspond to faculties. Hence, from the existence of a faculty we can infer the existence of an object, even though we have no experience of it. The correspondence of faculties and objects depends not on a *species sensibilis impresa* but upon the analogy between the mind and God, for 'our mind is the best image and specimen of divinity': 'Accordingly, whatever truth or goodness exists in us exists preeminently in God. And pursuing this view, I believe that the divine image is in turn imparted to the body.'⁹ In this fundamentally Platonic view the soul turns towards the exterior, which it finds mirrored within itself, and the correspondence between knowledge and its objects is presented as an application of finality.

The mutual correspondence of faculties and objects and the infinite multiplication of both brought an objection from Rossi, as it did from Herbert's contemporaries. Richard Baxter, for instance, offered the comment, similar to Descartes's, on Herbert's infinite faculties that he was not willing 'to think that I have as many different faculties as there are different plants in my Garden'.¹⁰ It may be a logical and technical weakness of Herbert's epistemology but it is at the heart of his account. Knowledge for Herbert is not *reactio* but *actio*; it is not mere passive reception but active creation and association. In this view of perception lies Herbert's basic discomfort with a purely intellectual and empirical approach. In this respect he shares a view essentially similar to that of a group of thinkers later in the seventeenth century, the Cambridge Platonists, whose questioning of the empiricism and materialism of Gassendi and Hobbes was based on Plato's axiom in the *Theatetus* that 'knowledge does not consist in impressions of sense, but in reasoning about them'. According to Ralph Cudworth, the most 'philosophical' of their number, the weakness of the empirical doctrine of knowledge is that it starts from an analysis of sense perception instead of an analysis of judgement. Hobbes for instance believes he is giving an account of knowledge when he explains mind as motion, as the vibration of cells in simple reaction to external stimuli; but the Cambridge Platonists quote Plotinus against him to the effect that sensation is a power exercised by the soul on material forces. John Smith, though arguing not against Hobbes specifically but against 'Epicurus and his followers', objects to a theory of knowledge which does not account for consciousness itself. To what, Smith asks, do the empiricist's 'apparitions' and 'seemings' appear? The mere impression affecting the mind cannot in itself account for our consciousness of this impression.¹¹ On the contrary, it was argued, it is only because there is something in us higher than and prior to sensation that we become aware of sensation and are able to pass judgements concerning it. Herbert would have substantially agreed, and had he had the opportunity would doubtless have benefited from the clarity of the discussion.

Cudworth's particular example is not of a speculative statement but the kind of concrete example so favoured of the empiricists, a white triangular surface. He argues that to sense alone there is merely the appearance of an individual thing, without any distinction, a simple impression. In order to make anything of this the mind has to analyse and resolve this undifferentiated whole, taking notice of its whiteness, its triangularity, and so on. All this, the empiricist would say, is quite possible on the basis of experience. But there remains the judgement of actual external existence, without which the object would remain, Cudworth says, merely 'a notion or objective cogitation'. By 'objective' here Cudworth is using the terminology of his time, for which we need to substitute the word 'subjective', objectivity, in our sense, being itself a function of the judgement Cudworth is demonstrating.[12]

The point here is that the claim being made by both Herbert and the Cambridge Platonists is that the influx of sense impressions must be referred to and measured by enduring thought patterns already 'written in our soul'—that is to say, Common Notions. It is only because we can think such 'unified essences' (in a phrase of Ernst Cassirer's) that we can relate and interpret particulars, compare them with each other, and anticipate 'general nature'. A further implication of such a view is that the general is not derived from the particular, but rather that particulars appear to us in the light of the general, so that knowledge is not a process of imitation but a deductive process of anticipation. Since genuine knowledge is, to use a favourite word of Cudworth's, 'prolepticall', cognition must be an act of spontaneity. The mind cannot stand in relation to any object or pass judgement on it without indirectly expressing its own essence and revealing its original nature. Hence objective knowledge implies an act of self-knowledge: 'Look into your own faculties and you will find God, virtue, and universal eternal truths'.[13]

Such a relation of correspondence can only hold if universal nature has a certain form or hierarchy in the order of which the human soul has a determinate place and grade. In opposition to mechanistic philosophers who, in his view, reverse the true order of being by deriving the spiritual from the corporeal, and to the empiricists who derive the intellect from sense perception, Herbert holds as axiomatic the doctrine of Plotinus (from whatever source it may have reached him) and of the Florentine Neoplatonists that form is the absolute *prius* in respect of matter: the whole is prior to the parts and cannot be derived from them. Since the soul, according to the familiar Neoplatonic tag, is 'form', it is composed of something entirely different from matter and cannot be derived from matter. Its existence and the knowledge which it possesses cannot be explained from the existence of objects alone. If there is such a totality of being of which we are part, just as we are aware of our individual ego so we are made aware of our place within a more comprehensive power. Through the 'inner court' of consciousness we become aware of ourselves; and by our sense perceptions and our ability to universalise we become aware of what is beyond us and of which we are yet a part. Herbert puts it this way: 'So while the inner consciousness, if we attend to it, shows that the whole of what affects us exists within us, external perceptions on the other hand teach that these feelings are not confined to us, but are capable of extension outside us. The infinite is everywhere and every part refers to some element of the whole.'[14] And if the Reader fails to grasp this, Herbert can only suppose that the Reader's 'intelligence is at fault'.

Since, according to this view, the spiritual faculties of the intellect can comprehend and influence the transitory world of matter, while mere sense perception cannot understand the domain of the intellectual faculties, Herbert is especially careful to distinguish between the spiritual and the physical faculties. The spiritual are 'analogous with God', the physical are 'analogous with the world';[15] 'every spiritual faculty of the intellect,' he says, 'has two objects, a particular and a general', but 'the physical faculties embrace only singular objects'[16] and are 'usually particular and changeable in their expression'.[17] Mind is always active, and whatever is passive in us is related to the body.[18] It therefore becomes absurd to put together all the objects of sense and derive from them a comprehensive theory of nature: as Cudworth succinctly put it, 'No Effect can possibly Transcend the Power of its Cause'.[19] Although Sir Thomas Browne's *Religio medici* (1643) was written, like Herbert's work, too early for the author to have the materialism of Hobbes specifically in mind, Browne, as a good Hermetical Platonist, equally asserts his belief in the primacy of spirit over matter, and in a manner as unmistakable as Herbert or the Cambridge Platonists. Like Herbert, Browne could be a serious and practical empiricist—Herbert was a keen and knowledgeable botanist; and when a whale was stranded on the Norfolk coast, Browne was there, tramping out over the cold salt flats to test his notions of spermaceti. Yet for either man to neglect first causes would be unthinkable. The first cause cannot be derived from others but must be grasped as a whole; while one may observe the particular workings of nature, one is bound also to proceed from the whole to the parts. 'Had Aristotle', Browne comments, 'been as curious in the enquiry of this cause as he was of the other, he had not left behind him an imperfect piece of Philosophy, but an absolute tract of Divinity.'[20] Behind Browne's sentiments, as behind Herbert's, lies the Plotinian doctrine of an animating spirit and regulating force that descends from the One through *nous* into the world-soul of nature. Speaking of angels, Browne is led to this speculation:

Now, besides these particular and divided Spirits, there may be (for ought I know) an universal and common Spirit to the whole world. It was the opinion of Plato, and it is yet of the Hermeticall Philosophers. If there be a common nature that unites and tyes the scattered and divided individuals into one species, why may there not be one that unites them all?[21]

This was a question which Herbert also put, and he found his answer among 'the Hermeticall Philosophers'. Let us follow his thoughts on the *analogia* that unite and tie 'scattered and divided individuals' and on 'an universal and common Spirit to the whole World'.

Magica sympathia

There is a good deal of evidence which would appear to suggest that Herbert showed a great interest in the occult sciences. The books in his personal library, which covered practically the whole range of learning of his day, included (as one would expect from such a bibliophile) a number of books on occult philosophy, among them Cornelius Agrippa's *De occulta philosophia* (1550), Michael Psellus's *De operatione daemonum* in a Paris 1615 edition, and the *Ars magica* in a Frankfurt 1631 imprint. It is impossible to say what proportion of his total library the books (over nine hundred) now contained in Jesus College Library, Oxford, represents; a further 230 volumes are in the Powis Castle collection, but a number, perhaps a significant number, of the books in his original library must have been dispersed.[22] It is obvious from the very large number of medical works that Herbert took his own ill health with melancholic seriousness; whether he was so attached to the functions of a *magus* is not so probable. In his autobiography he is eager to display his medical knowledge but he makes no mention of any talents he might possess in the occult sciences. On the contrary, he makes a joke about Dr Dee, the most celebrated occultist of the day, in the course of describing his relative, Sir William Herbert, who was the intimate friend of Dr Dee and worked closely with him. Sir William, Lord Herbert slyly tells us, was 'a man much conversant with books, and especially given to the study of divinity, insomuch, that he writ an Exposition upon the Revelation, which is printed; though some thought he was as far from finding the sense thereof as he was from attaining the philosopher's stone, which was another part of his study'.[23] Nevertheless, Herbert does not reject the theoretical basis of the magician's art. When his portrait was painted by Isaac Oliver (*c.* 1610–15) the youthful Herbert is shown, in full fashionable dress, reclining at the source of a symbolic spring. In the background the squire is preparing his master's armour and his caparisoned horse stands ready. Prominently displayed at the centre of the portrait is the knight's shield, bearing the legend *Magica sympathia*—a motto which might be rendered not only as 'sympathetic magic' but 'the theory of analogy' or as 'universal correspondence'. In the philosophy of occultism Herbert would have found one manifestation of the idea of correspondence between man, the cosmos, and God which came to have such a dominant place in his metaphysics. 'Other thinkers', Rossi remarks, 'had alluded to analogy, had deduced it as a consequence of their own systems; but in Herbert it becomes the first fundamental, the very basis of human knowledge.'[24]

Traditionally enough, Herbert speaks of man as the microcosm of the universe; but he goes further by claiming that every individual being that we can apprehend (whether through the exterior or interior faculties) possesses an analogy or correspondence with some feature of the mind. The correspondence of faculties and objects is explicitly based on this assumption: 'Our minds clearly correspond to God and our body to the world, and the principles of all the differences in the world are inscribed in man. This is the basis of my proposition that the number of differences in the faculties correspond to the number of differences in things.'[25] For example, the entire system of the world is reproduced in the motions and structure of the body, whose passions are analogous to that part of the firmament 'where hurricanes, whirlwinds and meteors rage'.[26]

In his autobiography Herbert recommends a young man to ground himself in the Platonic and Aristotelian philosophies, and adds: 'After which it will not be amiss to read the *Idea medicinae philosophicae*, written by Severinus (Danus), there being many things considerable concerning the Paracelsian principles written in that book, which are not to be found in former writers'.[27] Peter Severin was physician to the King of Denmark, and his work, published at Basle in 1571 and elsewhere later, contained the sum of Paracelsian analogy.

But this physiological application is perhaps the crudest aspect of Herbert's use of *analogia*. More interesting is the way in which he describes the acts of the mind as rays of light which pierce the apertures of the sense organs and apprehend the things to which they are related in accordance with their reciprocal analogy, so that every aspect of apprehension is related to a feature in things. The theory explains the nature of the *conformatio* in which a faculty is in conformity with its object—a view which is different from the traditional conception that cognition must conform to objects, and also different from the opposite Kantian view that objects, as cognised, must conform to cognition. But such a view is of course dependent on suppositions of cosmic harmony and of correspondence between truths and beings, implying an image of the universe as a great series of infinitely reflecting mirrors. Herbert would have found such a conception in the natural magic of Agrippa (sceptic though Agrippa may have been), in the Pythagorean wisdom of Nicholas Cusanus, the Hermetic–Platonic philosophy of Ficino, the occult concordances of Pico, Cardanus's doctrine of 'subtilty', in Telesio, Patrizi, in Paracelsus's 'light of nature' and his secret signatures, or in Kepler's 'cosmographic mysteries'—in fact almost anywhere in the great pantheistic, panpsychistic speculations which proliferated over the whole of the preceding epoch.

Most often of course such views of the universe as a living whole which is unified throughout all its apparent diversity by analogical harmonies were the justification for Renaissance magic and occultism. Ficino, for instance, arguing analogically, explains how there is an intellect of the world and a body of the world, and between them the soul of the world; in the soul of the world there are corresponding 'seminal reasons' which reflect exactly the ideas in the *Mens*, which in turn are reflected in the body of the world, in matter. Everything is joined together by congruities which, Ficino says, Zoroaster called divine links and Synesius magic spells. Magic therefore consists of the manipulation of signs and images which unite the highest divine world with the soul of the world and the world of sense. Because the All is One, the *Magus* can pull the strings of occult sympathies which run through all nature.[28] The idea of 'natural magic' and the concept of analogy itself had their *locus classicus* in the *Corpus hermeticum*, in which Stoicism was fused with Neoplatonism along with various ingredients of Jewish origin. *Corpus hermeticum* is the name given to a collection of documents—about seventeen in number—most of which were written in the third and fourth centuries A.D. Besides each of the books, or *libelli*, of the *Corpus*, the extant 'Hermetic writings' include also the Latin *Asclepius*, excerpts in the *Anthologium* of Stobaeus, and fragments quoted by Lactantius, Cyril and others. The *Asclepius* was formerly attributed to Apuleius (it is in fact a translation of a Greek original, now lost); the *Anthologium*, a large collection of pagan Greek writings, was compiled *c.* 500 A.D. The Renaissance editors and commentators believed the common author of these writings to be 'Hermes Trismegistus', who was thought to have lived before Pythagoras and Plato and from whom the 'Platonic' philosophy and theology ultimately derived.[29] Numerous writers of the sixteenth century had summarised and evaluated the *Corpus* until it became so absorbed into Renaissance speculative philosophy that its basic doctrines came to be commonplaces of Renaissance thought. Ficino, Patrizi, Paracelsus, Pico, Bruno, all of them names to conjure with, were deeply influenced by the Hermetic writings. In spite of Isaac Casaubon's scholarly *coup de grâce* when, in 1614, he dated the Hermetic texts somewhere at the end of the first century A.D. instead of before Moses and Pharaoh (and he was, considering the time-span involved, very close), the Hermetic philosophy lost the prestige of its supposed antiquity only gradually. Herbert, who enjoyed the privilege of conversations with Casaubon in Paris, was fully aware of this 'exposure' and possessed a copy of Casaubon's spectacular exercise in historical criticism. The new dating affected matters of fact and scholarship, and nobody could seriously now invoke Hermetic authority, but as an imaginative and symbolic gesture the Hermetic writings were already irretrievably absorbed by Casaubon's generation, whatever their precise provenance. Eighty editions of the Hermetic writings appeared before 1500, and twenty-two editions have been counted from 1471 to 1641.[30]

What sort of philosophy was to be found in the Hermetica? The best known part of the *Corpus, Mercurii Trismegisti poemander*—'The Divine Pymander'—included all the *libelli* of the *Corpus hermeticum*, though in fact the name 'Poemander' refers only to the first *libellus* specifically, but since Ficino first used the title in his translation of 1471 it was generally used to denote the whole *Corpus*. Since each of the *libelli* is more or less distinct and independent, most of them by different hands and sometimes flatly contradicting each other, it is hardly possible to summarise neatly 'the Hermetic philosophy', for the term is really something of a convenient fiction. Certain characteristics, however, stand out clearly. Two of its cardinal doctrines are: the idea of the substantiality of the incorporeal world and man's involvement in it by virtue of his incorporeal soul (with the insistence on the final destiny of the soul in the transcendent world); and the idea of 'correspondence', of a definite and involved relation between the different parts of creation—both of which doctrines are basic to *De veritate*. But embracing all these doctrines is the over-riding conception of unity in diversity. It is dependent on the following chain of relationship—'God, Cosmos, Man'. 'The Cosmos is contained by God, and Man is contained by the Cosmos; the Cosmos is the son of God, man is the son of the Cosmos and grandson, so to speak, of God.'[31] In the next *libellus* this becomes: 'Everywhere God will come to meet you, everywhere he will appear to you; for there is nothing which is not God'.[32] And this notion of the interrelation Man : Cosmos : God is expressed in the old saying, *hoc dixi, omnia unum esse et unum omnia*—'All things are One, and the One is all things.' Similar ideas are to be found in the other primary source of Renaissance Neoplatonism, the works of Plotinus. Plotinus also holds that God is the 'One', the highest principle, pure reality and complete actuality, and from the 'One' Mind or Intelligence emanates downwards, as it were, by the agency of the World Soul. God is therefore both the 'One' and the 'All', the principle of unity, self-sufficiency and immutability, and at the same time the source and the informing energy from which being flows through all levels down to the lowest.

In both the Hermetic writings and in Plotinus there is a logical difficulty, for God is conceived as self-contradictory, as both One and All. The Renaissance solution to this difficulty, and already adumbrated in Plotinus, involved a characteristic *tour de force* which Herbert follows very closely. In order to reconcile the contradition within God's nature recourse was sometimes made to a concept of a secondary deity, a kind of 'demi-urge', called by Pico (after Hermes, Plato and Zoroaster) the 'First Mind'.[33] But Pico saw himself as a Christianising Platonist and such a conception militates against the traditional theology of a transcendent God, and he is at pains to point out that the secondary deity is expressly 'not the Son of God,' 'He not being a Creature, but one essence, co-equal with the Creator'.[34] The classic solution of the dilemma was the theory of the *coincidentia oppositorum*, a 'meeting of extremes in the Absolute', by means of which God can be conceived as both 'One' and 'All', as perfect and yet other, as transcendent and at the same time immanent.[35] Hence God is a being who embraces all the diversity of the universe within himself, though himself without parts; in whom the mutable world lives and moves, though he himself is immutable. The most frequently recurring image to express this paradox is the image of God as a sphere whose centre is everywhere and whose circumference nowhere—a formula which turns up again and again in Neoplatonic thought as a paradoxical and yet, for that very reason, profoundly satisfying explanation of the relation of God to the world, the world to God, and man to both. Ficino attributes the image to Hermes, although it is in fact first found in a pseudo-Hermetic treatise of the twelfth century, from which it was culled by Cusanus.[36] With this notion behind him Cusanus states that 'God ... envelops all in the sense that all is found in Him; He is the development of all in the sense that He is found in all'. Hence centre and circumference, maximum and minimum, infinite and finite, are one.[37] However objectionable as logic such a procedure might be, it conformed to a principle defined by Proclus as 'the whole in the part' and to Plotinus's *Anima est tota in toto et tota in qualibet parte*.[38] If therefore we take the most extreme of opposites it follows that they will possess a relation of balance and harmony; throughout the creation there are always antitheses, always relationship, always there is part and counter-part—a notion which Cusanus set out to demonstrate in a startling manner by showing that one pound can counterbalance a thousand pounds by its distance from the centre of the scales, thus proving that all opposites may be reconciled within the infinite which is everywhere.[39]

How does Herbert adapt ideas of this sort? He characterises the 'great amphibium' man, who, in the words of the Hermetical Sir Thomas Browne, inhabits 'divided and distinguished worlds':

Infinity cannot be grasped except through the idea of the finite, nor eternity save through the form of time. We possess indeed faculties in the soul which correspond to these notions; those in fact which are themselves eternal and those which we desire to exist for ever. Nevertheless the intellect, under the guidance of its Common Notions, leads us to perceive that infinity surpasses our comprehension, that eternity is not capable of measurement by our order of time. Here it behoves us to have a little patience for a while until we are freed of our body and the world. We seem indeed too refined in relation to gross objects, too gross in relation to refined spheres.[40]

But there is inherent in our God-implanted faculties of faith and the instinct for religion (which Herbert calls the 'unique and ultimate *differentiae* of man') the means of resolving all oppositions and all paradoxes. Our instinct for God partakes of infinity itself, and through it

we are not only transported to loftier realms but are enabled to bring these down to our level. They [religion and faith] serve to unite distant spheres; and accordingly their dwelling is in man, who is himself poised between the higher and lower realms ... the illimitable power of religion and faith combines and unites not only lower and higher orders, but also the past and the future. And there is nothing, we rightly believe, they cannot bring into harmony.[41]

And so the circle of relationship is completed:

Everything we can imagine exists in the infinite, and everything beyond this. God is beyond all things, and alone independent of all. He transcends transcendence, and fills, informs and encompasses the infinite itself in the vastness of His unity. This is proved by the fact that just as we encounter the finite and universal order in the infinite, so in all that is finite can we find some traces of the infinite. Thus everything seems capable of being divided into an infinity of parts, but since it must be in the end resolved into a unity (the ultimate characteristic of the infinite) infinity and unity appear to meet.

The 'coincidence of opposites' theorem, releasing all manner of fruitful analogies and correspondences, is important in Herbert's thought as a dialectical instrument in the defining of truth and the unification of knowledge and the related concern, in Herbert, of promoting religious toleration. The notion lurks too behind the theoretical assumptions of 'metaphysical' poetry as a distinctive style and is nowhere better illustrated than in Herbert's verse. For example, in his 'love poem', 'Restrained hopes' the lady whom the poet addresses is too great for him, too noble in beauty and all perfection; and yet by means of an intellectual trick reminiscent of Cusanus's weighing experiment Herbert 'composes' the opposites of beloved and rejected, of beauty and unworthiness, perfection and imperfection, and because everything that exists has its opposite, a relation must maintain between the two extremes. On these grounds the lover, however unworthy, may yet lay some hopes:

> As there is nothing yet doth so excell,
> But there is found, if not its parallel,
>   Yet something so conform, as though far least
>   May yet obtain therein an Interest,
> Why may not faith and truth then join so well,
> As they may suit her rare perfections best?[42]

In these lines—whose conclusion may at first sight make one wonder, as so often in Herbert's verse, if it is not some quite different argument which is being clinched—he wittily introduces into the composing of beloved and rejected (the dramatic point of the poem) the unexpected conjunction of 'faith and truth', which are perhaps here treated (as in *De veritate*) as possible opposites which may through 'something so conform', or proper conformity of the faculties, ultimately 'join so well'. Many other poems are made up of a similar play of opposites which are resolved at length into a 'golden mean'. In his Marvellian sonnet, 'Made upon the Groves near Merlow Castle,' there is a very exact balance of light and shade, heat and cold, burning and freezing, resolved to 'one even temper':

> You well compacted Groves, whose light & shade
>   Mixt equally, produce nor heat, nor cold,
>   Either to burn the young, or freeze the old,
> But to one even temper being made,
> Upon a Greene embroidering through each Glade
>   An Airy Silver, and a Sunny Gold . . .[43]

The succeeding poem in the collection, *To the C. of D.* (to either the Countess of Dorset or the Countess of Devonshire), has a precisely similar logical structure, playing upon the 'contraditions' of 'delight' and 'state', 'Love' and 'gravity', chastity and virtue, 'sweet neglect' and 'reverend respect', the 'understanding' and the 'heart', and love and honour.[44] In *The Brown Beauty* Herbert enlarges on the theme in a very explicit fashion:

> While the two contraries of Black and White,
> In the Brown *Phaie* are so well unite,
> That they no longer now seem opposite,
>   Who doubts but love, hath this his colour chose,
>   Since he therein doth both th' extremes compose
>   And as within their proper Centre close?[45]

In his formal philosophy the conception of the One and the Many, of whole and part, does not perhaps appear with the same immediate clarity as it appears in his poetry nor with the air (which is very apparent in his verse) of having been lifted straight out of Plotinus or Ficino.[46] His approach is more subtle and provides a show of independence. Yet there remains a body of assumptions without which the structure of *De veritate* would collapse. Like so many Renaissance minds, Herbert, in spite of the appearance of some hard-hitting pragmatism, responds to the idea of truth as to a *mysterium fascinosum* whose ultimate characteristic is the unification of all diversity. Towards the paradoxical opposites of the finite and the infinite he advances the resolution of the *coincidentia*. In the section of *De veritate* entitled 'On Possibility' he constructs a rhetoric which is reminiscent of both the language and the enthusiasm of Giordano Bruno. Herbert asserts the possibility of a future state beyond death for the soul—a theme he constantly stresses throughout *De veritate*—and justifies such a belief in a Brunoesque fashion by referring to the possibility of infinite worlds and hence infinite possible states of the soul. Arguing analogically, he suggests that just as the embryo in the womb has no knowledge of life after birth and yet discovers that a second world exists, so 'why should there not be a third and a fourth state, and many more if there are no limits to infinity?' This possibility exists because the human soul partakes of infinity, evidenced by its ability to conceive the infinite; and this ability is significant of the soul's final destiny because, as Herbert repeats on many occasions, nature does nothing in vain.

The compass of the soul embraces not merely a man's height in the ordinary sense, but the limit of his faculties. And since the faculty of sight reaches to the sun and even to the stars, while the understanding and the will refer to the infinite and eternal, is it to be supposed that in spite of our aspirations we do not reach and grasp them?[47]

Moreover, on the journey from 'the womb of this lower world' the soul will pass through the ceiling of heaven (which, Herbert adds, appears to be blue because of its distance, 'as experts in optics tell us') and emerge into the regions of the stars that 'have been erected not merely to sparkle, but to be new worlds'; 'and at last . . . the infinite itself will unfold'.[48] The speculation on the infinite is pursued by manipulating the *coincidentia oppositorum*:

What reaches and illimitable depths may there not be in the infinite? You may gain some idea of them by reflecting that there is no number which can fill or empty it. It cannot be increased by addition or diminished by subtraction, but at one moment passes into the Nature which is its own, at another returns to infinity. At every point it is identical, and occupies no space nor is limited by any boundary.

He goes on:

It is true that a small urn holds our ashes, but the whole visible world cannot afterwards comprehend the soul, and in view of its sublime nature it may be the only object we do not comprehend in this world. The authors may therefore be right ... in maintaining that so far from the infinite being capable of any addition, it extends to, and reaches, every point of space.[49]

The 'authors' here are evidently Lucretius (*De rerum natura*, I, 951), Cusanus (*De docta ignorantia*), and Bruno (especially *De l'infinito universo e mondi*, dialogue II). The ultimate characteristic of the infinite is, Herbert repeats, unity. Although everything may be divided into parts, all parts 'must in the end be resolved into a unity'. And, at the centre and circumference of all that is, God 'transcends transcendence, and fills, informs, and encompasses the infinite in the vastness of His unity'.

It seems more than probable that Herbert derived these ideas from Bruno, a copy of whose *De l'infinito* (Venice, 1584) was in Herbert's library. For Bruno the innumerable worlds he imagined were all divine centres of the unbounded universe, and this infinitely extended All was still One. The unity of All and One is constantly celebrated in Bruno's work: 'the *summum bonum*, the supremely desirable, the supreme perfection and beatitude, consists in the unity which informs the All'.[50] In his *De la causa, principio e uno*, for example, Bruno argues that all diversity and difference is not diversity and difference of 'Being' but of various modes of 'Being': 'Multiplicity results from a multiplicity of modes of being, which is one; multiplicity and difference is pure accident, pure figure, and pure alteration of substance; all things are in the universe and the universe is in all things ... because all things concur in a perfect unity.' All that we see which exhibits difference, transformation, figure, colour, is, Bruno maintains, nothing but a diversity of appearance; each particular thing is a mutable, transitory mode of what is immutable and eternal: 'All contraries coincide in the One'.[51] Thus Herbert writes, in the colour symbolism of his *Sonnet of Black Beauty*:

> When all these colours which the world call bright,
>   And which old Poetry doth so persue,
> Are with the night so perished and gone,

> That of their being there remains no mark,
> Thou still abidest so intirely one,
> That we may know thy blackness is a spark
> Of light inaccessible, and alone
> Our darkness which can make us think it dark.[52]

This is the language of men who will not be laughed 'out of the Philosophy of Hermes' by 'the severe Schools'. For example, Sir Thomas Browne's declaration that *'Natura nihil agit frustra*, is the only indisputable Axiome in Philosophy' leads him, like Herbert, to wonder at the function of those unbounded faculties of the soul, and makes him conclude that 'we carry with us the wonders we seek without us'[53] So too Thomas Traherne, drawing on the Hermetic wisdom as transmitted by Cusanus and Bruno, says 'Nothing is vain, much less infinity. Every man is alone the centre and circumference of it. It is all his own, and so glorious, that it is the eternal and incomprehensible essence of the Deity.'[54] Traherne's sense of the infinity of space and the spiritual infinity of the soul pervades his work:

> His Omnipresence is an Endless Sphere,
> Wherein all Worlds as His Delights appear.
> His Beauty is the Spring of all Delight,
> Our Blessedness, like His, is infinit.
> His Glory Endless is and doth Surround
> And fill all Worlds, without or End or Bound.[55]

Such 'transcendence' as responses like this affirm is ambiguous. Herbert, like Bruno, seems to be reworking Stoic and Neoplatonic doctrines of a World Soul. Certainly, as M. H. Carré observes, such an idea was 'well adapted to provide an alternative to the medieval insistence on transcendence . . . it expressed a fundamental desire of the Renaissance to unite the human and the divine'.[56] Like Bruno, Herbert consequently approaches very close to pantheism, for it is a standing danger of such a vast and all-embracing view of the deity to reverse the Nicene formula and to mistake the creation for its Creator. 'What is Nature,' enquired Seneca, 'if not God and the Divine Reason inherent in the entire world and in all its parts?'[57] While Herbert took especial care to equate Nature not with God but with 'Divine Providence', Bruno was quite prepared to ask, What is God, if not Nature?[58] Herbert is here in accord with the Florentine Neoplatonists Ficino and Pico concerning the relationship between the creation and the Creator: God for them is active and manifest in the universe but not identical with it; he may be perceived through his creation, but it is dependent on him while he is independent of it. If Bruno cannot find God anywhere he concludes that it must be because God is everywhere, and turns to a mystic pantheism which finds an immanent God in an infinite Nature. Herbert retreats from pantheism in this sense, and that one should be defending, as it were, the so-called 'Father of English Deism' from a possible charge of pantheism is of course not without its own peculiar interest.

The desire 'to unite the human and the divine' is conspicuously present in Herbert as an attack on the scholastic insistence on transendence. His Common Notions are conformities between Natural Instinct in man and its spiritual objects, and it is a vital point in his doctrine that they are expressions of our practical rather than our theoretical understanding. They are a means of preparing a ground upon which the individual might establish a belief which squared with his conscience, his reason and credibility, and with his instinct. Truth is founded on Common Notions; the Common Notions are founded on Natural Instinct; Natural Instinct governs our analogy with God and with the world. As a criterion of truth the theory of Common Notions based on universal analogy is a reply to Montaigne's contention that 'diversity is the most universall quality'. Herbert, recognising this diversity, maintained that it was an appearance only, integrated by means of signs, correspondences and reflections into the total structure of the universe—a structure which was therefore approachable and comprehensible. In the very opening paragraph of his introduction to *De veritate* Herbert reviews the contemporary 'philosophy of Nature' which is, he says, 'composed of irreconcilable and fortuitous principles' (that is, the philosophy of the sceptics), and he claims that Nature itself is not like this at all; rather, 'some spirit of truth pervades this shapeless and monstrous chaos of beliefs, informing its very errors with life and motion' (*anima quaedem veritatis permeet*), and it is this spirit (his choice of the world *anima* is significant here) that he proposes to 'examine, to clarify, and to defend'.[59] Herbert would have endorsed the ancient Hermetic warning that 'If anyone attempts to separate all things from the One, taking the term "all things" to signify a mere plurality of things, and not a whole made up of things, he will sever the All from the One, and will thereby bring to naught the All'.[60] According to Herbert's metaphysics, the existent, eternal, universal and self-evident truth is, to be sure, scattered in many different things so that there are as many truths as there are differences in things; but these differences in things are made known to us by faculties inherent in us as epitomes of the universe. Although everything seems capable of division, so that we are tempted to recognise diversity as the universal datum, this 'infinity of parts' must in the end be 'resolved into a unity'.

By means of this assumption Herbert is able also to attack pure nominalism. We can discover not only simple truths, that is to say truths relating to particulars, but also composite truth concerning general ideas, for the intellect asserts the truth when particular truths are in right conformity with each other. This composite truth acquaints us with the true nature of things: 'Composite truth . . . is concerned with universals. Its governing principle is that the intellect expresses the truth in universals when particular truths are in proper conformity with one another. Composite truth is of special importance because it fastens on the universal aspect of things . . .'[61] And yet, since the core of Herbert's doctrine is that truth is the intuition of the manifold analogies by which reality is unified, we find ourselves in a philosophical world in which the 'ordinary Peripatetic doctrine' of the relations of universals and particulars is subsumed in the organic relations (those 'Paracelesian principles' for which Herbert commends Severinus) of the Whole and its parts. It is worth noticing that Herbert does not of course attempt to demonstrate or prove the theory of analogy, or that there is an absolute unity of whole and part, or that mind must be prior to matter; he seems to take these propositions for granted as axioms which, like his own Common Notions, 'it is not legitimate to dispute'. Such 'proof' as there is lies in the recognition that knowledge is something other than what the materialists and atomists might say, which we intuit by contemplating items of knowledge and recognising their nature.

Plastic virtue

Herbert has a curious name for the force which animates his holistic universe: he calls it the 'plastic power', or 'plastic virtue'. The term first occurs specifically in *De veritate* in the section on the Internal Senses, where Herbert is speaking of the nature of mind and body and of the analogy between them:

I call bodily structure that definite system of principles which in order to produce the human organism coalesce and remain latent in the humours as in minerals (for the humours correspond to the elements). Anyone who refuses to look for the law by which these principles combine with our own in the mind or Harmony of the world, that *plastic power* which reduces different kinds of food to one form, may learn to know it through his inner consciousness.[62]

The function of the 'plastic power' seems very much like that of Natural Instinct in one of its aspects; that is, it is that power which tends towards 'the preservation of the individual, of species, of kinds, and of the universe'.[63] There are two important functions of Herbert's use of the concept. The first is to combat materialistic and mechanistic physico-theologies (in which engagement Herbert shows himself remarkably prophetic of the way scientific thought was to develop in the seventeenth century); and the second and most important for Herbert personally, is to affirm, by an appeal to natural processes, the immortality of the soul.

As a 'biological' principle of conservation, 'plastic virtue' bears similarities to Montaigne's 'common sense' or 'sens naturel'. When Montaigne describes the activities of bees, the nests of swallows, or the spider's web—all models of orderliness and planning reflected directly in action—the key word is 'judgement', the power 'naturall and without teaching' given to all creatures by a benevolent Mother Nature. All creatures have the capacity to order the world and themselves for the preservation of their being, which they have by 'a kind of natural instinct'—an instinct which Montaigne insists is of more value to our protection and contentment than our distinctively human faculties of reason, imagination and art. Although Herbert's use of the principle is particularly associated with his arguments for immortality, he also presents it as a general ontological law. In all the lower forms of life on earth there is discernible everywhere, he says, an impulse directing life towards self-preservation; we see in Nature, in animals and plants and even in elements, an impulse which according to differences of species produce behaviour directed towards the same end.[64] This impulse is a faculty which 'aims at self-preservation in the elements, the zoophytes, and even in the embryo'.[65] The conclusion must be that it would be truly remarkable if this impulse did not manifest itself in ourselves. What is a biological force in Nature becomes a spiritual force in man, but since Herbert regards Natural Instinct in man as psychologically continuous with the lower forms of life on earth, this tendency in man preserves its instinctive character and its intuitions are not always understood by the rational or discursive faculty: 'It must be remembered that it is in the nature of Natural Instinct to fulfil itself irrationally, that is to say, without foresight. The elements, minerals and vegetables give no evidence of possessing foresight, and yet display knowledge strikingly directed towards their own preservation.'[66]

The peculiar term 'plastic virtue' is Herbert's designation for a notion which came to him from many varied sources. It was most probably suggested by the theory of *rationes seminales* or *logoi spermatikoi* of the Stoics, chiefly Cicero and Seneca, and, through the agency of Ficino's translation of the *Enneads*, from Plotinus. In Stoic writers the term is more or less equivalent to the idea of 'Nature', or 'God as efficient cause', the universal and unconscious creative force, and is very like the *natura naturans* in Neoplatonism, or the Stoic 'cosmic fire'.[67] The word *plastikos* occurs in the *Enneads*, and in 1678 Ralph Cudworth translated *logos spermatikos* from the *Enneads* as 'Spermatick Reason or Plastick Nature'.[68] In Ficino himself Herbert would have found the theory of *spiritus*, upon which Ficino's conception of magic is based; magic consists in guiding and controlling the influx of *spiritus* into *materia*, chiefly through talismans. The spiritual cosmology here is that between the soul of the world and its body there is a *spiritus mundi* which pervades the universe and through which stellar influences come down to man, whose own spirit receives them, and to the whole *corpus mundi*. This is the *spiritus*, Ficino says, of which Virgil spoke: '*Spiritus intus alit, totamque infusa per artus / mens agitat molem et magno se corpore miscet.*'[69] Herbert's own theory seems to gather up and imply the functions of the seminal reasons, of the scholastic 'vegetative soul', the Aristotelian *appetitus naturalis*, and of the Plotinian notions of *plastikos* and the *anima mundi*—'the world's common soul' to which Herbert refers in his verse, for instance in his *Elegy for the Prince*. It is in fact an amalgam of various animating principles which he now puts forward under a novel designation.

His emphasis on the necessity for such a principle is especially remarkable because it anticipated by two decades the doctrine of 'Plastick Nature' which was to become so important, later in the seventeenth century, to thinkers like Henry More and Cudworth. The earliest noted use of the term 'plastic' in this sense is in Henry More's *Psychozoia* of 1642, where 'plastick might' is given as an attribute of aether.[70] Herbert was using the term in 1624. Like the

Cambridge Platonists' use of the concept, Herbert's original
development of it was impelled by a desire to combat mechanistic
arguments which reverse the order of mind and matter—was
proposed, that is, in order to uphold a view of the universe which
was God-centred, God-animated and God-sustained, subject at
every turn to the impress of the Divine Providence and in which all
created things moved as within a continuum of divine activity. The
doctrine, which appeared later under a number of names, such as
the Spirit of Nature, the *vis formatrix*, or the 'hylarchic principle', was
of special use to Cudworth and More, for it is crucial to the problem
posed by the Cartesian dualism of substances of interaction between
corporeal and incorporeal substance. In a well known passage
Cudworth points to the dilemma. 'For unless there be such a thing
admitted as a Plastick Nature' there seem to be only two
alternatives: either everything in Nature occurs by chance and
without a directing Mind, or 'God himself doth all Immediately, and
as it were with his own Hands, Form the Body of every Gnat and
Fly'.[71] His concern with plastic nature has therefore a definite
philosophical significance, for it provides an argument against
Descartes and Hobbes by asserting that there is no automatic
mechanism in nature which does not move towards its final cause in
direct dependence on God; that there is 'no Being which does not
bear the seal of mind, whose secret analogy, heard by the spirit
alone, pervades the universe'[72] Just as Herbert had done, Cudworth
observes this 'Energetick, Effectual and Operative Cause' acting in
plants and animals, and if this 'Plastick Nature' creates and
preserves 'so many Microcosms' there must also be a 'general
Plastick Nature in the Macrocosm, the whole Corporeal Universe,
that which makes all things to conspire everywhere, and agree
together into one Harmony'.[73]

The emphasis here must be upon Lord Herbert's
perception—whether he was wholly or only partly conscious of its
implications—of a crucial theological and philosophic difficulty
inherent in a mechanistic philosophy of nature and in the empirical
method itself. Herbert was of course writing before the impact of
Cartesianism made itself felt—Descartes's influence in England can
be dated from 1637 when Sir Kenelm Digby sent from Paris a copy
of the *Discours* to Hobbes—and he is not so acutely aware of the
dilemma which Cudworth and others saw so clearly. Yet he
constantly underlines the importance of Natural Instinct as the

agent or intermediary of Mind, or the will of God; and intimately related to this mediatory property of Natural Instinct is its power to preserve life. It is worth noting that Spinoza's doctrine of *conatus*, the striving towards self-maintenance of all particular things within the order of Nature, is very similar to Herbert's theory. Spinoza states that each particular thing exhibits a characteristic tendency to cohesion and to the preservation of its identity, a 'striving, in so far as it lies in it self to do so, to persist in its own being'.[74] The importance of the the idea is that it qualifies a merely atomistic or mechanical account of the physical world such as Spinoza found in Descartes, whose philosophy—fatally as Spinoza thought—has no equivalent of the notion of *conatus*. Stuart Hampshire, in his exposition of Spinoza's philosophy, has suggested that the idea of individual self-preservation 'is exactly the concept which biologists have often demanded as an essential to the understanding of organic and living systems'.[75]

Herbert's Natural Instinct, in its 'plastic' capacity, preserves the whole universe—'Unless a law inwardly demanded and not drawn from the universal wisdom of nature did not avert the mutual destruction of things, they would all conflict with such violence that they would instantly fall into ruins'—in such a way that the general order depends on the preservation of individuals, so that there is a particular and a general providence working from individual to species to genera and finally returning upon itself from the universe as a whole to the individual[76] Herbert, as usual, insists on this as much for ethical as for metaphysical reasons. The immediate distinction he makes between general and particular providence is that of Nature and Grace; and, putting the two together, he states that 'there is therefore a supreme Providence composed of universal Providence or Nature, and particular Providence or Grace, and controlling both'.[77] Now the lesson to be drawn at once from this is that we should not extol Grace by abusing Nature, for 'if this Grace is universal it is part of Common Providence'. Clearly, Herbert's argument is an attempt to solve several (probably too many) problems at the same time. By means of Natural Instinct, or particular Providence, or Grace, or *plastica vis*, the conservation of all life is guaranteed, the goodness of general Providence is upheld against those, chiefly Calvinists, who would separate the two domains, Grace is reconciled with Nature, immanence and transcendence are brought together, ethical determinism is refuted, the belief (primary to Herbert) that 'all men have the means of access to God' is justified, and the ultimate end of all our strivings is shown to be 'Eternal Blessedness'.

Herbert is, as he points out himself, arguing throughout by means of analogy—a methodology which was, incidentally, highlighted in the next century in Bishop Joseph Butler's celebrated *Analogy of Religion* (1736), in which Butler is concerned chiefly to show that the constitution of the world is analogous to and of a piece with revealed religion, and that the deists, by attempting to base religion on natural theology alone and by seeming to imply that God, apart from the initial creative act, has no further concern with the life of the cosmos, are erroneous. Butler, like Herbert, stresses the importance of probability as a guide to judgement and opposes himself to those who, he says, form their 'notions of the constitution and government of the world upon reasoning, without foundation for the principles which they assume'. Lord Herbert, the 'father of the deists', had made the same qualifying point about reasoning with equal if not more vehement insistence. The gesture Herbert makes with his theory of 'plastic virtue' is significant in that it suggests a refusal to abandon the government of the world to second causes, a desire to preserve the coalitions of Nature and Grace, Cause and Effect, Corporeal and Incorporeal; and suggests too an emphasis on those 'foundations' which must lie beneath all so called 'reasoning'—foundations which Cudworth saw in 'as it were a Diaphanous and Crystalline Globe, or a kind of Notional World, which hath some Reflex Image, and correspondent Ray, or Representation in it, to whatsoever is in the True and Real World of Being'[78] and which Herbert, expressing himself more soberly, found established in the Neoplatonic 'hierarchy of Nature'.

The immortality of the soul

In the course of explaining the kind of analogical and intuitional knowledge of which man is capable, Herbert also expounds at length his views about the soul's nature and its final destiny. The two most important human faculties, those of Natural Instinct and the Internal senses, have as their ultimate object of concern 'Eternal Blessedness', and Herbert's repetition of the necessity for a state of blessedness in the world beyond death is so insistent that *De veritate* might equally be called a celebration of the soul's immortality as an exposition of truth.

Yet the two topics are not entirely unrelated. The nominalist division between 'truths of faith' and 'truths of reason', memorably expressed in Pomponazzi's words in his defence against the charge of heresy as 'I believe as a Christian what I cannot believe as a philosopher', became focused specifically on the question of the soul's immortality. In his *Tractatus de immortalitate animae* (1516) Pomponazzi argues, following at some points Averroes and at others the opinions of Alexander of Aphrodisias, that immortality is a fiction: the ability of the soul to exist without the body is undemonstrable, whereas the soul's utter dependence on bodily senses is quite amenable to proof. He rejects the ontological and moral arguments put forward by Aquinas and the most recent Platonists, and reaches a Machiavellian ethic which sees virtue as its own reward and vice its own punishment; to justify virtue it is not necessary to propose immortality, though rulers have obviously recognised the usefulness of the belief in promoting virtue, restraining vice, and thus easing the difficulties of government. Following the Averroists and the nominalists, he separates thought into faith and reason and points out that it is quite possible for Pomponazzi the Christian to believe immortality while Pomponazzi the philosopher denies it.[79]

Such denial of personal immortality, even under this apparently schizophrenic guise and the protection of the 'double truth', was a signal mark of atheism not only because it refused to accept the authority of the Scriptures on the point but also because the government of the world by God's providence, and indeed God's very existence, could be brought into question at the same time. Hence the immortality of the soul was the chief banner under which the campaign against atheism and religious scepticism was conducted. Throughout the Renaissance and far on into the seventeenth century argument and counter-argument waged back and forth with monotonous repetition and left in their wake a vast literature of tracts and treatises, among which we may number *De veritate*.[80] Herbert's own personal and obsessive concern with the issue is strikingly reflected in the catalogues of his library. The books remaining in Jesus College Library, Oxford, include, among others on the subject, Pontanus, *De immortalitate animae ex sententia Aristotelis* (Rome, 1597); Julius Caesar La Galla, *De immortalitate animorum*

(Rome, 1621); Jean de Silhon, *De l'immortalité de l'âme* (Paris, 1634) (the second discourse of which is a 'Refutation du Pirrhonisme et des raisons que Montaigne apporte pour l'établir'); Antonius Sirmondus, *De immortalitate animae* (Paris, 1635)—besides a copy of Iamblichus's *De mysteriis Aegyptiorum, Chaldaeorum, etc.* (Venice, 1497), with the following notes in Herbert's hand: '*Homo est anima utens corpore.* Proclus. *Qui movi ausus est se immortalem novit.* E.H. *Nullum est in nobis quod dubium istud immortalitate animae moveat (excitet) nisi timor mortis.* E.H.' The National Library of Wales catalogue cites *Le Phaedon de Platon traitant de l'immortalité de l'âme* by Jean de Divresme (?), 1553.[81]

Supplying the many arguments which recur to support immortality there are obvious common sources, particularly the proofs of the Angelic Doctor, Aquinas, that the soul's intellectual functions demonstrate its incorporeality and hence, by analogy with the known nature of other incorporeal beings, its immortality. For example, Guillaume Houpelande, writing in 1489, repeats the Thomistic proofs, quotes the views of Plato, Hermes Trismegistus, Seneca and Cicero, stresses the innate desire for justice which can find satisfaction only in another world where the divine justice may be fulfilled, and emphasises the Stoic *consensus gentium* as an indisputable proof.[82] A further importance source is in the Neoplatonic arguments showing how the soul can be separated from the body in ecstasy, how it is independent of physical infirmities, and how it is necessarily spiritual and immortal because of the structure of the universe. In a popular work like the three books of hexameters by Palearius, *De immortalitate animorum*, first printed in 1536 and frequently reprinted afterwards, all the various arguments can be seen in full display; the poem proves God's existence, celebrates immortality and the bliss of the soul when released from the bonds of the body, describes its flight on the wings of desire towards its source and creator, and demonstrates its eternity by its powers of abstraction and its comprehension of contraries, infinities, and universal forms. The work was specifically directed against atheists, and was often printed as a corrective appendix to Lucretius.[83]

The *consensus gentium* 'proof' was a key argument, but one which Pomponazzi dismissed out of hand. In answer to the objection that if the soul were mortal almost the whole world would be deceived, since all religions hold the soul to be immortal, Pomponazzi replied that this was indeed precisely the case. Citing Plato against the Platonists, he argued, with crushing logic, that

> if the whole is nothing but its parts, as many think, since there is no man who is not deceived, as Plato says in the *Republic*, it is not wrong, nay, it is necessary to admit that either the whole world is deceived or at least the greater part. For assuming that there are only three religions, those of Christ, of Moses, and of Mohammed; then either they are all false, and thus the whole world is deceived; or at least two of them, and thus the greater part is deceived.[84]

In these words, incidentally, he puts forward a powerful argument for Renaissance syncretism. His particular point was echoed by Bertrand Russell, who suggested that if we suppose three religions and if all three are to have an equal chance of being true, each must be more likely to be false than true.[85] But the issue of immortality need not be affected by this argument since, as men like Herbert assert, there are fundamental religious instincts in all religions and the affirmation of the soul's immortality is common to them all. However untrue they may be, they will not be untrue for *that* reason. Herbert in fact uses an argument similar to Pomponazzi's against Calvinist ideas of predestination and their implicit denial of the efficacy of repentance, for unless wickedness can be abolished by penitence and faith in God, 'there does not exist, nor ever has existed, any universal source' of grace; 'if this *were* the case, God has created and condemned certain men, in fact the larger part of the human race, not only without their desire, but without their knowledge'. This idea is 'so dreadful' that the assertion of universally available truth and its location in the Common Notions is for Herbert imperative.[86] And the same dreadful consequence would also attend denial of immortality, since Herbert declares that it would be 'strange and unworthy of Divine Providence' to provide us with capacities incapable of fulfilment, and we would be involved in the most unthinkable cosmic deceit.[87]

For, together with Pomponazzi's famous treatise, the other most significant and comprehensive discussion in the Renaissance of immortality was the *Theologia platonica de immortalitate animorum* of Marsilio Ficino, in which great reliance is placed on the appeal to our natural capacities. Ficino's *Theologia* is the most systematic and formal presentation of Renaissance arguments for immortality and its general approaches should be summarised. Two of Ficino's most important principles are those of *primum in aliquo genere* and of *appetitus naturalis*. The first of these is a general ontological law according to which there is in every genus a highest member or *primum* which contains in itself the characteristic essence of the genus, and all other members of that genus reflect its attributes in a definite hierarchy. Since the totality of being is conceived as a kind of genus also, God, or Being and Goodness itself, may be called the *primum* of that genus. All things below God receive being and goodness from him as source and cause of all, so that all movement and desire is towards God as the final and highest end. The second, and related, principle of *appetitus naturalis* asserts that the human soul is directed by an innate desire towards some end peculiar to it, and that this end must be capable of attainment; and since the final end is said to be infinite truth and goodness, it can be attained only in an after life for which the soul must necessarily be equipped. Following these principles, Ficino argues that the desire for God, and hence for spirituality and immortality, is based on the soul's essence: 'The goal and end of mind is Truth and Goodness itself, namely God; towards God it moves like fire, with an essential instinct'.[88] And since the soul has been directly created by God, God himself must have implanted that natural instinct: 'Men seek God's form, therefore this appetite is given by God'.[89] Hence the human soul, which has a natural desire towards the eternal, has itself an eternal nature.

From this another proof follows, based on a further ontological principle that nothing in nature is superfluous or vain. 'Every natural movement', Ficino states, 'is able to reach its goal at some time, and every preparation related by nature to a form is able to acquire that form at some time'.[90] The application of this axiom to the natural movement of the soul towards God at once demonstrates its immortality. Ficino also uses a Pauline kind of argument to the effect that no other creature despises present blessings for the sake of future blessings, and if man alone enjoys neither present nor future then he is indeed the most miserable and stupid of all animals. But this is impossible and the hope of immortality is assured.[91]

Ficino's chief metaphysical argument is dependent on the definition of the soul and the nature of the objects it comprehends. The soul of man is considered to be a self-existing substance which has a unique place in the hierarchic order of the universe, and according to the principle of affinity, of microcosm and macrocosm, there is a definite relation between knower and known. In the realm of pure thought we are led to a necessary affinity between the soul and the incorporeal, intelligible entities which it contemplates, and to the conclusion that the soul itself must be an incorporeal, intelligible entity: 'As we cannot perceive invisible things with the use of our sight, so we cannot think incorporeal things with the use of a corporeal instrument, or seek, enquire, find and preserve things separated from matter, space and time with the use of a nature bound to body, place and time'.[92] It follows that the soul which conceives these eternal and immutable objects of thought must itself be eternal and immutable in its essence.

An obviously important aspect of the discussion concerned the definition of the soul, exactly what it is, and where it can be said to reside. Various arguments of great complexity were put forward. A characteristic Neoplatonic solution is rehearsed in an English work by John Woolton, Bishop of Exeter, *Treatise of the Immortality of the Soule* (1576, and dedicated to the Countess of Bedford). Woolton quotes from St Augustine that 'the soule cannot be said to be bodye ... for the soule is spreade throughout the body which it quickneth', and from Justin Martyr that the soul 'never dieth'.[93] 'For death can but touch that which is animated or made a living creature by the soule, but the same beeing the fountayne or origen of life can not die.'[94] Woolton is evidently well versed in the Platonists: 'I am not ignorant', he says, 'of that olde sentence: *Anima est tota in toto, et in qualibet parte tota*', and goes on to describe the action of the soul on the body as like the 'brightnes from the sunne beames, which is dispersed into every part of the ayre round about'.[95] He refers triumphantly to that 'Mercurius Trismegistus, who lived not long after Moses'—to the Hermetic philosophy that had such a decisive and formative influence on the Platonic theology of Ficino—and who 'writeth thereof divinely and very sweetely, after this manner: "Onely Manne of all earthly creatures is deemed to be of two natures, Mortall in respect of the body, but Immortall in respecte of the soule" '.[96]

Undoubtedly the two most popular works in England dedicated to confounding atheism were *The Books of the Resolutions* by the Jesuit Robert Parsons, and Phillipe Mornay's *A Work Concerning the Trueness of the Christian Religion*. Parson's *Resolutions* (as the work is generally called) was first published, in part, in 1582, acquiring the new title of *A Christian Directory Guiding Men to their Salvation* in subsequent printings in 1585, 1598 etc. The *Resolutions* were

available in three versions authorised by Parsons, in two rival
Protestant versions, in one unauthorised Catholic version, and even
it seems one late edition in Welsh.[97] Mornay's work, translated into
English by Sir Philip Sidney and Arthur Golding in 1587, first
appeared in Antwerp in 1581; although there were only four English
editions before 1640, frequent references to it in Elizabethan
literature testify to its popularity.[98] Mornay favours Platonic and
Hermetic authorities and he justifies the belief in immortality
accordingly; in chapter xiv of his book he gives an interesting
Anselmic kind of argument, suggesting that the very concept of
immortality is itself proof of immortality, and man's ability to reason
about it is a refutation of those who deny it—a characteristically
Renaissance response which, since God is said to be revealed in the
deepest elements of man's soul, can gather in every unwarranted
intuition and propose it for truth, for, as Ficino had said, 'All is
possible'. Robert Parsons, like Mornay, gives a list of 'common
notions' affirming God's existence, among them some metaphysical
proofs, almost identical with Mornay's, dependent on the
supposition that 'every multitude or distinction of things proceedeth
from some unity', just as the complex functions of the microcosm,
man, proceed from 'one most simple unity and indivisible substance,
called the soul'. This soul 'is a spirit and immaterial substance,
whose nature dependeth not on the state of our mortal body', a
substance which is by the 'consent of all learned men' immortal. The
metaphysical argument is substantially reinforced by moral
considerations of reward and punishment, arguments from the
natural 'appetite of some more high and excellent object' than that
of beasts, and the conclusions of Plato and Plotinus that the final end
of man is union with God.[99]

The widespread diffusion and influence of these two treatises, with
their summaries of all the unassailable proofs, emphasises the
overriding importance of the question of immortality in theological
and philosophical controversy. However anxious Lord Herbert may
have been that some of his propositions in *De veritate* might cause
alarm and hostility in certain quarters, he could be confident that
his strenuous support of the soul's immortality would at least be well
received, and he joins his voice with the voices of overtly Christian
apologists in affirming the necessity for personal immortality and a
final destiny in the realm of Eternal Blessedness. Herbert repeats in
his own way the arguments of *primum in aliquo genere* and of *appetitus*

naturalis, claiming that every natural impulse and every Common Notion is directed towards immortality, and 'Natural Instinct itself, which has its origin both within us and outside us in self-preservation, aims at Eternal Blessedness as its final end'.[100] The faculty he calls Natural Instinct seems more or less identical with the notion of *appetitus naturalis,* for it is the 'immediate instrument of Divine Providence' which 'pervades and informs all things'. All particular objects and particular goods are subordinated to the ultimate *primum* which is their final end.

Of all the traditional arguments for immortality, those to which Herbert seems most attracted and of which he makes the greatest use are of a Platonic, Stoic or Hermetic character. There is, for instance, relatively little insistence on the ability of the mind to abstract and universalise and to resolve logical problems as an indication of the soul's incorporeality, partly because Herbert does not rate logical thought very highly and partly because the soul's nature is already known to us by a Common Notion. The nearest he approaches to this sort of strategy is in his assertion that there are as many faculties in the mind as there are existent or possible objects, and that from the existence of a faculty we can infer the existence of an object, even though we have had no experience of it.[101] This is one way in which Eternal Blessedness may be proved to exist, and it is akin to Ficino's principle of affinity and the relation of knower and known. 'Our mind', Herbert says, 'is the best image and specimen of divinity.'[102] As for the famous maxim of Aristotle, *nihil est in intellectu, quod non prius fuit in sensu,* made much of by Averroists, Paduans and Lucretians, the Common Notions engraved in the mind attest the contrary; the statement is only meaningful if we add that every external feature of things has an internal parallel, for if we confine knowledge to sense perception we overlook the inner analogies and the conceptual elements in apprehension. Herbert frequently stresses the argument based on the proposition that nothing in the universe is in vain, and it is repeated or implied with such persistence that it becomes a characteristic Herbertian doctrine: 'Experience and reason teach us that the divine wisdom does not fail us in matters of necessity, nor pour out its gifts superfluously'.[103] From this principle Herbert applies his theory of 'plastic virtue' and of eternal conservation to the destiny of the human soul.

One of Herbert's favourite ideas was that the individual in its growth passes through separate 'lives', seminal, embryonic, earthly, and celestial. In *De veritate* he begins with the embryo, which could scarcely be capable of conceiving a new life beyond its mother's womb and which yet finds that 'the veil, so to speak, is lifted, and it issues forth, discovering, whether it wishes or not, a new world of objects'.[104] The purpose of the argument is obvious. From this organic sequence Herbert deduces the existence of a future life in which the human capacities of 'hope, faith, love and joy', which are never adequately fulfilled on earth, will find completion. The agent of this organic process, though generally called Natural Instinct in *De veritate*, is sometimes called *plastica virtus*, as his Latin poem *De vita humana disquisitio*, which summarises the theme of immortality already elaborated in *De veritate* and in *Religio laici*. Later in his life Herbert returns to this same topic once more, and includes a version of this poem in his autobiography, where his comments on it constitute one of the very few revelations in that work of Herbert the philosopher. Having reiterated the progress, under the impulsion of 'this *plastica* or *formatrix*', from womb to manhood, and having asserted the necessity of a 'perfect, eternal, and infinite' world in which 'hope, faith, love and joy' can 'indeed acquiesce', he concludes with the conviction that the God who is the object of these faculties would never allow them to be 'placed in vain, or remain long unrequited'.[105]

Pomponazzi's amusing and ingenious objection to this point of view takes up the familiar notion of man the great amphibium, 'of twofold nature,' in Ficino's words, 'and a mean between the mortal and the immortal', and compares this hybrid with the mule, blandly pointing out that 'the mule also, though it has all the organs of generation' cannot attain what it aspires to, 'although it desires it exceedingly'.[106]

In asserting immortality Herbert is naturally led into more rhetorical and less precise forms of speech than may seem proper to a detached investigation of the nature of truth. An occasional image or illustration, so rare in his solid treatise, may diffuse a sudden and unexpected colour. As an analogy to the human soul he invites us to 'consider the rose in winter', which

does not continue to thrive in virtue of its roots, nor of its stems, nor even of its seeds, but, hidden within the bosom of nature, in virtue of its own power of fertility. Consider, if possible, not the physical circumstances but the product, even though it may scarcely be seen until all causes meet and the rose itself emerges.[107]

It is an image which brings to mind Herbert's own manipulation of 'causes' in his *Elegy over a Tomb*, and also the gracious opening of Carew's *Song*: 'Ask me no more where Jove bestows, / When June in past, the fading rose; / For in your beauty's orient deep / These flowers, as in their causes, sleep.' In more assertive vein, Herbert declares that

if the worm which is born of the corruption of the body can gaze at the sun and rejoice in it, can you believe that you are destined to be enshrouded in eternal darkness? Be assured, your state is better than that which is born of corruption. The eye can perceive a little of this, but faith grasps greater marvels. Contemplate the system of things. Eternal Blessedness is the necessary object of Natural Instinct, the sovereign law of which consists in the self-preservation of soul and body; and this pervades all that exists.[108]

A similar belief in the ultimate unity and incorruptibility of creation informs, as one would expect, Herbert's many speculations, within the poetry as well as in *De veritate* itself, on immortality. In his verse there is a sense of definite Hermetic, Neoplatonic patterns of continuous creativity: the 'impression' of beauty and goodness upon formless material is in part the subject of *The Idea* and of *The Green-Sickness Beauty II*; the dissolution of the elements in death is treated at length in *A Meditation* and elsewhere, together—as in the *Ode upon a Question moved* and the *Elegy over a Tomb*—with the further fate of the dispersed elements in reforming and regenerating the universe. *A Meditation upon his Wax-Candle burning out*, for instance, suggests the familiar comparison of man's life with a candle and uses it as a sounding-board for what appear to be Hermetic ideas. The soul, like the candle flame, has a natural affinity with the realms above; the melting of the wax prefigures the body's decay. Each element of which it is composed will be resolved into its 'Proper principle', that is, earth to earth, water to water, etc. These terrestrial parts will lie in ashes; but

> Thy more sublime to higher Regions flies,
> The rest b'ing to the middle wayes expos'd.

The 'middle wayes' are the intermediate spheres through which the soul will pass on its way to the higher regions, and to them the soul will render up its integuments and the elements be dispersed to their originals. In the first *libellus* of the *Hermetica* the soul's ascent is described: the disembodied soul, having resolved its gross body into air, water and earth, rises above the sublunar world and mounting through the planetary spheres gives back to each planet in succession the evil passion which it had received from that planet until cleansed from all corruption it takes its place in the incorporeal realm.[109] Herbert then abandons the figure of the candle to make a direct affirmation of faith:

> Much more our Souls then, when they go from hence,
> And back unto the Elements dispense
>   All that built up our frail and earthly frame,
> Shall through each pore & passage make their breach,
>   Till they with all their faculties do reach
> Unto that place from when at first they came.

This seems to be a poetic re-working of a similar passage in *De veritate* where he points to the decay of our 'physical house' but the survival of its inmate, the mind.[110] Herbert concludes the poem *in propria persona* with a statement that repeats his own *Epitaph for Himself*:

> And therefore I, who do not live and move,
> By outward sense so much as faith and love,
>   Which is not in inferior Creatures found,
> May unto some immortal state pretend,
>   Since by these wings I thither may ascend,
>   Where faithful loving Souls with joys are crown'd.

The *Ode upon a Question moved, whether Love should continue for ever?*—probably Herbert's best known poem—is in its formal aspects a remarkable display of craftsmanship and subtlety. Beneath its grace and artistry however lies that complexity, or individuality, of thought characteristic of Herbert. The convention of this kind of 'casuistic dialogue on love' may be traced through Sidney's eighth song of *Astrophel & Stella*, Fulke Greville's Sonnet 75 of *Caelica*, George Wither's *Fair Virtue*, Sonnet III, and of course Donne's *The Extasie*.[111] In Herbert's *Ode* the conventional pastoral setting is formal and stiff, with particular emphasis on nature's pattern which binds all things into 'an harmony of parts'. Against this background the figure of Melander offers a proof of the eternity of love which is predictably Platonic. The key to Herbert's argument in the poem is to be found in the proposition in *De veritate* that 'It is then reasonable to believe that the faculties with which we are born do not perish at death'.[112] Yet the poem itself modifies a rigorous Platonism and, like *The Extasie*, 'composes' the apparent opposites of carnal and spiritual. Herbert argues, in the poem, that if the guilt of sin never dies then the joy of virtuous love cannot but survive; if this were not so, Heaven's laws would be in vain, 'When to an everlasting Cause /

They gave a perishing Effect'. And if bodies rise again, sense cannot be excluded. Even in the transcendent world beyond death

> These eyes again then, eyes shall see,
>   And hands again these hands enfold,
>   And all chast pleasures can be told
> Shall with us everlasting be.

It is therefore much more than 'the faculties' that 'do not perish at death'; for if we read on in *De veritate* we find Herbert distinguishing between decay and dissolution which is only apparent and that which is final. Our earthly structure may be dissolved, he says, but through 'a plastic or motive power' our best faculties are restored together with the matter and elements with which they were invested.[113] Death, then, is the state in which 'All imperfection is refin'd'. And the philosophy of the *Ode* is a reflection of the same assertive philosophical optimism.

The final answer to the question moved rests not in fact on the proof of the immortality of the soul but on propagation—or rather, the arguments for the immortality of their love take on a practical form without losing their intellectual implications.

> So when one wing can make no way,
>   Two joyned can themselves dilate,
>   So can two persons propagate,
> When singly either would decay,

so that 'Each shall be both, yet both but one'. *De veritate* is again relevant here, where Herbert speaks of the faculty of love, which is

above all sensitive to the divine beauty and goodness, and afterwards to all the divine attributes . . . The common object of this faculty is physical love. For this reason the feeling which relates to the perpetuation of the species, so long as it is not infected with unlawful lust or concupiscence, is humane and may spring from the faculty which seeks the general good.[114]

Herbert is reworking, both here and in the *Ode*, arguments from Ficino's *Commentary on the Symposium*, made most familiar to us in Spenser's *Hymn in Honour of Love*, and the poem's conclusion turns out to be rather like the theme of Shakespeare's first group of sonnets, or George Chapman's Ficinean exercise on love and generation in *Andromeda liberata*. Melander justifies the physical act by the quality of love, demonstrating that it must be the impulse only of the intellectual and spiritual faculties. Through this, Herbert's Melander participates, somewhat coyly one might feel, in

the convention which allowed such dialogues to be read (as Donne's
Extasie may be read) as an argument towards seduction, yet takes
refuge in the protection afforded by the promotion of 'the general
good'.

Herbert is in fact rehearsing once more the theme of self-
preservation and of the eternally generative force of the universe
which lies at the heart of Neoplatonic speculation from Hermes
Trismegistus on, effecting the conservation of species, genera, and
the universe itself.[115] Herbert's Melander and Celinda are, as it
were, participants in the operations of *appetitus naturalis*, of the Stoic
and Hermetic World Soul by which all things are generated, and of
Natural Instinct; they are conforming to the principle which, as
Ficino expressed it, affirms that

anything that performs an act is induced to action by a natural appetite for
propagating its own perfection, in order to generate something as like itself
as possible, as is manifest in elements, plants and animals, where it appears
that the natural appetite is directed towards the good, that is, towards life,
existence and similar things, not towards their opposite.[116]

And so Herbert too asserts this same doctrine of a paradoxical, all-
pervading conservation, taking it at times peculiarly to himself and
infusing it with his own form of personal vanity: 'Nothing, in a word,
which endows a man with true singleness of mind and even fine
looks, fails to survive. Old objects and even new ones survive and no
portion of matter or element with which we invest ourselves under
the will of God disappears.'[117]

Herbert is, then, echoing in his arguments for immortality a host
of voices raised in its support, and dependent on a metaphysical view
of the nature of life's fundamental processes. His contribution is, as
always, distinctive and idiosyncratic. The 'poetic mythology' of immortality which Herbert offers, whether in the poetry itself or in *De
veritate*, assumes that the soul is a substance independent of the body,
and shows a particular preference for paradoxes borrowed from
Platonic or Neoplatonic philosophy, especially the Platonic
paradoxes of 'the One and Many'. In comparison with manifestly
Christian apologists (and poets) Herbert has a distinctively different
emphasis—at times he seems to disregard the Christian concept of
personal immortality and stresses instead a kind of physical immortality which affirms survival in the universal soul of the elements dispersed from the human body. There is little specific evidence of the
redeeming Christian belief that the body and soul together would be

revived at the Resurrection, but rather the Platonic or Brunonian idea that being and reality continuously move in infinite circles, beyond space and beyond time. Where the orthodox Christian response tends to move on two planes of reality, the sensible and the spiritual, the human and the divine, mediated by the fact of the Incarnation, Herbert's Platonising instinct tends to separate the two realms in order finally to assimilate them by making the divine and spiritual world (so often figured in Herbert's 'mythology' in the stars) the ideal replica of the sensible and human world.

Herbert's Platonising strain, a Platonic *ascesis* which climbs up from the sensible to the intelligible, in contrast to the Christian sense of 'incarnation' which merges the spiritual in the sensible, has led some readers to regard him as, in fact, a materialist. W. K. Jordan speaks of a 'cold materialism which pervaded all of his thought' and locates it specifically in Herbert's discussions and poetic exercises on the theme of immortality.[118] Robert Ellrodt, in his illuminating criticism of Herbert's poetry, distinguishes perceptively between the 'acute sense of the mystery of the Incarnation which is a fundamental aspect of the religious sensibility of Donne, George Herbert and Crashaw' and Herbert's World Soul, his natural theology, and his pantheistic inspiration. Emerging from such a comparison and contrast, however, is the questionable and misleading general conclusion that 'Lord Herbert's philosophical theory reveals a new orientation which was to substitute for a universe based upon the correspondence of contrary qualities—such as cold and hot, dry and moist—a universe based upon mathematical relations of quantity, the universe of Galileo and of Newton'.[119] It would seem that the pressures of an already established historical model involving Herbert's generally accredited function as rational deist have influenced such a judgement. The so-called gesture of 'cold materialism' may of course with equal justice be diagnosed in any number of Platonising apologists, from Ficino to Pico to Sir Thomas Browne to Joseph Butler. Sir Thomas Browne, for example, pointing to the many Types of the Resurrection, forsakes his apocalyptic vision for a moment and invites us to speak 'naturally and like Philosophers' and admit that 'the forms of alterable bodies in these sensible corruptions perish not'. 'A plant or vegetable,' he says,

consumed to ashes to a contemplative and school-Philosopher seems utterly destroyed, and the form to have taken his leave for ever; but to a sensible Artist the forms are not perished, but withdrawn into their incombustible part, where they lie secure from the action of that devouring element . . . This is that mystical Philosophy, from whence no true Scholar becomes an Atheist.[120]

In the opening section of Butler's *Analogy of Religion* (1736) Herbert's thesis is precisely repeated as a fundamental 'analogical' argument for immortality: 'that we are to exist hereafter in a state as different (suppose) from our present as this is from our former is but according to the analogy of nature'; destruction, Butler insists, does not necessarily imply death; our 'destruction' 'may immediately in the natural course of things put us into a higher and more enlarged state of life''.[121] Such arguments from probability and analogy, like Herbert's general argument or the evidences of Berkeley's vegetables which 'left to rot in the earth rise up again with new life and vigour',[122] may be ultimately futile, as Kant was to demonstrate in his penetrating criticism of such attempts to transfer terms like 'indivisible' and 'composite' from the material world, where they have meaning, to the immaterial world, where they have none.[123] Yet the impulse here is that vision which sees the universe as types and emblems bespeaking God's creative will and continuous activity, and which is held up—by the 'irreligious' Lord Herbert as strenuously as anyone—for a lesson to atheists and unbelievers.

Notes to Chapter IV

1 *D.V.*, p. 247; Carré, p. 330.
2 See W. Windelband and H. Heimsoeth, *Lehrbuch der Geschichte der Philosophie*, 14th ed. Tübingen, 1950, pp. 341f.; Edwin A. Burtt, *The Metaphysical Foundations of Modern Science*, London, 1932; and Joseph A. Mazzeo, 'Universal analogy and the culture of the Renaissance', *Journal of the History of Ideas*, 15, 1954, pp. 299–304.
3 Rossi, I, pp.. 293–5.
4 Rossi's argument is partly in opposition to that of A. Carlini, whose *Herbert di Cherbury e la Scuola di Cambridge* (in *Rendiconti della Reale Accademia dei Lincei*, 5.A. vol. 26, Rome, 1917) claimed extensive influence on Herbert of Ficino; Carlini also found in Herbert the influence of Bacon and of Campanella. Rossi denies these influences, at least to the extent Carlini claimed, and most effectively in the case of Campanella, since Carlini unfortunately believed *De veritate* was first published in 1633. In fact it antedates Campanella and hence Carlini's 'evidence' is nonsense. See Rossi, *Alle fonti del deismo e del materialismo moderno*, Florence, 1942. Rather, Rossi finds the sources of many of Herbert's most important ideas in Telesio and Patrizi. See Rossi, I, p. 285.
5 *D.V.*, p. 29; Carré, p. 106.

6 *D.V.*, p. 27; Carré, pp. 105–6.

7 *D.V.*, pp. 27–8; Carré, p. 105.

8 *D.V.*, p. 54; Carré, p. 132.

9 *D.V.* p. 70; Carré, p. 150.

10 Richard Baxter, *More Reasons for the Christian Religion, and No Reason Against It* part II: *Animadversions on a Tractate de Veritate*), London, 1672, p. 80.

11 Cf. Hobbes: 'Whatsoever accidents or qualities our senses make us think there be in the world, they be not there, but are seemings and apparitions only; the things that really are in the world without us, are those motions by which these seemings are caused' (*Treatise of Human Nature*, 1650, II, 10). For Cudworth's argument see *The True Intellectual System of the Universe*, London, 1678, pp. 730f.; for Smith see *Select Discourses*, ed. Worthington, London, 1660, *Discourse Concerning the Immortality of the Soul*, chap. vi. The chronology of Smith's writings makes it unlikely that Smith has Hobbes in mind, though Basil Willey describes Smith as an anti-Hobbist writer (see his *The English Moralists*, London, 1965, chap. xi). In fact Smith, in the essay on *The Immortality of the Soul*, does not mention Hobbes at all; this is not surprising, for Smith died in 1652, within a year of the publication of *Leviathan* and two of the *Treatise of Human Nature* and the *De corpore politico*.

12 See J. H. Muirhead, *The Platonic Tradition in Anglo-Saxon Philosophy*, London, 1931, second impression 1965, p. 45.

13 *D.V.*, p. 43; Carré, p. 121.

14 *D.V.*, p. 87. Carré, p. 167.

15 *D.V.*, p. 75; Carré, pp. 155–6.

16 *D.V.*, p. 63; Carré, p. 142.

17 *D.V.*, pp. 116–17; Carré, p. 196; cf. also *D.V.*, p. 87; Carré, pp. 167–8.

18 Herbert does however add a qualification: 'Whatever is passive in us is physical; but this does not mean that whatever is active must be mental. For objects and their images retained in memory are active. The idea of beauty excites us, not to speak of the idea of ugliness' (*D.V.*, p. 72; Carré, p. 152).

19 Cudworth, *True Intellectual System*, bk. I, 4, p. 728.

20 Sir Thomas Browne, *Religio medici*, 1643, I, 14.

21 *Religio medici*, I, 32.

22 See Fordyce and Knox.

23 *Autobiography*, ed. Lee, pp. 40–1.

24 Rossi, I, p. 360.

25 *D.V.*, p. 89; Carré, p. 169.

26 *D.V.*, p. 91; Carré, p. 171.

27 *Autobiography*, ed. Lee, p. 49.

28 Ficino, *Libri de vita* (1489), bk. III: *De vita coelitus comparanda*, i, In *Opera*, Basle, 1576, 2 vols. consecutively paged, pp. 532–3. See also Frances A. Yates, *Giordano Bruno and the Hermetic Tradition*, London, 1964, pp. 64–9.

29 See W. Scott, *Hermetica*, Oxford, 1923–4, 4 vols., I, introduction.

30 See Scott, *ibid.* I, pp. 32–3. Isaac Casaubon's critique is in his *De rebus sacris et ecclesiasticis exercitationes XVI. Ad Cardinalis Baronii Prolegomena in Annales*, London, 1614, pp. 70f.

31 *Libellus* X.14b. References are to W. Scott's edition.

32 *Libellus* XI(ii).21.b.

33 John Picus, Earl of Mirandula, *A Platonick Discourse*, I.v.vi. in Thomas Stanley's *The History of Philosophy*, London, 1743, p. 207. For the basic Hermetic theory of *demiurgus*, see *Hermetica, libellus* I.

34 *A Platonick Discourse*, I.v.

35 Plotinus, *Enneads*, V.2.i. and V.4.i. in *Plotinus's Complete Works*, trans. K. S. Guthrie, London, 1918, Cf. A. O. Lovejoy, *The Great Chain of Being*, Cambridge, Mass., 1936, p. 83.

36 See Frances A. Yates, *loc. cit.*, p. 247.

37 Cusanus, *De docta ignorantia*, II,iii; I.xxi, etc. Trans. Fr. Germain Heron, London, 1954.

38 Proclus, *Elements of Theology*, ed. and trans. E. R. Dodds, 2nd ed., Oxford, 1963, prop. 67; Plotinus, *Enneads*, IV.2.

39 Cusanus, *De staticis experimentis*, one of the four short works included in his *Idiota*. Cited by Edgar Wind, *Pagan Mysteries in the Renaissance*, London, 1958, p. 183.

40 *D.V.*, p. 27; Carré, p. 104.

41 *D.V.*, pp. 174–5; Carré, pp. 255–7.

42 *The Poems*, ed. G. C. Moore Smith, Oxford, 1923, pp. 81–2.

43 *The Poems*, p. 54.

44 *The Poems*, p. 55.

45 *The Poems*, p.60.

46 Moore Smith, in his commentary on the poems, suggests a number of probable Platonic and Plotinian references. F. J. Warnke has painstakingly listed some Platonic and Neoplatonic analogues, particularly from the *Timaeus* and the *Symposium*, and from Ficino's *In Convivium Platonis de amore Commentarium*. See his dissertation *This Metaphysick Lord: A Study of the Poetry of Herbert of Cherbury*, Columbia University, 1954, pp. 154f.

47 *D.V.*, p. 244; Carré, p. 327.

48 *D.V.*, p. 246; Carré, p. 329.

49 *D.V.*, p. 247; Carré, p. 330.

50 Bruno, *De la causa, principio, e uno*, dial. V. In *Dialoghi italiani*, ed. G. Gentile and G. Aquilecchia, Florence, 1957, pp. 341–2. English translation by S. Greenberg, *The Infinite in Giordano Bruno*, New York, 1950, pp. 77f.

51 Greenberg, *loc. cit.*, pp. 41–2.

52 *The Poems*, p. 38.

53 *Religio medici*, I, 15.

54 Traherne, *Centuries of Meditations*, V, 3.

55 Traherne, *Centuries, Poems, and Thanksgivings*, ed. H. M. Margoliouth, Oxford, 1958, II, p. 180.

56 M. H. Carré, introduction to *De veritate*, p. 33.

57 Seneca, *Of Benefits*, IV,vii.

58 E.g. Bruno, *Spaccio della bestia trionfante*, 1584, dial. III, in *Dialoghi italiani*, pp. 781–3.

59 *D.V.*, p. 1; Carré, p. 75.

60 *Hermetica, libellus XVI, iii.*

61 *D.V.*, p. 29; Carré, p. 107.

62 *D.V.*, pp. 88–9; Carré, p. 169: *Quomodo principia ista cum nostris cohaerent, rationem ex Animae, sive Harmonia mundi qui petere recusat, ex vi illa plastica diversas*

eduliorum naturas in unum compingente, sensu interno edoctus excogitet.

63 Definition of 'Natural Instinct', *D.V.*, p. 44; Carré, p. 122.

64 *D.V.*, p. 41; Carré, p. 119.

65 *D.V.*, p. 60; Carré, p. 139.

66 *D.V.*, p. 42; Carré, p. 120.

67 E.g. Cicero, *De re publica*, III, i,1; *De natura deorum*, I,xx,53. An argument very similar to Herbert's occurs in Seneca, *Epistulae morales*, 102, and in Antoninus, *Meditations*, lib. ix, 3.

68 *Enneads*, V,i,10; III,ii,16. Cudworth, *True Intellectual System*, 1678, p. 163. For a survey of different meanings and functions of 'seminal reason' see under 'raisons seminales' in E. Bréhier's index to his edition of Plotinus, Paris, 1938, VI,ii. On Ficino's contribution, see W. C. Curry, *Shakespeare's Philosophical Patterns*, 1937, p. 40.

69 Ficino, *Opera*, 1576, p. 535; Virgil, *Aeneid*, V, 726–7.

70 See W. B. Hunter, 'The seventeenth-century doctrine of plastic nature', *Harvard Theological Review*, 43, 1950, pp. 197–213. It seems probable also, as Moore Smith notes in his dating of Herbert's poems, that the Latin poem *De Vita Humana*, which uses the phrase, was composed much earlier than 1645, the date it was first printed.

71 Cudworth, *True Intellectual System*, p. 147.

72 *True Intellectual System*, p. 151. See Lydia Gysi, *Platonism and Cartesianism in the Philosophy of Ralph Cudworth*, Bern, 1962, p. 23.

73 *True Intellectual System*, p. 167. Cf. Henry More, on 'The Immortality of the Soul', in *A Collection of Several Philosophical Writings*, London, 1662, pp. 120–1, where he describes, very characteristically, this 'Plastick Power' as 'an unresistible and unperceptible pleasure, if I may so call it, arising from the congruity of Matter to the Plastick faculty of the Soul'. Cf. also his rhapsodic gloss on *Physis* (which he uses in *Psychozoia*, 41) in *Philosophicall Poems*, Cambridge, 1647, pp. 345–6.

74 Spinoza, *Ethics*, part III, prop. vii.

75 Stuart Hampshire, *Spinoza*, London, 1951, p. 60.

76 *D.V.*, p. 57; Carré, pp. 135–6.

77 *D.V.*, p. 57; Carré, p. 136.

78 *True Intellectual System*, p. 638.

79 Pomponazzi, *Tractatus de immortalitate animae*, Bologna, 1516, trans. W. H. Hay II, in *The Renaissance Philosophy of Man*, ed. E. Cassirer *et. al.*, Chicago, Ill., 1948.

80 For bibliography of this limitless topic, see J. G. T. Grässe, *Bibliotecha psychologica*, Leipzig, 1845; Henri Busson, *La Pensée religieuse francaise de Charron à Pascal*, Paris, 1933, pp. 29–31, 119–21. Busson gives a select list which 'montre la hantise que ce problème a exercée sur les cerveaux de 1600 à 1660'.

81 See Fordyce and Knox, and National Library of Wales, MS 5298 E.

82 See Henri Busson, *Les Sources et le développement de rationalisme dans la littérature française de la Renaissance*, Paris, 1922, rev. ed. 1957, pp. 147–48.

83 A. Palearius, in *Opera omnia*, Lyons, 1552. Cited by Don Cameron Allen, *Doubt's Boundless Sea: Skepticism and Faith in the Renaissance*, Baltimore, Md., 1964, pp. 172–3.

84 Pomponazzi, trans. Hay, *loc, cit.*, p. 363.
85 Bertrand Russell, *Histrory of Western Philosophy*, new ed., 1961, p. 769.
86 *D.V.*, p. 218; Carré, p. 299.
87 *D.V.*, p. 54; Carré, p. 132.
88 Ficino, *Theologia*, in *Opera omnia*, 1576, p. 99. On Ficino, see P. O. Kristeller, *The Philosophy of Marsilio Ficino*, New York, 1943; and Josephine L. Burroughs on Ficino's 'Five Questions Concerning the Mind', in *The Renaissance Philosophy of Man*, *loc. cit.* pp. 188–90.
89 *Opera omnia*, p. 306; Kristeller, *loc. cit.*, p. 338.
90 *Opera omnia*, p. 318; Kristeller, p. 340. Cf. Aristotle, *Politics*, 1253a–1256b.
91 *Opera omnia*, p. 318f; Kristeller, p. 343.
92 *Opera omnia*, p. 627, *Epistolarum*, Lib. I to Cavalcanti; Kristeller, p. 328.
93 Woolton, *Treatise*, fol. 14r–14v. Woolton gives St Augustine, *Epistola ad Hierono, et de quantitate animae*, chap. i as his reference.
94 *Treatise*, fol. 40r
95 *Treatise*, fol. 42r
96 *Treatise*, fol. 56r. Woolton cites *Pimandri*, cap. I. Cf. *Hermetica, libellus* I, and *Asclepius*, I, 10.
97 For the complex bibliography of this work, see E. R. Strathman, *Sir Walter Ralegh: A Study in Elizabethan Skepticism*, New York, 1951, pp. 65–7.
98 According to Strathman (*loc. cit.*, p. 73, n. 18) the *Catalogue général de la bibliothèque nationale* lists nine editions in French before the first English edition, and the book was also available in Latin and Italian.
99 Quotations from the 1598 edition of *A Christian Directory*, chap. ii, pp. 20–89.
100 *D.V.*, p. 63; Carré, 143.
101 *D.V.*, pp.34–5; Carré, p. 112.
102 *D.V.*, p. 70; Carré, p. 150.
103 *D.V.*, p. 45; Carré, p. 123.
104 *D.V.*, p. 243; Carré, p. 326. Cf. *D.V.*, p. 46; Carré, pp. 124–5, and elsewhere; and the similar progress described in *Religio laici*, ed. Hutcheson, New Haven, Conn., 1944, pp. 109–11.
105 *Autobiography*, ed. Lee, pp. 35–6.
106 Pomponazzi, trans. Hay, *loc. cit.*, p. 335.
107 *D.V.*, p. 87; Carré, p. 167.
108 *D.V.*, pp. 109–10; Carré, p. 189.
109 *The Poems*, ed. Moore Smith, pp. 83–5.
110 *D.V.*, p. 46; Carré, p. 123.
111 *The Poems*, pp. 61–6. See also George Williamson, 'The Convention of The Extasie', in *Seventeenth-Century Contexts*, London, 1960, pp. 63–77.
112 *D.V.*, p. 46; Carré, p. 123.
113 *D.V.*, p. 92; Carré, p. 172.
114 *D.V.*, pp. 116–17; Carré, pp. 196–7.
115 For further reflections of the doctrine of perpetual generation and the instinct of self-preservation, see *Hermetica, libellus* XII,ii,16–19; Pico's Hermetic *Conclusiones*, v and vi, in *Opera omnia*, Basle, 1572, p. 80; Cornelius Agrippa, *De occulta philosophia*, 1533, II, 56; Campanella, *Sonnets*, iii, in *The*

Sonnets of Michelangelo Buonarroti and Tommaso Campanella, trans. J. A. Symonds, London, 1878, p. 121; Giordano Bruno, *Cena de le ceneri*, 1584, dial. V, in *Dialoghi italiani*, 1957, pp. 154–6; William Gilbert, *On the Loadstone* (*De magnete*, 1600), trans. P. Fleury Mottelay, London, 1893, book IV,xii, p. 309.

116 Ficino, *Theologia, Opera omnia*, p. 137; Kristeller, p. 187.

117 *D.V.*, p. 92; Carré, p. 172.

118 W. K. Jordan, *The Development of Religious Toleration in England, 1603–1640*, London, 1932–40, p. 437.

119 Robert Ellrodt, *Les Poètes métaphysiques anglais*, Paris, 1959–60, p. 44; p. 33.

120 *Religio medici*, I, 48.

121 *The Works of Bishop Butler*, ed. J. H. Bernard, London, 1900, II, pp. 13–14; p. 26.

122 Berkeley, *Alciphron*, dial. VI, in *Works*, ed. Luce and Jessop, London, 1950, III, p. 241.

123 See Kant, *Critique of Pure Reason*, trans. N. Kemp Smith, London, 1933, pp. 241f.

V
AUTHORITY AND FAITH

He is a fool that believes he knows neither what nor why.

Owen Felltham, *Resolves*

Herbert as publicist

It has been suggested that Lord Herbert's philosophy is in fact little more than a preparation for his specifically religious views, that it is a system of metaphysics and a theory of knowledge developed almost solely in order to erect the additional sections on religion which close *De veritate*. Herbert's nineteenth-century critic Charles de Rémusat, for example remarked that 'Toute religion comme toute philosophie suppose une théodicée. Celle de Lord Herbert est d'autant plus importante qu'on peut conjecturer que c'est en cherchant la vérité qu'il a trouvé sa philosophie.'[1] Rossi takes the matter rather further, claiming that Herbert's philosophy is that of the dilettante (a judgement which Rossi also makes on the poetry); Herbert is not a philosopher (though he asks some good questions) but a scholar: 'The philosophy of the scholar is eclecticism, and eclecticism, considered philosophically, is dilettante philosophy, the philosophy of those who are not philosophers at heart, who are not tormented by the great problems but are placid lovers of truth who appreciate an elegant solution without asking if it has any vital importance'.[2] A much earlier critic, Thomas Halyburton, came to a similar conclusion, at least by implication. Writing in 1714, Halyburton observes of *De veritate* and *De causis errorum* that 'these two books are for the most part philosophical, and written with some Singularity of Notion' (he means he cannot understand them—'they are scarce intelligible to any save metaphysical readers'), and says that he is concerned with them only because it is Herbert's 'avow'd Design in them to lay a Foundation for his peculiar Notions in Religion'.[3]

The history of the editions of *De veritate* certainly lends support not necessarily to the view that Herbert was somehow merely playing at 'philosophy' for some predetermined end and that it held no real interest for him, but at least to the view that later on his deepest concern as a publicist focused most sharply on the problems of religious belief. The expansions in the main part of the work in the course of its various editions were few and minor and were confined almost exclusively to the second edition of 1633. The sections on religion, however, received several additions and this expansion did not stop with the second edition. In the final 1645 text Herbert took the opportunity to supplement further his exposition of the five points of religion.[4] Rossi's researches among Herbert's papers disclosed a longish passage in the original MS of *De veritate* which had the effect of easing the transition from the theory of knowledge to the natural religion—from the Zetetics to the Common Notions—which is so abrupt in the later MSS and in the printed editions.[5] It is perhaps significant that when Herbert came to revise his text for a new printing he looked primarily to the sections on religion rather than to improving the clarity of his philosophical argument. It might seem that having got the metaphysics off his chest, as it were, Herbert could then go on without encumbrance to discuss his specifically religious convictions, repeating the theory of the five common religious notions and referring any sceptical reader of *Religio laici* and *De religione gentilium* back to the formal elaboration of Common Notions in *De veritate*.

But perhaps a distinction between philosophy and religion should not be pressed too hard. There is not for Herbert any meaningful line to be drawn, neither in the sense in which there might be for Pomponazzi and the Averroists (Herbert's epistemological and religious optimism is far too strong) nor in the sense in which there might be for a modern. The scholastic character of Renaissance thought makes it hazardous to separate out philosophical and religious issues; even the 'double truth' assumes that the *problems* are all one. What Herbert does do—as Ockham, or Reginald Pecock in the fifteenth century, or Pomponazzi, Bodin, Bacon, and a host of other writers had done—is to draw a distinction between reason and faith as modes of acquiring knowledge and truth and to attempt to assign to each their respective provinces. If the attempt purports to be, as Herbert's is, most concerned with 'truths of understanding, not truths of Faith', the procedure will naturally take the form of an epistemological enquiry. But the religious dimension is not thereby abandoned. What happens—as with Locke's controversial attempt to secure the 'great ends of religion and morality' later in the century—is that the meaning of knowledge, including religious knowledge, is brought under a new scrutiny and is examined by criteria from which religion had hitherto been held exempt. Herbert's enquiry is clearly a defence of truth; but it embodies, again like Locke, a defence of religious truth.

In view of Herbert's reputation and the use to which his arguments and methods were put by later controversialists, such a claim may require some clarification, for Herbert is not usually thought of as a defender of the faith. Nor indeed is he, when by 'faith' is understood solely the claims of the Church (and which Church?) with, as Herbert sees it, the double appeal of the priesthood to authority and revelation for its various sanctions. Having laid his 'philosophical' foundations in *De veritate*—the theory of analogy and unity, the role of Natural Instinct, the appeal to Common Notions and universal consent, and the assertion of the uniformity of reason in all men—Herbert directs his enquiry to the problem of the rights of external authority and the grounds of true inward faith. One of the paradoxical criticisms to which Herbert lays himself open is that he may be praised on the one hand for perceiving that an epistemological examination of the nature of truth-claims was vital to the situation of his age, and reproved on the other hand for indulging in a form of abstract and highly metaphysical argument (the fact that it may also be unsystematic and unstructured supports the reproof) which *ipso facto* disqualifies him from any true religious instinct or understanding. The implications of this paradox will no doubt be apparent throughout this discussion.

Why, we may want to wonder naively, *did* Herbert write *De veritate*? We may admit, but then lay aside, the psychological argument that, characteristically, he wished to do something difficult, distinguished and impressive to secure his fame—so of course did Milton. Apart from reading it with some care, we can perhaps approach that apparently simple question by looking at what Herbert was thought to be up to, and what he did with *De veritate*. As we have seen, he amended and expanded the text, concentrating on the articles of religion, though the appearance of *De causis errorum* with the 1645 edition of *De veritate*, the translation of part IV and the beginning of part V of Descartes's *Discours*, the translation of Hobbes's *De principiis* (apparently an early draft of his *De corpore*), and some rough notes towards an aesthetic theory, demonstrate that Herbert's philosophical interests were still very active.[6] The original edition of 1624 was published in Paris at Herbert's own expense, after he had shown it to those eminent Arminians Daniel Tilenus and Hugo Grotius and had received their warm encouragement. Herbert also received from Grotius complimentary copies of his *De jure belli et pacis* (1625) and *Excerpta ex tragediis et comoediis graecis* (1626) together with a letter from Grotius about the former.[7] Herbert himself was clearly esteemed by the contemporaries of his younger years: the verses of Jonson and Donne offer unstinted praise, though Donne, in his *Elegy for the Prince*, wittily vies 'with Sir Ed: Herbert in obscureness'. Of Herbert's two verse satires, one, *Of Travellers*, was addressed to Jonson, and the other, *The State Progress of Ill*, concerned with the problem of evil and how to regulate the 'beast' in mankind, was in all likelihood addressed to Donne and for which he received in exchange the verse epistle *To Sr Edward Herbert, at Julyers*, rehearsing a similar theme.[8] There seems to have been a reciprocal traffic of ideas, poems and books between Donne and Herbert. The occasion, noted in a subtitle, of Donne's *Good-friday, 1613, Riding Westward* was 'Riding to Sr Edward Herbert in Wales'.[9] Herbert possessed—probably he had been given it by Donne—a copy of Vorstius's *Responsio ad Matthaeum Sladum* bearing the signature J. Donne and the tag from Petrarch which Donne regularly wrote on his books, *per Rachel ho servito e ñ per Lea*. A manuscript copy of *Biathanatos* was presented to Herbert in April 1619, the gift accompanied by a letter from Donne in which he hoped a shelf might be found for it in Herbert's library, 'where Authors of all complexions were preserved': 'If any of them grudge this book a room, and suspect it of new or dangerous doctrine, you who know us all, can best moderate'.[10] At no time was Herbert himself thought of as harbouring 'new or dangerous doctrine'; he seems to have been regarded, by Jonson and by Donne, as the wise and trusted observer who would understand, and participate in on his own account, the intellectual adventures of his contemporaries. Donne's theological views and his sense of ecclesiastical allegiance were hardly similar to the course that Herbert's thought was to take, but Herbert's religious sensibility, even granted the marked difference that must have been apparent in him compared with the celebrated piety of his mother Lady Magdalen and, in retrospect perhaps, with the path that his brother George was to follow, was never brought into question.

De veritate became widely known only after the second edition of 1633, and subsequently assisted by the French translation which appeared in 1639. The 1633 edition had an *imprimatur* from the Arminian Archbishop Laud, and Herbert took active, and successful, measures to publicise his work further. He gave an armful of copies to the diplomat Elias Diodati, who passed them to Mersenne and Gassendi in Paris, Peiresc at Aix, and Campanella at Rome shortly before Campanella took refuge in France.[11] Samuel Hartlib sent a copy—he may have bought it or been given it by Herbert—to Descartes early in 1638. Herbert also seems to have enlisted his brother's help, for Sir Henry made a gift of *De veritate* to Richard Baxter and also gave a copy to John Evelyn.[12] We do not know how, but copies also reached the Vatican, possibly of the 1624 edition, for early in 1634 Gassendi heard from Diodati that the Pope, Urban VIII, had highly praised it, though that did not prevent it from being placed on the Index of Prohibited Books.[13] We have already encountered the response of Gassendi and of Descartes, the one reserved and dismissive, the other cautious but favourably sympathetic. Herbert it seems, was anxious to have the opinion of Campanella and would have valued it greatly but, apart from the knowledge that he did not approve of the condemnation at Rome, nothing is known of Campanella's verdict. Mersenne took an active hand in assisting with the dissemination of Herbert's work; it is extremely likely that it was Mersenne who translated it into French (though it is still possible that Herbert may have done so himself), and Rossi has disclosed evidence that it was certainly printed by Mersenne (clandestinely and with no place of publication, though at Herbert's expense) and distributed by him. A letter of 1640 from Joachim Hübner, a friend of Samuel Hartlib, to Comenius mentions Mersenne as the translator—though he too may have been only guessing. But the correspondence between Mersenne and Herbert on the subject at least makes the publication arrangements clear.[14]

Mersenne, a pious if liberal Catholic, set little store apparently by the fact that the book had been on the Index for some years, but set about disseminating it in a vernacular translation. As his earlier writings show, Mersenne could be as harsh as the next monk or cleric on thinkers he regarded as unorthodox; but as he grew older he became less concerned with orthodoxy and more concerned with promoting religious peace and reunion. He clearly saw *De veritate* as a work to aid the cause. In August 1639 he wrote to Herbert to say he had given the French translation to many of his friends 'and clever men', and that if, as he hoped, he went to Italy that year he would like to take some copies with him 'to give to certain cardinals and to other honourable people I may happen to meet'.[15] Mersenne in fact never made the journey, but someone, perhaps Herbert, had managed to get copies of *De veritate* to Italy before 1634, and when in 1635 the papal emissary Gregorio Panzani was in England to bend Charles I's mind towards Rome, Herbert took the opportunity (he was at the time working in rooms at Whitehall) to have a private talk with him about *De veritate*, and professed to recognise (though no doubt in terms of religious anthropology, as it were) the 'Church of Rome as the mother of all the churches'. Panzani tried to persuade him to submit to the Holy Office and ask for the errors of his book to be corrected so that an amended edition could be printed and circulated.[16] He claimed to have had Herbert's agreement, and although apparently nothing came of the project, it is clear that Herbert hoped that *De veritate* might help to bring about a reconciliation between the Anglican and Roman Churches.

When Mersenne, through whose hands so much fascinating material passed, was sent in 1639 a copy of Comenius's great encyclopaedic project, the *Pansophiae prodromus* (1637, 1639), he wrote back enthusiastically offering his assistance.[17] Comenius's work was composed of a Neoplatonic scheme of 'ideas in the mind of God' with which the whole created world, appropriately catalogued, must necessarily be in harmony. Mersenne at once recognised an affinity between such an analogical *schema* and Herbert's endeavours to establish Common Notions, and promptly suggested to Comenius that his labours would be reduced if he read Herbert: 'not a few of these you could get out of that heroic *De veritate*, written by the illustrious Edward Herbert'.[18] For Common Notions, he later wrote to Comenius, 'are the sacred store and anchor, to which we must constantly refer, and for which that treatise of Lord Herbert's *De veritate*, which you have doubtless seen, will provide help'.[19]

There was, then, in the mid seventeenth century a great deal of activity, on a European front, in the cause of religious peace, drawing in both Catholics and Protestants. The eirenic aims of Comenius and his friends Hartlib and Dury were primarily concerned with achieving some kind of Protestant reunion, but in

their correspondence with Catholics like Mersenne they obviously
had hopes of amending Catholic opinion. On both the Catholic front
and the Protestant, *De veritate* advanced its claims as peacemaker,
actively promoted by Herbert and encouraged by the most liberal
minds on both sides: Hartlib had sent *De veritate* to Descartes,
Mersenne had sent it Comenius; Hübner, who had assisted Hartlib
in the publication of the *Prodromus* (a copy of which was in Herbert's
library and with the author of which Herbert later corresponded),[20]
sent to Herbert a long comment on *De veritate* in 1640 and wrote to
Comenius about Mersenne's translation of it.[21] The conclusion
inexorably emerges that Herbert wrote *De veritate* for eirenic and
reunionist purposes, that it was conceived not only as a
philosophical and disinterested enquiry into modes of knowing but
as a strategic weapon, directed to a readership of learned,
discriminating and liberal philosophic minds, implied both in its
Latin form designed to reach a European coterie, and in the
gathered audience assembled by Herbert himself and by Mersenne,
Hübner and others on his behalf and on behalf of the cause of
religious peace. He was, in other words, regarded highly and
accepted, during his lifetime at least, without suspicion by both
liberal Catholics and by Arminian Protestants such as Grotius,
Tilenus, Laud, and Gerard Vossius, who was entrusted with the
publication of Herbert's *De religione gentilium*.

Authority and tradition

Herbert's contemporary readers could hardly have been unaware of
the salvoes of criticism, let off at frequent intervals throughout
Herbert's writings, against the clergy themselves as the ostensible
guardians of religious truth. Later readers have often found these
broadsides more shocking, embarrassing, or more puzzling than the
contemporary readership evidently found them. W. K. Jordan sees
in Herbert 'a fearlessness born of unbelief and a darkly hostile
detestation of clericalism',[22] a remark which risks a *non sequitur* since
anticlericalism need not of course imply unbelief. 'Detestation of
clericalism' and vigorous attacks on the Church's claim to spiritual
authority is vividly apparent in the movements of Reform (both
Erasmus and Luther, it may be recalled, had a number of
uncomfortable things to say); the notion that the clergy may be

engaged in exploitation, self-aggrandisement and the amassing of power (while their flock is encouraged to rest in a reverential deference to history, tradition and the voice of the doctors of the Church) runs through English thought from Langland and Chaucer to John Colet's celebrated Sermon to Convocation (1511), through the movements of dissent, to John Selden's notorious *Historie of Tithes* (1618) and, without straying into the by-ways of revolutionary deism, to Locke's blunt assertion that 'priestcraft and tyranny go hand in hand'. When William Stephens, one of the earliest historians of deism, reviewed the turmoil of the first part of the seventeenth century, he did not find it hard to understand the cynicism which the grand tour of Catholic Europe would induce once Englishmen returned to the England of sectarian prophets, Archbishop Laud, and Presbyterian and Independent factions; many, he thought, said 'let my Soul be with the Philosophers' rather than in the pockets of the clergy, whatever their colour.[23]

We are sometimes encouraged to imagine that, had the true nature of Herbert's criticisms been appreciated, they would have brought down on him far greater clerical wrath even than that which fell on his friend Selden (the King was persuaded to permit the Court of High Commissions to summons Selden, and the offender was obliged to submit, offer expressions of regret, and to promise not to reply to the plethora of clerical invectives his treatise had provoked). Herbert's work was certainly less directly accessible than Selden's and its readership was automatically selective; but there is also the difference that Selden, with aggressive scepticism, had focused on the peculiarly sensitive matter of the economic base of the clergy. Herbert was never so specific (except against Calvinism and predestinationists). Moreover, while Herbert seeks to protect the laity from what he sees as the contradictory and possibly disingenuous truth-claims of the clergy, Milton grates at the

> Blind mouthes! that scare themselves know how to hold
> A Sheep-hook, or have learn'd ought els the least
> That to the faithfull Herdsmans art belongs!
>
> (*Lycidas*, 1638)

In Milton's anticlericalism there is no 'unbelief', and though every critic may have his own bias—Milton's Independence, Selden's Erastianism, Bacon's concern for 'the advancement of learning', or Herbert's reunionist ambitions—attacks on the clergy and the institutions of priesthood, though they may provoke anger or discomfiture, were part of the air which all men, clergy and laity alike, breathed. Selden's reflection that 'religion is made a Jugglers paper; now 'tis a horse, now 'tis a lanthorn, now 'tis a brat, now 'tis a man.To serve ends Religion is turned into all shapes'[24] is another version of Bacon's cold observation that 'those which held and persuaded pressure of consciences were commonly interested therein themselves for their own ends',[25] and bears similarities to Herbert's own pungent comments.

The attack upon that form of authority resting in revelation was not, however, so easy to accommodate, for it appears to strike at the heart of the Church's profession. And in one of the most persuasive and closely reasoned sections of *De veritate* Herbert takes up this very issue. His criticisms on both counts are, if somewhat lacking in finesse, astringent and pointed. But the charge of irreligion is difficult to sustain; the impatience with authoritarian religion no doubt reflects on Herbert's failure to appreciate the corporate element in religious life (as it does too in Milton, for example), rather than on his own religious instinct; and his strictures on the claims made by those with revelations do not preclude in Herbert any sense of the mysteries of faith, and even less do they necessarily suggest an exclusion of the possibility of specifically religious insight and truth gained through revelation.

Let us look at Herbert's objections, first to 'authority', and secondly to 'revelation'. The invocation of authority appears to him as a kind of coercion inconsistent with the nature and dignity of man. Authority, the refuge, he says, of the ignorant and prejudiced, is altogether pernicious in its effects and is without reasonable grounds since the Common Notions 'imprinted in the mind' provide us with the only authority we need. The criterion of religious truth is within a man, and each man's conclusions are, for practical purposes, both as good as and necessarily the same as another's. In Herbert's attitude to authority there are resemblances to Bacon's attitude towards 'cobwebs of learning' and the obfuscation of the mind through adherence to the Idols. Herbert's psychological empiricism of 'Look into your own faculties . . .' leads to this kind of warning: 'However true any book may be in respect to the truth of object, your own truth must be derived from yourself'; or again, more sombrely, 'the supreme Judge requires every individual to render an account of his actions in the light, not of another's belief, but of his own'.[26] In his invective against authority he employs

sometimes a rather ponderous irony, sometimes a battering-ram of
amplificatio, and always an aloofness bred of the assumption of
superior scholarship calculated to disarm criticism. He is led to
make some frankly exaggerated claims for his own methodology,
declaring that the 'plausible tales' and 'vulgar inventions' we are
commanded to believe, 'would never have occurred if the test I
advocate had been used'.[27]

It is the sort of criticism which might bring to mind the similarly
contemptuous comments of Hobbes's *Leviathan* on the priesthood
and the 'kingdom of Darkness', but Herbert's motives are not those
of Hobbes. His suspicion of all vested authority would seem to be the
result of his deep concern for (as Harold Hutcheson puts it) 'the
ordinary welfare of the ordinary man'. Herbert speaks with some
passion of the 'wretched terror-stricken mass' whom he sees
harangued from pulpits everywhere with fallacious arguments and
empty rhetoric, tormented 'in spite of the protests of conscience and
the inner consciousness, by the belief that all who are outside their
particular church are condemned'.[28] It seems to him that the
priesthood, absorbed in promoting their own interests and enlisting
disciples, are indifferent to this torment. Of the Calvinists he wryly
comments: 'I noted those men were rather Inquisitive through the
help of their Teachers whether they were of the number of the Elect
then studious to work out theire Salvation'.[29] Behind his strictures
there lies always a positive and abiding concern for what seems to
him fundamental and central in religious experience and a scorn for
what is merely adventitious: 'your own truth', he insists, 'must be
derived from yourself'. The Church, he argues, in its aspect of a
fallible and human institution has led the individual religious
consciousness into a chaos of sects and divisions, all claiming divine
sanction and all appealing to authority and revelation. As
Archbishop Tenison dryly observed in his *Argument for Union* (1683),
one needed to distinguish not only between Anglican and Catholic
but between 'Presbyterians, Arians, Socinians, Anabaptists, Fifth-
Monarchy Men, Sensual Millenaries, Behmenists, Familists,
Seekers, Anti-nomians, Ranters, Sabbatarians, Quakers,
Muggletonians and Sweet Singers'.[30] The English situation in the
earlier years of the century would have equally impressed on the
layman the urgent need to distinguish, and Herbert, when in 1608
he left his family and taking Aurelian Townshend as his companion
went to France, would have seen enough of the bloody controversies

of the Catholics and Huguenots. In the sectarian strife which he would have heard warring and skirmishing round him, the Christian profession was so fragmented and discredited that his sympathy goes out immediately to the laity caught in the cross-fire of ecclesiastical faction.

The object of his invective is not of course religion. Time and again in his work there breaks through a plea for a 'true religion' of inwardness, and the proper consent of the mind to the propositions of religious doctrine. The manner in which it is couched in Herbert's peculiar jargon need not mislead us. In the section of *De veritate* on the External Senses Herbert digresses from his discussion of the faculty of hearing to remark that

It has been well said that the blind who hear are wiser than the deaf who see, for hearing is the sense by which a man learns; as long as by faith you do not mean reliance on authority, but what springs from the proper conformity of the faculties. For this is within us, while the essential nature of the former is external to us. It is in this way that I chiefly distinguish the truth of things from that of the intellect. When you experience conviction or an inward act of consent, as a result of certain doctrines, consider whether the object in question has been brought into conformity as a probablity, a possibility, or as an eternal truth. For it may happen that a rash use of discursive thought, whereby these points have received insufficient attention, may bring everything to confusion, with the result that what is probable or possible will be taken for the truth and vice versa. It is important, then, to consider these facts, unless we prefer credulity to true belief.[31]

Again he presses the distinction between credulity, or acquiescence in 'authority', and true belief, or a recognition of the fundamental common religious notions, when he asks how anyone can

read the huge mass of books composed with such immense display of learning, without feeling scorn for these age-long impostures and fables, save in so far as they point the way to holiness? What man could yield unquestioning faith to a body which, distinguished under the name of the Church, wastes its time over a multitude of rites, ceremonies and vanities, which fights in so many parts of the world under different banners, if he were not led to perceive, by the aid of conscience, some marks of worship, piety, penance, reward and punishment?[32]

There are several points worth noting here. Herbert's contempt for 'display of learning' both scholarly and theological reveals the same ambition as Sebastian Castellio's claim that in inviting religious assent 'we must begin with those things which are clear to all peoples' and avoid those 'inexplicable enigmas' intruded after the days of apostolic simplicity.[33] It is the voice too, as we shall see, of Guillaume Postel and of Jacob Acontius; and in the seventeenth century of William Chillingworth, and of Joseph Glanvill's plea for a statement of belief which would consist of 'few but simple and essential articles';[34] of Locke's firm conviction that 'if schisms and heresies were traced up to their original causes, it would be found that they sprung chiefly from the multiplying articles of faith, and narrowing the bottom of religion by clogging it with creeds, and catechisms and endless niceties about the essence, properties and attributes of God',[35] and embodies the maturer judgement of William Law in the latter half of the eighteenth century that 'Christendom, full of the nicest Decisions about Faith, Grace, Works, Merits, Satisfactions, Heresies, Schisms, &c., is full of all those evil Tempers which prevailed in the Heathen World'.[36] In none of these men, nor in the tradition they represent, is there any mind whatever to demolish the whole structure of Christian belief, but merely to pare down to the minimal and assured fundamentals. Herbert's Baconian contempt for learning in this sense is one expression of his concern for the layman's interests. He would doubtless have agreed with A. G. Dickens's remark that 'a national church cannot become a club for religious athletes',[37] and no more for learned peacocks.

Secondly, there is in the passage quoted the emphasis, characteristic of Herbert, upon practice rather than creed, upon the 'way to holiness' and the fulfilment of religious duty as contained in five common religious notions, suggesting a predominantly ethical drive and an impatience with dogma that is akin to the later teachings of the Cambridge Platonists, to that ideal of 'virtuous mediocrity' which Simon Patrick praised in the Cambridge men, in contrast to 'the meretricious gaudiness of the Church of Rome and the squalid sluttery of fanatic conventicles'.[38] It is worth noting too Herbert's phrase 'disguised under the name of the Church'; his attack is directed not towards religion but the accretions and distortions fostered by authoritarian self-interest and ignorance on what seem to him fundamental beliefs. A man has a right to expect a reasonable justification of any belief to which his assent is demanded by external authority: a bishop's mitre, Herbert would say, or a cardinal's hat are not sufficient grounds for such assent, and no more are a cart-load of citations from Aristotle, Aquinas, or anyone else: 'Let us trust Divine Providence above any tradition'.

There is an apparent paradox in Herbert's impeachment of 'authority'. For very often the voice of authority may be compared, as Hooker compares it, with 'the general and perpetual voice of men' which is 'as the sentence of God himself'³⁹—a statement which Hooker, incidentally, substantiates with references to those prototypes of 'natural religion', Ficino's *De christiana religione*, the works of Cusanus, and Telesio's *De rerum natura*. Seen from one point of view Herbert's position is as authoritarian as one could wish, for it admits of no argument. His stress however, made with repeated insistence, shifts the grounds of that authority from an external to an internal compulsion. Yet to dismiss tradition and the authority of the accumulated wisdom of the writings and practice of the Church, and to then claim universal consent as a criterion of truth and a basis of allegiance, when that tradition and authority claims to embody such a consent, would seem to invite confusion. Herbert's reply to this sort of objection is, first, that the whole drift of his argument is to show that, as the progress of Reformation schismatics proves, what is universal in the doctrines of particular Churches has been abandoned for stratagems and trifles; if this were not so, they would not be particular churches but one, universal Church. Secondly, his position reflects a long-standing Renaissance argument over the distinction between natural and posited law, between universally operative principles and varying human custom. It would be a mistake to assume that by Common Notions Herbert means custom, however much custom may appear to embody what is universally held to be so; for custom is by its very nature relative. As Montaigne had pointed out: 'Law and justice, if man knew any, that had a body and true essence, he would not fasten it to the condition of this or that countries customes'.⁴⁰ Meric Casaubon, speaking of religious and philosophic principle, notes that the ancient philosophers and the Fathers of the Church warned those who 'seek the *truth*, to beware of *custome*: and to this purpose *Tertulian* would have us remember, that *Christ* called him selfe *veritatem, non consuetudinem*: *truth*, not *custome*, be it never so generall, or so ancient'.⁴¹ Custom suggested establishment, the *mores* of the constituted circle of power, the guarantee of institutional continuity. To the conservative or Erastian mind it was the great ally. Later in his work the conservative Casaubon defers to practical, civil considerations and reminds his reader that laws 'grounded upon *custome*, are thought by many as the most acceptable, so the most naturall and obligatorie

Lawes that are: as being not the invention of any single man, but of long Time and experience'.[42] And Hooker had defended episcopacy by showing that natural law and reason were in all important matters as true as revelations of the divine will as the Scriptures. The particular pressure on Hooker was the radical puritan and Calvinist split between nature and grace, which he attempts to refute by drawing together rational, natural law and divine law, for 'God being the author of Nature, her voice is but his instrument'. His argument, as a recent commentator points out, was an intellectual triumph, but it failed to convince the puritans: 'For Hooker to assert that positive laws cannot bind universally, to assign church government to the realm of positive law, and yet to bind men to episcopacy, must have seemed to the Puritans not only the indulgence of a false assumption but the drawing of a contradictory conclusion.'[43] But Hooker's advocacy of tradition and the accumulated wisdom of man as enshrined in custom indicates, even granted the appeal to Nature, a view of such 'authority' as an indispensable safeguard for the order of society.

The strategy of reform, on the other hand, takes a very different view of custom, and ranges against it the considerable guns of reason, nature, truth, or (without paradox) common notions. Prominent in the arguments championing reforms in the Church is the appeal to nature, to the inwardness of religious experience and the sanctity of the individual conscience, and the natural diversity of parts which bespeaks a unity of the whole, as the most persuasive counters to the religious customs of established institutions and the claim of such institutions to an exclusive possession of the path to salvation. In the first of his antiprelatical tracts, *Of Reformation in England* (1641), Milton—of whom it has been wittily said that he himself 'was a sect'—distinguishes clearly between truth and custom, 'for Custome without Truth is but Agednesse of Error'. And Herbert explains for us why custom should be of so great power in the world, and especially in religious life:

I observe that though no tenets, so far as they are untrue, are universally held, popular errors are very often wont to spread widely whenever they contain a large admixture of truth. For this reason there is nothing which so preoccupies the mind as Religion; even though it should be false. For our minds possess no more ancient nor more essential kind of correspondence than that which is established with God.[44]

With the appeal to nature (or 'Natural Instinct'), then, went an attack on custom, and this is essentially Herbert's position, with the attack directed particularly at the institutional claim to exclusive salvation. He therefore gives a new and deep resonance to the phrase 'Catholic Church'. In his *Religio laici*, first printed in the 1645 edition of *De veritate* (together with *De causis errorum*, an *Appendix ad sacerdotes de religione* and some Latin poems),[45] he persuades the layman, or 'Wayfarer' in this earthly life, to use his reason to 'search out doctrines which are analogous to the internal faculties, and then afterwards those about which there is most agreement'. The result of this search will obviously be the discovery of the chief religious notions. 'By these truths alone,' Herbert declares, 'is this universe governed, and disposed to a better state; these therefore consider the catholic truths of the church'.[46] Herbert in fact makes 'the Church' so literally and determinedly 'catholic' that it becomes a vague and amorphous concept to which it is difficult to give any precise content—and this would seem to be exactly what he wished to happen, for the more clear-cut and dogmatic a religious institution is the more effectively it can pursue its characteristic occupation of intimidation, compulsion and persecution—a view later endorsed by Locke, for whom persecutions 'are generally made to gratify the pride, the ambition, or the interest of the clergy'.

Although Herbert's literary passion is relatively cool (*De veritate* is an intensely 'learned' treatise, though not—to Herbert's credit—in the way he himself despised), the question of ecclesiastical authority rouses him to some of his most impassioned rhetoric. *Religio laici* breaks into some truly aggressive passages, excellently rendered in Harold Hutcheson's translation, which display both his polemic at its best and the motives of his attack. He begins, as is his custom, with a broadside at the schoolmen; although they are fashionably discredited, Herbert is directing his barbed point at contemporary church government, both Catholic and Protestant, for the implication is of course that such tyranny is already rampant:

Yet because ... the schoolmen every one, clad in whatever garb or robe, wearing whatever cap or hood, have allowed no religion to be adorned with any but their own faith and their own miracles (or at least none that did not included these), if they banish every doctrine which does not enter by this gate, and if finally they keep the keys for themselves and themselves alone, Good God! what tyranny they will introduce![47]

The consequent fragmentation of the Church and the bewilderment of the Wayfarer is sharply drawn by means of a series of questions

which are laid like mines under the basic assumptions of the
Church. Although Herbert as usual names no names, the particular
object of his attack is the scholastic 'Calvinism' of Theodore Beza,
Calvin's successor in Geneva, and the 'Calvinist' articles formulated
at the Synod of Dort in 1619. These were: predestination not
dependent on faith; limited atonement; the total depravity of man;
irresistible grace; and the impossibility of falling from grace. The
decrees of the Synod were in part the result of the labours of the
puritan William Perkins, whose *A Golden Chaine concerning the Order of
the Causes of Salvation and Damnation, accord to God's Word*, proposed a
rigid determinism and the full rigour of predestination. It was
Perkins's work which provoked Arminius's refutation of the dogma
of election, and ultimately the condemnation of Arminius by the
Synod.[48] Herbert makes his own Arminian position clear, but his
questions could be embarrassing enough to any seventeenth-century
churchman:

Or shall he [the Wayfarer] believe firmly in these miracles because they
were thus possible, and although objectors maintain with equal pertinacity
that they were not possible? Or place the same faith in that writers only
heard and in those they actually saw? Or because priests boast of having
received revelations from God, immediately grant that they have uttered a
law for himself as well? Shall he moreover shut himself up so completely
within some church that he will consider all men outside it damned
eternally? . . . Or under the name of God worship a divinity which has
deliberately and painstakingly created and permeated souls doomed to
perish? Or which for its mere good pleasure has destined the greater part of
the world to the everlasting punishment of Hell? Shall he, finally, demand
no other reason of all things than that proceeding from the faith and
traditions of the priests?[49]

A similar strain is taken up by the Cambridge Platonists, for whom
the dogma of predestination was neither intellectually nor morally
defensible. John Smith protests emphatically in *The Nature of Legal
and Evangelical Righteousness*;[50] Henry More shudders at 'the Black
Doctrine of absolute Reprobation'; and Benjamin Whichcote (he
might be echoing Lord Herbert) claims that it 'is not worth the
name of religion to charge our consciences with that, which we have
not reconciled to the reason and judgement of our minds, to the
frame and temper of our souls'.[51]

When Herbert turns his attention to priests in particular his irony
is sharper and his voice bitter. The Wayfarer will find the priestly
orders

however quarrelsome and clamorous about their faiths, however busy sowing contentions not only among themselves but among neighbouring nations, conspiring together none the less about these matters: everywhere to interpose and to maintain their authority; to allow nothing they teach to be so much as doubted; to confine what is most important to abstruse and difficult passages which they interpret; to restrain the most lawful pleasures which they themselves have not appointed; to deny obstinately that heaven can be approached without their influence; to threaten anathema and eternal punishments against those who differ; briefly, conspiring that neither entering nor leaving this world should be quite lawful without their aid.[52]

With a similar vision of the situation, if with a contrasting voice of quieter irony, Sir Thomas Browne too comments on this folly:

Thus whilst the mercies of God doe promise us heaven, our conceits and opinions exclude us from that place. There must be therefore more than one Saint Peter; particular Churches and Sects usurpe the gates of heaven, and turne the key against each other; and thus we goe to heaven against each others wills, conceits and opinions, and, with as much uncharity as ignorance, do erre I feare in points, not onely of our own, but one anothers salvation.[53]

Entirely consistent with his beliefs Herbert himself refused on his death-bed the aid of the priesthood, preferring to leave this world without their permission—a fiercely independent spirit which never left him:

> *Me totum bonitas bonum suprema*
> *Reddas: me intrepidum dabo vel ipse*

> Make me, Eternal Goodness, wholly good:
> Myself I'll answer for my hardihood.[54]

The burden of Herbert's general message is akin to that of Donne's *Satyre III*, 'Of Religion', a poem which one can imagine Herbert had read many times. Curiously, in an age so profoundly religious as the 1590s, Donne's youthful poem is a satire not of religion but of religious indifference, and he represents an early and unorthodox point of view. The indifference he diagnoses is of two kinds: there are those for whom no Church can possibly be true and those who regard them as all the same; but there is another sort of indifference, the willingness to submit to any convenient Church, led by upbringing or legislation or by apathy, without exercising any truly religious motive—the acquiescence in 'authority'. Into the dominant tone of the age, the presumption of *knowing* all the important truths, Donne introduces a kind of Cartesian doubt. At the heart of his response lies the Reformation stalemate on the question of a criterion of truth. The enquirer is encouraged to 'Seeke true religion'; but the question inevitably comes, 'O where?' Some find it in Rome; some find it in the 'plaine, simple, sullen, yong, / Contemptuous, yet unhandsome' religion at Geneva, and others, hearkening to 'Some Preachers, vile ambitious bauds' who 'bid him thinke that shee / Which dwells with us, is onely perfect', rest in the Church of England. For the layman the burden of choice is all but overwhelming: 'but unmoved thou / Of force must one, and forc'd but one allow; / And the right':

> To adore, or scorne an image, or protest,
> May all be bad; doubt wisely; in strange way
> To stand inquiring right, is not to stray;
> To sleepe, or runne wrong, is.

'Foole and wretch,' Donne warns, 'wilt thou let thy Soule be tyed / To man's lawes, by which shee shall not be tryed / At the last day?' And he concludes with the challenging couplet, 'So perish Soules, which more chuse mens unjust / Power from God claym'd, than God himselfe to trust'.

The *Satyre* raises a host of issues, among them the inadequacies of religion by 'authority', the confusion of conflicting truth-claims, the dangers of religious indifference, the necessity for religious heroism and independence, the nature of ecclesiastical allegiance, and the wide difference between the institutional Church, or Churches, and the invisible Church of true believers. Although Donne's vision of Truth—

> On a huge hill,
> Cragged, and steep, Truth stands, and hee that will
> Reach her, about must, and about must goe,
> And what the hills suddennes resists, winne so

—is far different from Herbert's, which finds the question more simply resolved by the observation of one's own faculties and an acknowledgement of the self-evident and non-contradictable, Herbert is in many respects taking up and investigating further these issues and making some of them peculiarly his own.

There has probably always been a tension in Christianity between individual, unique and intimate contact with God and the regularising, institutionalising and externalising of those contacts. 'Faith' and 'Church' are both historically and logically at odds with one another; and the expression of the relationship may vary from the massive institutionalism of the Roman Church, the Gospel revivalism of the radical Protestant sects, to the final move towards dissociation of a Lord Herbert or a Milton. Both Donne and Herbert, in their view that the Church is more than an institution, are of course in perfect accord with most Protestant opinion. 'All visible Churches upon earth', says William Perkins, 'are subject to Apostasie',[55] and the militant puritan John Preston, using language remarkably similar to Herbert's though his final injunction is rather different, urges Christians 'to take nothing merely upon trust, not to think things are so only because the Church hath said it; this foundation is too sandy for us to build our Faith upon, that should be built upon the Rock which is the Word of God'.[56] Herbert, who has nothing to offer on the vexed and vital question of scriptural interpretation (he would almost certainly have agreed with Selden's exasperated remark, '*Scrutamini Scripturas*: These two words have undone the world'),[57] takes a different direction and urges his layman to avoid that particular contentious trap and take hold first of all on the Common Notions of religion which are recognised by the 'truly *Catholic Church*, which neither fails nor ever will fail, and in which alone *Divine Universal Providence* triumphs': (1) there is a supreme God; (2) He is to be worshipped; (3) virtue and piety are the chief parts of religious worship; (4) men have always been aware of their vices and crimes, which must be expiated by repentance; and (5) there is reward or punishment after this life.[58]

Herbert's procedure raises, in fact, the more radical doubt whether membership of any visible and particular Church at all is really essential to salvation. But even this apparently destructive and dismissive exercise need not imply religious indifference or lack of religious faith. The question Herbert puts may be regarded as both practical, necessary, and theologically impeccable; where the central viewpoint is that the true Church is *invisible*, what power has the *visible* Church to enforce allegiance? It is not a novel question by any means, nor is it at all the special property of Lord Herbert; Donne had put the same point, speaking in the voice of Erasmus a century before, and had allowed the tail of his sentence to carry an even more subversive sting: 'We must be so far from straitening salvation to any particular Christian church of any subdivided name, Papist or Protestant, as that we may not straiten it to the whole Christian church, as though God could not in the largeness of his mercy, afford salvation to some whome he never gathered into the Christian church'.[59]

Revelation and faith

The source from which, ultimately, both institutional dogma and individual faith must draw their inspiration is the recognition and acceptance of divine revelation. The question which Herbert approaches is not *whether* such revelation can be recognised and accepted, but *how* is the appeal to it to be distinguished from the Church's or the individual's particular self-interests? It is important to stress that he does not reject revelation; but he does insist that it must be a personal affair, valid only when it comes directly and specifically, and that in the documentation of historical revelations we must examine the nature and the circumstances of the particular revelation before according it our faith. Neither a man, whoever he may be, nor an institution has the right to foist their own revelations on the majority of men, let alone maintain them by violence. As is so often the case Herbert is so deeply engaged with the ethical question that he ignores, or chooses not to see, consequences in other directions. Such a view of revelation appears to cut deep at the heart of Christianity and Herbert, although he professes orthodoxy, nowhere mitigates the difficulties. At the forefront of his thought is the pressing need to distinguish between revelation and mere authority, bearing always in mind that warning which, as Montaigne put it, reminds us that 'Whatsoever is told us, and whatever we learne, we should ever remember, it is man who delivereth, and man that receiveth: It is a mortall hand, that presents it, and a mortall hand, that receives it. Onely things which come to us from heaven, have right and authority of perswasion, and markes of truth'.[60]

How then are we to decide what is from heaven and what from man? The framing of such a question implies that there *are* two realms to be distinguished, and the answer must lie in our rational, decision-making, discriminating faculties. This is in fact an orthodox enough point of view, for the traditional position (as expressed in Aquinas and Hooker) is that there is a reasonable basis for Christianity and, as Hooker assured the puritans who were caught in their circle of self-authenticating scriptural authority,

'Scripture teacheth us that saving truth which God hath discovered
unto the world by revelation, *and it presumeth us taught otherwise that
itself is divine and sacred*'.[61] Our instrument is the faculty of
reason—for Herbert both in the sense of our intuitive knowledge and
Natural Instinct, and in the sense of *discursus*. Herbert begins his
investigation by saying that 'certain assumptions which underlie our
notions of revelation ought to be examined'. In the course of the
examination he juggles with the words 'faith' and 'reason', setting
them one against the other; *fide, implicita fide, rationem humana,
credulitas, discursus* all appear, and we would be advised to tread with
caution. The easy conclusion might be that Herbert is proposing an
intellectual dualism in which 'faith' is merely perfidious and to be
discarded. Certainly he has no time for a fideism which asserts that
there are *no* rational motives for assenting to divine revelation; but
since 'reason', in the primary sense of Natural Instinct, is that
faculty which identifies the divinity within us and which is a God-
implanted power of conforming our knowledge to the truth, and that
further, since its apprehensions are intuitive and immediate ('man
must embrace some beliefs that surpass his understanding'), the
term comes very close to what another writer might mean by 'faith'.
To deny the efficacy of reason, in this sense, in leading us to religious
truth would be the worst kind of blasphemy. The reader is warned
not to 'degrade the divine intellectual faculties', and is told that 'if
you prefer faith to reason [*si Fidem denique rationi praeponitis*] do you
not bring the entire edifice of the understanding to ruin by
wretchedly abusing the gifts of God?'[62] By 'faith' here he clearly
means 'fideism', or simple credulity and blind acceptance of the
proposals of the ruling power. The most impressive evidence of our
God-given reason is the existence of Common Notions, without
whose prompting 'it is impossible to establish any standard of
discrimination in revelation, or even in religion'. He then elaborates
on his sense of *implicita fide* (confirming Sir Thomas Browne's sense
of a 'humble, yet not implicit, faith' in *Religio medici*), and at the
same time resolves the paradox of 'custom' and 'consent':

Theories based upon implicit faith, though widely held not only in our own
part of the world but also in the most distant regions, are here irrelevant.
Instances of such beliefs are: that human reason must be discarded, to make
room for Faith; that the Church, which is infallible, has the right to
prescribe the method of divine worship, and in consequence must be obeyed
in every detail; that no one ought to place such confidence in his private

judgement as to dare to question the sacred authority of priests and preachers of God's word; that their utterances, though they may elude human grasp, contain so much truth that we should rather lay them to heart than debate them; that to God all things of which they speak and much more are possible.

He points out, with persuasive logic, that 'these arguments and many other similar ones, according to differences of age and country, may be equally used to establish a false religion as to support a true one'. He comments finally, ironically indulging a Greek pun, that 'anything that springs from the productive, not to say seductive seed of Faith will yield a plentiful crop.'[63]

There is here, quite clearly, a species of scepticism, directed strategically at the opposite response of pure fideism. There is the prerogative of doubt, the right to debate rather than swallow whole, the refusal to accept as God's what is proposed by man—a critical mind that insists on proper discrimination and that such discrimination is within the power of reason. It is a response to the sort of logic seriously advanced (for one example out of many possible examples) by the puritan Thomas Cartwright in Elizabeth's day, that God 'must have done' certain things: God does what is best for the Church, this is best for the Church, therefore God must have done it, and all opposition must knuckle under and accept this authority.[64] Early in *De veritate*, in his summary of the modes of truth, Herbert says that 'the truth of Revelation has a place among these truths, and I recognise it freely', but he adds, 'So long as what is put forward under this head is genuinely revealed. The traditions of historical faith are distinct from the deliveries of divine faith, not merely by the method by which they are perceived, but by the whole breadth of the sky; and sober revelations are no less distinct from wild experiments.'[65]

It is of crucial importance to the historical perspective to remember that Herbert is making his points in an age that had been, and was further to be, characterised by anti-intellectual sectarian prophesying; cults and sects were created by self-interested claims of revelation and divine promptings, each cult loudly desecrating the 'impostures' and 'fraud' of rivals and enemies. 'Implicite Faith' was to become the mark of fanaticism; Herbert's phrase 'wild experiments' was more than a figure of speech. The anti-rational posture of the puritans in Hooker's day was an important religious phenomenon for several generations, from the anti-intellectual stance of Thomas Cartwright to the Independent prophets of the 'Puritan Revolution', Coppe, Coppin, Muggleton, Fox, Reeve and many others. It was not until later in the seventeenth century that anti-rational '*Enthusiasts,* or true Fanaticks' were to be regarded, even by Dissenters, as a lunatic fringe among English Protestants. The wheel oddly comes full circle in the outburst of the curious Edmund Hickeringill, by turns Independent chaplain, Baptist, Quaker, 'atheist' and Anglican-deist who, in his attack on priestcraft and clerical knavery, characterises the priestly 'Ceremony-Monger' as a man whose 'Soul and Conscience is neither rul'd by Holy Scripture, Right Reason, nor by the Law of the Land but in despight of all these . . . only through Custom, Ignorance, blind Devotions, implicite Faith, and apish Imitation . . . by Avarice and Ambition'.[66] In Herbert's view the source both of historical confusions and of the proliferation of wild experimenters lay in the failure to recognise the role of reason in religion. His position is that a revealed statement can be accepted as true, however contrary it may seem to reason, so long as it can be shown that revelation occurred, and that it is not a question of possibility, probability, or falsehood. This, being a matter of fact, is to be established like any other factual matter. It therefore lies within the competency of the rational mind.

This position is, as has been suggested, essentially orthodox and within the tradition of Christian rationalism. It is very similar to the view of Herbert's friend Hugo Grotius, who pointed out the ease with which 'revelations' may occur. Grotius is speaking of paganism (and Herbert, it will be remembered, is of course discussing religion in general, not Christianity in particular) when he says that

The wisest among them [pagans] reject many of them [miracles], as supported by no sufficient Faith of Witnesses, and plainly counterfeit. Some which are reported to have been real, happened in secret, in the dark, in the presence of one or two, whose eyes, by the cunning of their priests, might easily be deluded. Others there are, which caused admiration only in such as were ignorant of things Natural, and occult properties.[67]

(It was nevertheless the kind of argument which, through suitable adaptation, could become the staple fare of later 'deists' like Charles Blount for example or John Toland on the subject of Christian miracles.) Grotius had also pointed out in his *Truth of the Christian Religion* (1624) that in matters of faith an appeal is necessary to common sense in assessing the validity of religious testimony; the same canons are to be used in the evaluating of religious as of secular texts. One has as much evidence, Grotius suggests, that what the Bible says about Christ is true as one does of the life of Socrates from the writings of Plato and Xenophon.[68] Herbert does not anywhere go explicitly as far as Grotius in proposing the historical validity of Christianity along these lines (nor on the other hand does he anywhere deny it)—Grotius's work was originally intended as a handbook for Dutch sailors to be used in converting pagans in foreign ports, and it is therefore not emphatic on those schisms within Christianity which are Herbert's special concern. But it is evident that what Herbert is attacking is not the truth of revelation but the authenticity of the assumption of revelation, which is a very different thing. 'We must proceed', he says, 'with great care in discerning what is actually revealed'.[69] His warning was, in terms of the spiritual history of the period, a signally apt one; and his attitude, like that of Grotius, is another step in the growth of historical criticism.

The Anglican Joseph Glanvill, in a sermon to the clergy in 1670, proposed, in an age which he and many others thought in desperate need of it, a 'seasonable Recommendation and Defence of Reason in the Affairs of Religion', and concerning the principles of 'pure Revelation' he argued that

Reason cannot prove them immediately; nor is it to be expected that it should: For they are matters of Testimony; and we are to no more looke for immediate proof from Reason of those things, than we are to expect, that abstracted reason should demonstrate, That there is such a place as China; or, that there was such a man as Julius Caesar. All that it can do here, is to assert, and make good the credibility, and truth of the Testimonies that relate such matters.[70]

Nor does Glanvill miss the important matter of motivation and the probability of clerical corruption; for he leans forward to 'speak a word to You, my brethren of the CLERGY, (Those, I mean of the Younger sort, for I shall not presume to teach my Elders)' and to confirm by implication the kind of warnings sounded first by Herbert in the 1620s:

You have heard, no doubt, frequent and earnest declamations against Reason, during the years of your Education; and Youth, we know, receives impressions easily; And I shall not wonder if you have been possessed with very hard thoughts of this pretended terrible enemy of Faith, and Religion: But did you ever consider deeply since, what ends of Religion, or Sobriety, such vehement defamations of our faculties could serve? And what Ends of a Party they did?[71]

Glanvill surveys the history of the church over the last few decades of schism, strife, civil war and bloodshed, and again implicitly commends Herbert's earlier general advice:

There is nothing, that I know, hath done so much mischief to Christianity, as the disparagement of Reason, under pretense of respect, and favour to Religion; since hereby the very Foundations of the Christian Faith have been undermined, and the World prepared for Atheism. For if Reason must not be heard, the Being of a GOD, and the Authority of Scripture can neither be proved nor defended; and so our Faith drops to the ground, like a House that hath no foundation. Besides, by this way, those sickly conceits, and Enthusiastick dreames, and unsound Doctrines, that have poysoned our Aire, and infatuated the minds of men, and exposed Religion to the scorn of Infidels, and divided the Church, and disturbed the peace of mankind, and involved the Nation in so much bloud, and so many Ruines; I say hereby, all these fatal Follies, that have been the occasions of so many mischiefs, have been propagated and promoted.[72]

Glanvill notes (and again he might be echoing Herbert) the importance of defining and distinguishing terms like 'reason', 'religion' and 'revelation'; 'The want of this', he says, 'hath been the occasion of a great part of those Confusions we find in Disputes'. Religion is defined 'under two Generals, Worship and Virtue', and the 'Principles of Religion' are of two sorts, '(1) Fundamental and Essential; others (2) accessory and assisting'. Glanvill lists four 'Fundamental Principles': (1) that there is a God of infinite perfection; (2) that we are sinners and exposed to his displeasure; (3) that God is our maker, and Author of all our blessings; and (4) that there is Moral Good; and Evil. There are others, he says, which are 'not so absolutely necessary' but are 'very incouraging and helpful', e.g. pardon, divine assistance in our endeavours, and punishment and reward in another world. Christianity embodies all these 'and superadding two other instances, Baptism, and the Lord's Supper': 'And though our Church require our assent to more Propositions; yet those are only Articles of Communion, not Doctrines absolutely necessary to Salvation'. As for the faculty of 'Reason', Glanvill more or less repeats Herbert in summary:

By the Principles of Reason we are not to understand the Grounds of any mans Philosophy; nor the Critical Rules of Syllogism; but those inbred fundamental notices, that God hath implanted in our Soules; such as arise not from external objects, nor particular humours, or imaginations; but are immediately lodged in our minds; independent upon other principles or deductions; commanding a sudden assent; and acknowledged by all sober mankind.[73]

In the application of Reason to Religion, Glanvill allows a degree of philosophical scepticism: 'the Divine Nature is infinite, and our Conceptions very shallow and finite'; moreover, 'we know not the Essence, and ways of acting of the most ordinary and obvious things of Nature, and therefore must not expect thoroughly to understand the deeper things of God'. And he makes the same sensible sort of point that Herbert had made: 'When some of these propositions of Faith and Religion are said to be Above reason, no more is meant, than that Reason cannot conceive how those things are; and in that sense many of the affairs of nature are above it too'. Equally though, ''tis not faith, but vain credulity to believe everything that pretends to be from God'.

Such a position might well become, through the pressures of disillusionment and change, the position expressed in John Toland's *Christianity not Mysterious* (1696) or William Stephen's oft-repeated question in *An Account of the Growth of Deism in England* (1696): 'That which is above Reason must be above rational Belief, and must I be saved by an Irrational belief?'[74] The complexity of Herbert's view, in the face of such a question, is at once apparent. As Herbert says, beliefs which rest on Natural Instinct also 'rest on pure Faith'.[75] The grounds of that faith may have been significantly shifted in the process of questioning, but the term 'rational theologian' may be misleading as applied to Herbert, since what he understands by 'belief' is rational in so far as it makes the objects of belief rationally comprehensible, in other words in conformity with our faculties—if they are not rational in this sense, they are not beliefs but opinions or errors; but it is also 'irrational' in so far as it makes the grounds for the object's rational appeal rest in a context which is, in the sense of being beyond demonstration, extra-rational, the realm, that is, of the instinctive and the intuitive. Herbert in fact embodies the paradox, unperceived by later controversialists, that if rationality consists of holding only justifiable beliefs, then it must always have irrational foundations.

A further aspect of Herbert's treatment of revelation relates to revelations to ourselves. His emphasis on this is not a mere diversion directed at the over-credulous or the Margery Kempes of the age, but is a sober comment on the 'inner voice of persuasion' and the putative visitations of the Holy Ghost. It would be inconsistent of Herbert to reject entirely this particular manifestation of the trust in the individual conscience from which Protestantism had drawn its profoundest impulses, and he is in no doubt that such revelation does occur. To be admitted as true however all the faculties by which we assess knowledge must have been consulted first, the revelation must be directly to ourselves, it must persuade us to some good, and we must distinctly feel the inspiration (*afflatus*) of God.[76] But having confirmed the fact of revelation in this way, Herbert blocks the flood-gate to sectarianism by saying that it is not therefore incumbent on us to intrude our revelation upon others.

The frequency with which Herbert's views here have been misunderstood makes the point worth labouring. His famous account, which he records in his autobiography, of the sign from heaven before the manuscript of *De veritate* was sent to press, has most often been taken as a mark of gross inconsistency and instability of mind. Herbert describes what happened as follows:

Being thus doubtful in my chamber, one fair day in the summer, my casement being opened towards the south, the sun shining clear, and no wind stirring, I took my book, *De veritate*, in my hand, and, kneeling on my knees, devoutly said these words:

'O thou eternal God, Author of the light which now shines upon me, and Giver of all inward illuminations, I do beseech Thee, of Thy infinite goodness, to pardon a greater request than a sinner ought to make; I am not satisfied enough whether I shall publish this Book, *De veritate*; if it be for Thy glory, I beseech Thee give me some sign from heaven; if not, I shall suppress it.'

I had no sooner spoke these words, but a loud though gentle noise came from the heavens, for it was like nothing on earth, which did so comfort and cheer me, that I took my petition as granted, and that I had the sign I demanded, whereupon also I resolved to print my book. This, how strange soever it may seem, I protest before the eternal God is true, neither am I any way superstitiously deceived herein, since I did not only clearly hear the noise, but in the serenest sky that ever I saw, being without all cloud, did to my thinking see the place from whence it came.[77]

Of this episode one anonymous commentator, describing *De veritate*, says that the 'supposed miraculous interposition' exhibits 'contradictions so singular as to point to this work as one of those great errors of a great mind'.[78] A much more recent critic assembles some of Herbert's more striking paradoxes and concludes that 'one can only compare him with a remarkably agile equestrian artist in a circus, leaping with nonchalance from a horse going in one direction to one headed the other way'.[79] One might defend Herbert negatively by pointing out the abundance of such paradoxes in the seventeenth century: that Sir Kenelm Digby of the Royal Society advertised, and sold, a 'powder of sympathy' that cured from a distance; that Boyle was still looking for the philosopher's stone; that Descartes vowed to make a pilgrimage to Loretto if the Virgin would assist his thoughts; or that Newton himself thought that God occasionally adjusted the minor irregularities of the solar system personally. But such criticisms also overlook the significance of Herbert's total religious awareness and betray a misunderstanding of his views on revelation. Even the judicious W. K. Jordan claims that 'the suspicion is perhaps justified that he made dexterous use of a pretension which the sects, whom Herbert disliked so intensely, were wont to employ for the advancement of their 'truth'. We cannot possibly credit Herbert with sincerity in this amazing statement.'[80] But it is scarcely sufficient to summarise, as Jordan does, Herbert's view as 'Nothing should be believed or accepted which violates the reason of the individual or which transcends reason'.[81] Herbert himself makes frequent representation on behalf of the opposite view. However deficient Herbert may be in his understanding of ecclesiasticism, his instinct for religious experience is lively and vigorous. In *De veritate* he makes the following assertion which bears directly on his own sign from heaven: 'When in a moment of intense faith we make a special appeal to God, and feel within us His saving power and a sense of marvellous deliverance, I do not doubt that the mind is touched by Grace, or particular Providence, and that since some new aspect of God is revealed, we pass beyond the normal level of experience.'[82]

Hooker, Herbert and Locke on religious knowledge

The subsequent progress of the relation between the claims of revelation and of reason is full of that characteristic seventeenth-century complexity and paradox. The attempt to heal the divisions between 'faith' and 'reason' opened up by nominalist and sceptical approaches was based largely upon the scholastic and humanistic evidence of the *lex aeterna*, the *jus naturale*, and the proof of the *consensus gentium*, and its classic exposition, Hooker's great synthesis of the Laws of God and the Law of Reason in the *Ecclesiastical Polity* (1593–7). Hooker refused to recognise a 'double truth' which set theology over against the arts, sciences and human virtues of man, but brought together the claims made by revelation and reason,

uniting them in the context of his majestic model of the universe. For
him, reason does not war with faith, nor Nature with Grace; the
spiritual does not do battle with the rational: 'if Nature hath need of
Grace', yet also 'Grace hath need of Nature'.[83] Bacon's advice that
we should render unto faith the things that are faith's betrays the
suspicion however that Pomponazzi may have been right; and when
he says that 'Sacred theology ought to be derived from the word and
oracles of God, not from the light of nature, or the dictates of
reason'[84] he confronts us with precisely the opposition—as though
the 'dictates of reason' had nothing whatever to do with the 'word
and oracles of God'—which both Hooker and Lord Herbert refused
to admit.

The spiritual worlds of Hooker and Herbert are not of course very
close, yet the affinities between the two men may be superficially
striking. Herbert's reliance on the Common Notions cannot fail to
recall Hooker's 'general and perpetual voice', for Hooker equally
maintains that man always had an inborn knowledge of God, proved
by the *consensus gentium*. Firmly within the tradition of Christian
humanism, Hooker regards all forms of knowledge as modes of
goodness since they derive from the wisdom of God, the ultimate
good. This is the central ethical premise of both the scholastics and
the Renaissance humanists, that the human will and the human
reason rest upon 'the intellectual presentation of the good'. Yet
Hooker, unlike Herbert, was a good Anglican and a firmly orthodox
Christian, so that he is careful to guard against the threat to revealed
religion which is concealed in this identification of truth with virtue.
As Herschel Baker has put it,

It was all too easy, as the seventeenth century was to learn, to slip down the
path of rational theology to deism, or even worse. Once the delicate
equilibrium between reason and faith was dislocated, or the claims of
natural knowledge permitted to usurp the prerogatives of revelation, then
there was a real danger to the sovereignty of God.[85]

This carefulness on Hooker's part is all-important. Compared with
his intricately moulded arguments, Herbert is brash, cavalier,
confident and distinctly carefree—he has no great edifice of
authority which he is pledged to support, no self-acknowledged
belief in the great Thomist structure of theology, and no concern
with the niceties of Church government. For Herbert Church
government can, to all intents and purposes, go hang. Yet curiously
enough what Lord Herbert endangers is certainly not the

sovereignty of God; with him, as in another form with Hooker, God's sovereignty is unassailable and is the very keystone of the Herbertian cosmos; what Herbert endangers, by his riding roughshod over the tenets of traditional theology, is the status of the Church and the Church's authority. And this is precisely what he intended and what he saw to be vitally necessary.

Hooker was naturally incapable of taking such a direction. Yet despite the rich cadences of his prose and the gentleness of his good manners, Hooker's 'sweet reasonableness' may be much exaggerated. Although Hooker taught, as he felt bound to teach to the puritan opposition, that reason could discover the essential truths of Christianity, he avoided the problem of defining what those truths were, and what areas reason could properly occupy. In the eyes of orthodox contemporaries Herbert's particular crime (in so far as he was read and understood) was that he did *not* evade this task, but gave substance and definition to the hints and nudges of theologians, bringing upon himself in consequence the later odium of 'deist', 'free-thinker', and worse. Yet Herbert's contribution was in some respects exactly what the doctrinal confusion of his age demanded and which Hooker had failed to provide. Hooker's teaching is in fact that rational freedom is not the prerogative of all men but the prerogative only of the Church.

Hooker's great synthesis did not of course, any more than Herbert's, 'end dispute', let alone make dispute impossible. The orthodox Dean of St Paul's, regarding reason much as Hooker had, as important but beneath revelation, aims most of his comments on the 'double truth' against the Roman Catholics, who are continually guilty of mingling philosophy and theology until men are forced to make 'philosophy and reason speak against Religion'; they are unaware that, unless truth is distorted, 'whatsoever is true in philosophy is true in divinity too'. True admiration and wonder stand between faith and reason 'and have an eye to both'.[86] To Donne faith and reason are almost like the two blades of a pair of scissors—but not quite, for reason is ultimately dispensable. He explains to Lady Bedford that 'reason is our soul's left hand, faith her right', and embroidered minutely on that text in his *Elegy for the Prince*, 'Look to me, Faith'—a poem composed, so Drummond of Hawthornden records Ben Jonson as saying, for Lord Herbert's benefit.[87]

In Sir Thomas Browne the separation comes alive again, but in

Browne—a doctor practising in an increasingly scientific age—the tone changes to a defensive apologetic for faith's flights to an 'O altitudo', and he quotes that maxim of Tertullian's, *certum est quia impossibile est*, that crops up so often in this period.[88] It indicates the kind of spiritual athleticism which Herbert had never really appreciated. Yet with the added impetus given to rationalism by Descartes and the criterion of 'clear and distinct ideas' the role of reason, working in the interests of faith, became magnified and confirmed. The Cambridge Platonists were, as John Tulloch said, 'characteristically *rational* theologians' who 'sought to bring every truth or doctrine to the test of Christian reason'. S. P. (probably Simon Patrick), one of their defenders, argues that it is absurd to accuse them of 'hearkening too much to their own reason', and proceeds to demonstrate how a man must have some reason for believing anything, whether it be 'a deduction from the light of nature', the principles of 'the candle of the Lord', divine revelation, Holy Scripture, historical study, Church authority, or a combination of any of these, 'for there is an eternal consanguinity between all verity; and nothing is true in divinity which is false in philosophy, or on the contrary; and therefore what God hath joined together, let no man put asunder'.[89] The specific role of revelation is supplementary; to 'the truth of natural inscription', John Smith writes in his *Select Discourses*, 'God hath provided the truth of divine revelation'. Truth, though single in itself, may be communicated to man in many forms, but all truth is ultimately grasped by reason, for it is reason that apprehends it. There is, to the Cambridge Platonists, no necessary conflict between faith and reason or between revealed and natural truth.

In Jeremy Taylor the rehabilitation of reason is equally unmistakable. In the opening of his vast *Ductor dubitantium* (1660) Taylor sees God not only in the workings of providence but in those laws engraved on our hearts: 'He rules in us by His substitute our conscience ... God sits there and gives us laws'. And conscience itself is 'nothing but right reason reduced to practice, and conducing moral action'.[90] And among the progressive theologians of the Revolutionary and Restoration periods—Tillotson, Glanvill, Stillingfleet, Tenison—the desire to eliminate the irrational from religion dominates, though the praise of reason is usually more in evidence than its definition. Gilbert Burnet joins, as Herbert had done, the prompting of the divine spirit and the testimony of reason, if by reason we mean 'the clear conviction of our faculties'.[91] Among the Latitudinarians many are Herbertian enough to claim that the mind, without appeal to any extraneous authority, can grasp in broad outline a religion which includes all the essentials of belief. In his essay detailing *The Agreement of Reason and Religion* (1676)—a slightly altered version of his earlier sermon to the clergy—Glanvill lists a mere three points, though augmented with four subsidiary and equally general points, the acceptance of which he regards as necessary to salvation: the existence of God, the providence of God, and the reality of moral distinctions.[92]

If much of this may seem to resemble the maturing of Herbert's original position, it is a little surprising to find that among the pioneers of deism—in whose company Herbert is generally assigned a leading place, not least by the deists themselves—there is a quite different tenor and drift. Charles Blount, who specifically claims Herbert's authority, presented his translation of the *Life of Apollonius of Tyana* (1680) in order to furnish himself with the opportunity of suggesting, through gibes and innuendoes, that the miracles of Christ were really much the same as the mendacities of Apollonius. Throughout Blount's writings there are indications of a view of religion as an expression only of the baseness, weakness and credulity of man—and he is speaking of that very capacity for 'religion and faith' which Herbert considered 'the unique and ultimate' distinction of man. And John Toland, in his *Christianity not Mysterious* (1696), diminishes reason to demonstration, describing it as 'that Faculty of the Soul which discovers the Certainty of any thing dubious or obscure, by comparing it with something evidently known'; he claims that reason in this sense (the sense which Herbert designated *discursus* and had so little faith in) is 'the only Foundation of all Certitude', and, with no hint of Herbert's important qualifications, he ridicules 'the famous and admirable Doctrine' which enjoins us 'to adore what we cannot comprehend'.[93]

In considering Locke's outstanding contribution to the debate, it becomes apparent that Locke's position is in many ways as paradoxical as Herbert's and that he is as easily to be accused of wishing to have his cake and eat it. As theological rancour declined and with the passing of the Act of Toleration on 24 May 1689 (though it expressly excluded Roman Catholics and Anti-Trinitarians), common sense finally triumphed, and nowhere more decisively than in John Locke. The essence of Locke's views on revelation and its relation to reason is contained in his famous *Essay Concerning Human Understanding* (1690), where Herbert's position is precisely restated: 'Whatever God hath revealed is certainly true; no doubt can be made of it . . . but whether it be a divine revelation or no, reason must judge'; or again, 'No proposition can be received for divine revelation, *or obtain the assent due to all such*, if it be contradictory to our clear intuitive knowledge'.[94] Yet these apparently clear, dogmatic and simple statements are fraught with the unexpected.

The problem of interpreting Locke's *Essay* is much the same as the problem of interpreting Herbert's writings, and depends on our holding clearly in the foreground the question, what is the basic purpose of the argument, and as a result of what pressures does it take its particular form? It is true that Locke's enquiry into human understanding occurs not by way of a preface to some major work, as in Boyle, nor as an almost accidental set of statements in a scientific treatise, as in Newton; it is not apparently a basis for a polemic against atheism and Roman Catholicism, as in Chillingworth's *The Religion of Protestants* (1638) or Tillotson's *The Rule of Faith* (1666), nor a foundation for natural theology, as in Wilkins's *Of the Principles and Duties of Natural Religion* (1675); nor is it offered as a basis for specifically scientific knowledge, the particular interest of Glanvill and Boyle. The *Essay* is a descriptive account of what goes on in the mind when knowledge, belief, and error occur: 'the exposition of these problems and their solution, based upon an appeal to the certainty of ordinary life and the doctrine of the levels of certainty, is the major purpose of the *Essay*'.[95] But in the course of Locke's enquiry there are a surprising number of statements, coming from the man so generally regarded as the father of empiricism, which one must either consider as mere anomalies or as expressive of yet another major purpose which, as in Herbert's case and despite some appearance to the contrary, may be defined as the defence and renovation of proper religious faith. And the 'anomalies' occur specifically in Locke's consideration of the validity and status of revealed truth.

As John Wilkins noted in his *Of the Principles and Duties of Natural Religion*, in securing a basis in reason for religion there are two forces to be opposed, scepticism *and* dogmatism. Before drawing any comparison between Locke's position on faith and reason and Herbert's, there are two aspects of Locke's thought to be considered which seem to fly in the face of Herbert's own arguments. The first is

Locke's scepticism, and the second is his celebrated demolition of the 'dogmatic' theory of innate ideas.

It would be a simple matter to quote extensively from the *Essay* to illustrate Locke's scepticism. The assertion of the weakness of human knowledge is imprinted on every page. It is not a work which, like Herbert's, makes the largest speculative claims on behalf of human reason, whether in the sense of demonstration or of 'Natural Instinct'. Locke severely limits the scope of the enquiry to 'those things which concern our conduct'. He is more concerned with the kind of knowledge man can lay claim to than the amount of knowledge. In the context in which Locke is writing and the growing but not always discriminate praise of reason, the *Essay* is something of a corrective. Yet it is no sceptical manifesto. The appearance of scepticism is related to Locke's mission of 'clearing away some of the rubbish that lies in the way of Knowledge'; and it is too the scepticism of an urbanity in which, as Basil Willey once put it, 'there is no more of the metaphysical flicker from world to world, none of the old imagery struck out in the heat of struggle or in the ardour of discovery'.[96] Among the rubbish that Locke encountered was the belief in innate ideas, which is, he says, 'an established opinion' that is 'commonly taken for granted'.[97] We have already considered one aspect of Locke's attack on the theory. A further aspect which is relevant here and which equally serves to show how chimerical an object of his attack Herbert would have been, is the manner in which Locke associates the belief with just that species of 'authority' Herbert laid siege to over fifty years earlier. Locke complains that 'even they who require men to believe that there are such innate propositions, do not tell us what they are'; the result is 'that different men of different sects' use the theory of innate ideas 'to support the doctrines' of their particular Church.[98] These are the men who 'stamp the character of divinity upon absurdities and errors'.[99]

Just as Herbert had objected to the 'authority' of priestly pronouncements, the superstitions of both Popery and Calvinism, and the pseudo-revelations of Protestant 'fanatic conventicles', so Locke (and he is not without precisely the above objections also) resists the clerical claim to authority embodied in his interpretation of the theory of innate ideas. Herbert, as we have seen, does not claim the existence of innate ideas (and consequently gives only examples of the utmost generality), only innate modes of thought; his Common Notions resemble more nearly Locke's items of that intuitive knowledge which 'like bright sunshine forces itself immediately to be perceived, as soon as ever the mind turns its view that way' and which is the basis of 'all the certainty and evidence of all our knowledge'.[100] Among the many critics who objected to Locke's polemic against innate principles the assertion, like that of John Edwards in *The Socinian Creed* (1697), of those 'natural impressions in all men's minds' which are 'the foundation of religion, and the standard of truth as well as of morality', is naturally in the vanguard. Ecclesiastical discomfiture expressed itself in sermons preached against the *Essay* and public denunciations of Locke from the pulpit; William Sherlock preached that Locke's treatise was, because it rejected innate ideas, 'atheistical'—despite Locke's own insistence that not one word of the *Essay* was the least damaging to Christianity. And John Edwards, in his defence of innate ideas in *A Free Discourse Concerning Truth and Error*, not perceiving that the trap was sprung, proceeded to satisfy Locke's demand for a list of innate propositions by listing precisely those cited in Book I of the *Essay* as examples to be rejected.[101]

The curious thing here is that Herbert's original advocacy of common religious notions, with their basis in Natural Instinct and 'the hierarchy of Nature', should be thought of as having provoked accusations of irreligion and atheism, whilst Locke's attack on innate ideas should, some seventy years later, provoke the very same response. The impulse behind both men is psychologically continuous in terms of the basic *purpose* of the argument, for both men attack ecclesiastical complacency and the appeal of the Church to a vested authority which is seen as dubiously based. The difference of course, as with the difference between Herbert's and Locke's epistemology, lies in the emphasis of the latter on that species of 'reason' which Herbert had regarded as only a handmaid to faculties higher than itself. The shift in the terms of the argument is significant of a shift of emphasis in religious sensibility, and particularly in the attitude towards sectarian schism and its foundation in conflicting claims of 'authority'.

It is easy to see from the vantage point of time that in England belief was already, even in 1624, moving slowly but irresistibly towards a rational theology and a 'reasonable faith'. It is also easy to forget that Herbert would not have seen it quite that way. However much Herbert was in fact in the mainstream of English religious thought he almost certainly would have felt himself to be a lone pioneer, an individual malcontent and eccentric facing the fragmentation of religion. For him, even though it can be demonstrated that ideas very like his own were current in European thought before *De veritate*, it was never simply a question of drifting with the stream but of cutting new channels; there were real and recalcitrant problems to which the eirenic offered by the common religious notions seemed the only solution. Although Herbert himself aroused little in the way of excited approval (one notices, and not only among those who pursued most vigorously the way he had opened up, the tacit assumption that in many respects he merely expressed 'what oft was thought'), his contribution of Common Notions was of importance both in ensuring that subsequent rationalism was not (*pace* Locke) empty of specific conclusions, and in offering the only effective challenge to the dogmatic and sectarian spirit of the age—so effective indeed that it has even been said, with some justice, that Herbert was 'merely advocating what history has been busy realising'.[102] By the end of the century and with the achievement of a toleration, the field of combat shifts. We are presented with the situation that, whereas Herbert was concerned to support religion against 'authority' with arguments drawn from the *experience* of common consent and the Common Notions, Locke is attempting to support religion with arguments now drawn from the *evidence* supplied by reasoning: once the old foundation of innate ideas is replaced by a surer one the superstructure of Christianity, Locke believed, would stand more securely than ever.

Yet the dilemma this puts Locke into is evidenced throughout the *Essay*. He is personally convinced of the absolute truth of Christianity and the simple demands of a faith drawn from the Scriptures; his *Reasonableness of Christianity* (1695) is governed by the conviction that the credal demands made on us by Christianity are few and simple and its morality harmonious with 'natural revelation'. At the same time Locke is equally convinced that the clergy, the trustees of that faith, have attempted to support it with the wrong sort of arguments, that is, those drawn from the theory of innate ideas, now vested with the aura of 'authority'. The dilemma is clear in Locke's discussion of the first of Herbert's common religious notions, the existence of God.

As Basil Willey remarked, 'Newton's great Machine needed a

Mechanic', and Locke generally relies on the argument from design, 'the visible marks of extra-ordinary wisdom and power', and the 'contemplation of causes and effects'; he makes frequent allusion to 'the steady workmanship of nature', and 'stupendous fabric' and 'magnificent harmony of the universe', as incontrovertible evidence of a Deity.[103] 'We more certainly know', he says, 'that there is a God, than that there is anything else without us.' It is an assertion made repeatedly and with a dogmatism that is not unlike Herbert's principle of non-contradiction. Such an assumption, Locke insists, is 'necessary', 'past doubt', and 'unavoidable' for any 'considering, rational creature'.[104] To contradict this would be to subvert one's claim to rationality: 'there never was any rational creature that set himself to examine the truth of these propositions that could fail to assent to them'.[105] With this conclusion we may compare Herbert's characterisation of the Common Notions as the products of innate modes of thought to which we are inexorably led unless we choose 'to strip ourselves of all humanity'. But the empiricist Locke, bereft of that hierarchic, metaphysical and symbolically fertile background which is the subsoil of Herbert's thinking, is left, in his argument from design, in a circle of reasoning which infers the existence of God from a perceived rational ordering of objects, and which justifies the 'rationality' of that order in terms of God's existence and intentions.[106] It is a problem congenital to and characteristic of deism (though Locke is no deist) in its approach to God through demonstrations rather than experience—a circle which Herbert (equally in this respect no deist) never falls into; his 'evidence' of the existence of God is not rational demonstration but mankind's shared experiential evidence of the inward workings of Natural Instinct. Nevertheless Locke, like Herbert, is asserting that if men 'reason rightly' (*mutatis mutandis*) they will ultimately arrive at those truths which support their very being. Thus Locke, through what can only be called the dogmatism of faith, avoids the bottomless pit of scepticism and avoids too, as in the case of his attack on innate ideas, the pitfalls of that sort of subjectivism which he sees practised by the clergy. When he added to his remark on the existence of God the significant rider that

> though this be the most obvious truth that reason discovers, and though its evidence be (if I mistake not) equal to mathematical certainty; yet it requires thought and attention; and the mind must apply itself to a regular deduction of it from some part of our intuitive knowledge, or else we shall be

as uncertain and ignorant of this as of other propositions which are in themselves capable of clear demonstration.[107]

it may be true that he 'thus disposed at a single stroke of the belief in innate ideas'; but, as Locke himself calmly said, 'this shakes not at all, or in the least concerns the assurance of faith; that is quite distinct from it, neither stands nor falls with knowledge'.[108]

The essential difference distinguishing faith from reason would seem to lie in the means by which a man acquires the information. Locke's attack on enthusiasm in religion would appear to include Lord Herbert, as one of those who 'have often flattered themselves of an immediate intercourse with the Deity, and frequent communications from the Divine Spirit'.[109] To rely solely on such sources of information is a way 'of illumination without search, of certainty without proof, and without examination'[110], but is to be noted that Locke is incapable of denying that it *is* illumination and certainty, just as his highest form of intuitive knowledge fills, without search or examination, the mind with its 'clear light'. Locke has, in the previous section of the *Essay*, just defined reason as 'the discovery of the certainty or probability of such propositions' as the mind receives 'by the use of its natural faculties; viz., by sensation and reflection'[111], and this means of acquiring knowledge he calls 'natural revelation', which is God's communication to us of as much truth as lies within the compass of our natural faculties. In contrast, faith is 'the assent to any proposition not thus made out by the deductions of reason, but upon the credit of the proposer, as coming from God, in some extraordinary way of communication. This way of discovering truths to men we call revelation'; or, 'natural reason enlarged by a new set of discoveries communicated by God immediately, which reason vouches the truth of, by the testimony and proofs it gives that they come from God'.[112] The similarity of this to Herbert's condition that reason should confirm the validity but not the truth of revelation, and his clear statement that through faith 'some new aspect of God is revealed' and 'we pass beyond the normal levels of experience', is evident. What is also evident is that Locke has, as a recent commentator points out, 'introduced, at the very end of the *Essay*, a new 'way of discovering truths' not formally considered within the boundaries of his epistemological discussion. Revelation stands outside the ordinary compass of human experience, and faith is explicitly associated with revelation.[113]

The dilemma in which this put Locke is conveyed, with some

poignancy, in Locke's correspondence with Stillingfleet. Locke tried to quieten ecclesiastical displeasure by insisting often that there was nothing in the *Essay* that could undermine the principles of Christianity. Since Locke is saying that there is no kind of knowledge that will ever disturb one's faith, the assertion is hardly surprising. The question Stillingfleet put to Locke is, however, a pertinent one: how, he asked, can Locke claim 'certainty' for the articles of faith he defends and yet not include them within his category of 'knowledge'?[114] There may be a resemblance between this question and asking Lord Herbert how he can undermine the validity of revelation and yet claim divine revelation. Despite important intellectual differences in their positions, Locke lays himself open to that same charge of confusion which Herbert had encountered, and it would seem for a similar reason. Both attack 'authority' as they see it manifested about them and both, with an eye to conduct rather than to creed, seek to establish the faith by which men of the seventeenth century lived upon a 'surer' foundation. And in this important sense Herbert's relation to revolutionary deism is as tenuous, and as embarrassed, as Locke's.

Notes to Chapter V

1 Charles de Rémusat, *Lord Herbert de Cherbury, sa vie et ses oeuvres, ou les origines de la philosophie du sens commun et e la théologie naturelle en Angleterre*, Paris, 1874, p. 181.
2 Rossi, I, p. 299.
3 Thomas Halyburton, *Natural Religion Insufficient: and Revealed Necessary*, Edinburgh, 1714, chap. XIII, p. 220.
4 See G. Gawlick's introduction to the reprint of *De veritate*, Stuttgart–Bad Cannstatt, 1966, pp. xxxiii–xxxiv, xlvi.
5 Rossi, I, pp. 423f.; III, pp. 414, 427f.
6 For the translation of the *Discours*, see Rossi, I, p. 477; II, p. 537; for the English version of Hobbes, Rossi, II, p. 538; and the aesthetic theory, III, pp. 442f.
7 See Fordyce and Knox. The letter and the books are at Powis Castle.
8 See Don A. Keister, 'Donne and Herbert: an exchange of verses', *Modern Language Quarterly*, 8, 1947, pp. 430–4.
9 Grierson, I, p. 336.
10 See Fordyce and Knox. The letter from Donne is now in the Bodleian, and is printed in Gosse's *Life and Letters of John Donne*, London, 1889, II, p. 125. The MS is neither in Jesus College Library, Oxford nor at Powis Castle.

11 Rossi, II, pp. 521f.; Gawlick, *loc. cit.* pp. xxif.
12 See *Correspondence de Mersenne*, VII, p. 436; *DNB*, 'Sir Henry Herbert'.
13 See Rossi, II, p. 497, and *Der Index der verbotenen Bücher*, ed. Joseph Hilgers S. J., Frieburg im Breisgau, 1914, p. 422, between whom there is some small discrepancy as to the exact date.
14 See Rossi, II, pp. 529–35.
15 *Correspondance de Mersenne*, VIII, pp. 476–7.
16 See Rossi, II, p. 490; pp. 498–9.
17 *Correspondance de Mersenne*, VIII, pp. 575–7.
18 *Correspondance*, VIII, pp. 576–7.
19 *Correspondance*, X, p. 264.
20 See Fordyce and Knox; Rossi, II, p. 528.
21 Rossi, I, p. 488; II, p. 528, p. 535. On Hartlib and Comenius, see C. Webster, *Samuel Hartlib and the Advancement of Learning*, Cambridge, 1970.
22 W. K. Jordan, *The Development of Religious Toleration in England*, 4 vols., London, 1932–40, II (1603–40), p. 443.
23 William Stephens, *An Account of the Growth of Deism in England*, London, 1696, p. 68.
24 Selden, *Table Talk*, published 1689, 'Religion', 15.
25 Bacon, *Essays*, 'Of Unity in Religion'.
26 *D.V.*, p. 137; Carré, p. 217; *D.V.*, p. 209; Carré, p. 290.
27 *D.V.*, p. 41; Carré, p. 119.
28 *D.V.*, p. 39; Carré, p. 117.
29 *Religio laici*, the unpublished first draft, MS 5295 E in the National Library of Wales Collection. Edited by Herbert G. Wright, in *Modern Language Review*, 28 (1933), pp. 295–307.
30 Quoted by A. R. Humphreys, *The Augustan World: Life and Letters in Eighteenth-Century England*, London, repr. 1964, p. 144.
31 *D.V.*, p. 136; Carré, pp. 216–17.
32 *D.V.*, p. 209; Carré, p. 290.
33 See Ferdinand Buisson, *Sébastien Castellion*, 2 vols., Paris, 1892, II, p. 494.
34 Glanvill, *Plus Ultra*, London, 1668, p. 139.
35 Locke, *Reflections upon the Roman Commonwealth*; see H. R. Fox Bourne, *Life of John Locke*, 2 vols., London, 1876, I, p. 149.
36 William Law, *Address to the Clergy*, 1764, p. 58.
37 A. G. Dickens, *The English Reformation*, Fontana Books, 1967, p. 436.
38 S.P. (presumably Simon Patrick), *A Brief Account of the New Sect of Latitude Men*, London, 1662, p. 11.
39 Hooker, *Ecclesiastical Polity*, bk. I, 1593, VIII, 3.
40 Montaigne, *Apologie*, *Essayes*, Everyman ed., vol. II, p. 296.
41 Meric Casaubon, *A Treatise of Use and Custome*, London, 1638, p. 20.
42 Casaubon, *ibid.*, p. 108.
43 Leonard Nathanson, *The Strategy of Truth: A Study of Sir Thomas Browne*, Chicago, Ill., 1967, p. 115.
44 *D.V.*, p. 7; Carré, p. 82.
45 *Religio laici*, see Rossi, III, p. 540. H. R. Hutcheson's edition and translation of the work, New Haven, Conn., 1944, entitles it *De religione laici*; Rossi calls it *Religio laici*. Rossi's title recognises that *De religione laici* is a

form imposed by the syntax of the joint title page (*Cui operi additi sunt duo alii tractatus: primus de causis errorum*; *alter de religione laici*) and that the title which appears on p. 127 and as the running title thereafter is *Religio laici*. It is in any case a neater form and matches titles such as Browne's *Religio medici* (1642), Sir George Mackenzie's *Religio stoici* (1665), the anonymous *Religio clerici* (1681) and of course Dryden's poem *Religio laici, Or a Layman's Faith* (1682).

46 Hutcheson, pp. 89–91.

47 Hutcheson, p. 119.

48 On the question of the progress of doctrinal Calvinism and of Calvin's influence in England, see Basil Hall, 'Calvin against the Calvinists', *Proceedings of the Huguenot Society of London*, 20 (1960–1), No. 3, pp. 284–301.

49 Hutcheson, pp. 119–21.

50 John Smith, *Select Discourses*, ed. Worthington, London, 1660.

51 Whichcote, *Moral and Religious Aphorisms*, ed. Samuel Salter, London, 1753, No. 315.

52 Hutcheson, p. 123. Cf. the long speech on religion that Herbert puts into the mouth of Sir William Fitz-Williams, in *The Life and Raigne of Henry VIII*, London, 1649, pp. 293f.

53 Browne, *Religio medici*, I, 56.

54 This motto appears in the portrait of Herbert riding the jennet presented to him by the Duke of Montmorency; Herbert says, 'This Motto by me'. The translation is Edmund Blunden's, *Votive Tablets*, London, 1931.

55 Perkins, *The Workes*, 3 vols., 1612–13, II, p. 287.

56 Preston, *Sermons*, London, 1630, pp. 19–20.

57 Selden, *Table Talk*, 'Bible'.

58 *D.V.*, pp. 208–26; Carré, pp. 289–307.

59 Donne, *Works*, ed. H. Alford, 6 vols., IV, p. 437.

60 Montaigne, *Apologie*, p. 277.

61 *Ecclesiastical Polity*, bk. III, viii, 13. My italics.

62 *D.V.*, p. 124; Carré, p. 204.

63 *D.V.*, p. 208; Carré, p. 289.

64 See e.g. Cartwright, *A Reply to an Answer to M. Doctor Whitgift*, 1573, p. 157; *Second Reply*, 1575, p. 50.

65 *D.V.*, pp. 6–7; Carré, p. 81.

66 Edmund Hickeringill, *The Ceremony Monger*, Edinburgh, 1689, p. 44.

67 *Hugo Grotius Against Paganism, Judaism, Mahumetanism*, London, 1676, p. 11.

68 Hugo Grotius, *The Truth of the Christian Religion, in six books*, trans. John Clarke, from Jean Le Clerc's 1717 Amsterdam edition, 9th ed., London, 1786. The work was originally published in Paris, 1624.

69 *D.V.*, p. 226; Carré, p. 308.

70 Glanvill, λογον ΘΡΗΣΚΕΙΑ, *or, a Seasonable Recommendation and Defence of Reason, in the Affairs of Religion; against Infidelity, Scepticism and Fanaticism of all sorts*, London, 1670, pp. 11–12; reprinted as essay V, 'The Agreement of Reason and Religion', in *Essays on Several Important Subjects in Philosophy and Religion*, London, 1676.

71 λογον, p. 29.

72 λογον, p. 1.
73 λογον, pp. 6–7.
74 Stephens, *An Account*, p. 20.
75 *D.V.*, p. 61; Carré, p. 141.
76 *D.V.*, p. 226; Carré, p. 308.
77 Sidney Lee, *The Autobiography of Edward, Lord Herbert of Cherbury*, London, 1886, pp. 248–9.
78 See *Herbert's Autobiography and History of England under Henry VIII*, World Library of Standard Books, London, 1880, p. 104.
79 Margaret Bottrall, *Every Man a Phoenix: Studies in Seventeenth-century Autobiography*, London, 1958, p. 65.
80 W. K. Jordan, *The Development of Religious Toleration in England*, II, p. 440, n.
81 W. K. Jordan, *ibid.*, p. 438.
82 *D.V.*, p. 229; Carré, p. 311.
83 Hooker, *Ecclesiastical Polity*, III,viii,6.
84 Bacon, *De augmentis*, IX,i.
85 Herschel Baker, *The Wars of Truth*, London, 1952, p. 91.
86 Donne, *Six & Twenty Sermons*, London, 1660, p. 91; p. 194.
87 Drummond quotes a conversation with Jonson: 'Done said to him, he wrott that Epitaph on Prince Henry ... to match Sir Ed: Herbert in obscurenesse' (*Jonson: Conversations with William Drummond of Hawthornden*, 1619, ed. G. B. Harrison, Bodley Head Quartos V, London, 1923, p. 7.
88 Browne, *Religio medici*, I,ix. Tertullian's paradox is: *mortuus est dei filius; prorsus credibile est, quia ineptum. Et sepultus resurrexit; certum est, quia impossibile est* (*De carne Christi, V*).
89 Quoted in John Tulloch, *Rational Theology and Christian Philosophy in England in the Seventeenth Century*, London, 1872, II, p. 41.
90 Jeremy Taylor, *Ductor dubitantium*, London, 1660, I,i,2; I,ii,1.
91 Gilbert Burnet, *Essay*, in *The Beginnings and Advances of a Spiritual Life*, in Scougal's *Life of God in the Soul of Man*, London, 1733.
92 Glanvill, *Essays on Several Important Subjects*, 1676, essay V, pp. 3–4.
93 John Toland, *Christianity not Mysterious: Or, A Treatise Shewing, That there is nothing in the Gospel Contrary to Reason, Nor Above it; And that no Christian Doctrine can be properly call'd A Mystery*, London, 1696, pp. 12–13; p. 24.
94 Locke, *Essay*, IV, 18, 10; IV, 17, 5 (my italics).
95 Henry G. Van Leeuwen, *The Problem of Certainty in English Thought, 1630–1690*, The Hague, 1963, p. 121.
96 Basil Willey, *The Seventeenth-century Background*, London, 1934, p. 268.
97 Locke, *Essay* I, i, 1–2; IV, 20, 8.
98 *Essay*, I, 2, 14.
99 *Essay*, I, 2, 26.
100 *Essay*, IV, 2, 1.
101 See John W. Yolton, *John Locke and the Way of Ideas*, Oxford, 1956, p. 62.
102 Hutcheson, Introduction, p. 42.
103 Locke, *Essay*, II, 2, 3; II, 9, 12; III, 5, 8.
104 *Essay*, I, 3, 9, 12, 23; II, 14, 31, 15, 3–4, etc.
105 *Essay*, I, 3, 17.

106 See Richard Ashcraft's illuminating article, 'Faith and knowledge in Locke's philosophy', in *John Locke: Problems and Perspectives, A collection of new essays*, ed. John W. Yolton, Cambridge, 1969, pp. 194–223.

107 Locke, *Essay*, IV, 10, 1.

108 *Mr Locke's Reply to the Bishop of Worcester's Answer to his Letter*, in *Works of John Locke*, 12th ed., 9 vols., London, 1824, III, pp. 146–7.

109 Locke, *Essay*, IV, 19, 5.

110 *Essay*, IV, 19, 8.

111 *Essay*, IV, 18, 2.

112 *Essay*, IV, 18, 2; IV, 19, 4.

113 Richard Ashcraft, 'Faith and knowledge in Locke's philosophy', *loc. cit.*

114 See *A Letter to the Right Reverend Edward, Lord Bishop of Worcester*, in *Works of John Locke*, *loc. cit.*, III, p. 30.

VI
HERBERT AND CHRISTIANITY

What's *Vice?* – Mere want of compass in our thought.
Religion what? – The proof of *Common-Sense*.
                                    Edward Young, *Night Thoughts*, IX

Paradox and history

The difficult and vexed question of Herbert of Cherbury's religious
responses, and particularly his relation to Christianity, is one that
presents teasing problems for the interpreter. What may be seen in
retrospect as Herbert's 'advanced rationalism' (without necessarily
invoking the term 'deism') was contained within a sense of worship
and conditioned by a vigorous religious, if not ecclesiastical, instinct.
John Aubrey records that Herbert had prayers said twice daily in his
house: events which, through their apparently paradoxical
occurrence, have led some to conclude not that there may be a
testimony to that 'pietie to God' for which his friend Ben Jonson
commended him[1], but that Herbert must have been some sort of
Machiavellist or Politique. Aubrey also records for us the story of
Herbert's deathbed, at which Herbert managed a final anticlerical
altercation with Archbishop Ussher; their mutual convictions being
embarrassing, the last sacrament was declined.[2] This combination
of prayers and the refusal of the sacrament has been taken as
evidence of 'the contradictions of Herbert's nature and behaviour',
just as the celebrated account of the sign from heaven has been
usually taken as an indication of his outrageous inconsistency
and—not to put too fine a point on it—his duplicity.[3]

However deficient Herbert may have been in his understanding of
ecclesiasticism, his openness to religious experience is difficult to
deny. In *De veritate* he makes the following unequivocal statement
which bears directly on his own sign from heaven: 'When in a
moment of intense faith we make a special appeal to God, and feel
within us His saving power and a sense of marvellous deliverance, I

do not doubt that the mind is touched by Grace, or particular Providence, and that since some new aspect of God is revealed, we pass beyond the normal level of experience.'[4] For all his rationalism Herbert is available to experience 'beyond the normal'; and the question is, how far, and in what directions, he is prepared to go. From one point of view his general attitude may resemble an extension of the ancient doctrine, supported by several texts in St Paul (e.g. Colossians II, 16–20; I Timothy IV, 1–5; Galatians II, 3–5; V, 13–15) and by Augustine's letter to Januarius, of the distinction between necessary and unchangeable things and *adiaphora*, things indifferent. In response to what they considered the arrogant dogmatism of the schoolmen, both Luther and Melanchthon had argued and developed this distinction. Herbert's strategy is in part to so reduce the number of necessary and unchangeable things requisite for true religion that a whole variety of possible and mutually co-existent ceremonies and creeds may be supported by the 'Catholick and Infallible' grounds he seeks to assert. Under the sixteenth-century conditions imposed on liberal Lutherans and Protestants the notion of *adiaphora* stood little chance of opening a path towards reunion. The early English Protestant George Firth who was martyred in 1533, partly at Thomas More's instigation, did not die for heretical articles on purgatory and transubstantiation but for his firm insistence on the principle that a particular doctrine on either of these points was not a part of a Christian man's faith 'necessary to be believed under pain of damnation'.[5]

In the later seventeenth century however the challenges presented by the concept to the charity and learning of Christians, and the growing awareness of its broader implications, stood a marginally better chance of success. Herbert certainly makes it clear that in his view the quality of a man's religious faith does not depend on how many dogmatic propositions he can swallow, nor on his ability to prostrate himself before the Trinity, the Bishop of Rome, or the Thirty-nine Articles, or before the imaginative and intellectual theologies of an Aquinas or a Calvin. 'Let us', he says in *De veritate*, 'trust Providence above any tradition.' Herbert is prepared to let his adiaphorism go very far indeed, and his motive appears to be that of a reunionist. How much, is the challenge he issues, can finally and without illusion be allowed to be hypothetical, tentative and imperfect? In posing such a challenge he may well appear to reach the point at which Christianity itself, in whatever form, becomes, in the face of the historically and anthropologically verifiable consensus of man's basic religious instinct, yet another *adiaphora*, a thing ultimately indifferent. I do not myself think that Herbert had consciously reached that point. He would undoubtedly have denied any such intention. Nevertheless, what is missing from Herbert's account of revelation in *De veritate*—and it is of course a glaring omission—is any consideration of specifically Christian revelation, for instance the cardinal Christian doctrine of the Incarnation. This gap in his discussion may account in large measure for the posthumous and intermittent reputation of 'the learned Lord Herbert' not merely as a deist but as an atheist. Certainly Richard Baxter thought there was something rather odd about it all.[6] The reasons for Herbert's omissions are perhaps not far to seek. Paradox is hardly tractable in a system based, like Herbert's, on clear, self-evident truths accessible to rational inquiry, nor does Herbert seem likely to admit that our intuitive knowledge may be paradoxical. 'Immensity cloystered in thy deare wombe' is not universally accepted, and does not easily lend itself to proof as a Common Notion. Nor need paradox conform to the principle of non-contradiction, since it may be affirmed and contradicted at the same time without doing violence to its central truth. Herbert, unlike for instance Montaigne, is not especially sensitive to blurred edges and indistinctions. At the same time, it is no doubt possible to argue that Herbert holds the Christian revelations as given and proceeds from there, deliberately ignoring particular issues and emphasising instead his vision of social rather than individual salvation. His abiding concern for personal freedom and his frequent stress on individual responsibility ('the supreme Judge requires every individual to render an account of his actions in the light, not of another's belief, but of his own')[7] results, as a kind of inverse proportion, in a corresponding lack of concern with personal and particular salvation. If, within the generous provision of Divine Providence a man can find God and Eternal Blessedness through self-determination, integrity and an implicit reliance on those Common Notions implanted in him by Natural Instinct, what need is there of all the Protestant machinery of personal conviction of sin, a personal experience of grace, a personal Saviour?

This stress on the clarity and simplicity of religious conviction is later reflected in Benjamin Whichcote's belief in the 'intelligible, rational, accountable' nature of religious experience and religious dogma.[8] Firmly assenting to the essentials of Christian doctrine but unable to allow *credo quia impossible* as a genuine religious attitude, the Cambridge Platonists (Whichcote, Henry More, Ralph Cudworth, John Smith, George Rust) concentrate their efforts, as Herbert had done, on the reinterpretation of the mysteries of faith in terms of a rational idealism which renders down paradox and obscurity to what is clear and distinct. Taking a point of view which extends beyond the confines of the Christian dispensation, Whichcote affirms that 'Religion has different Denominations and Names, from different Actions and Circumstances; but it is One thing, *viz*. Universal Righteousness: accordingly it had place, at all times; before the Law of *Moses*, under it, and since'.[9] On the question of the degree of acceptance of religious truths Whichcote warns that 'The longest Sword, the strongest Lungs, the most Voices, are false measures of Truth',[10] and one may be easily deceived into thinking this sort of remark 'a significant exception . . . to any attempt to seek truth in universally held common ideas . . . It neatly undercuts, for instance, the thesis of Lord Herbert of Cherbury in *De veritate*.'[11] Of course, it does nothing of the kind, for Herbert had said as much himself.[12] The puzzle is resolved in the preceding Aphorism in which Whichcote points out the disease to which Herbert had sought to minister: 'The more False any one is in his Religion, the more Fierce and furious in Maintaining it; the more Mistaken, the more Imposing: the more any man's religion is *his own*, the more he is concerned for it; but cool and indifferent enough for that which is God's'.[13] 'That which is God's' Whichcote defines as 'a Bond of Union': 'Men cannot differ, by true Religion; because it is true Religion to agree'.[14] One of the outcomes, especially significant with regard to the idealist's response to historical revelations, is that abstract and universal spiritual truths (or 'common religious notions') emerge as prior to and more fundamentally important than the particular historical events on which Christianity rests, so that those particular mysteries of faith come to be regarded as peripheral to spiritual truth and not of its essence—certainly not the first issues to be volunteered in debate.

The attitude of the 'natural theologian' towards Christ is characteristically ambiguous. A good example is Francisco Vicomercato, professor at the Collège de France from 1542 to 1567, a liberal laic in whose works of 'natural theology' (his *De principiis rerum naturalium,* Marburg, 1598, was in Herbert's library) the name of Christ appears only once. Herbert's own record is little better. The omission in his case however appears to be a consequence of a view of religious experience similar to that of the Cambridge Platonists. It is a curious thing that the name of Christ is mentioned very infrequently in their manifestly Christian persuasions, and that the doctrinal importance of the Incarnation and the Crucifixion is almost ignored, or at least minimised. The whole drift of their teachings was directed, in subtle ways, against the dominant theology of Calvinism, to which they advanced a questioning, critical attack that was all the more effective for ignoring the polity of Calvinism. The sacrifice for sin and the paradoxes of the Calvinist Atonement give way to a conception of salvation whose emphasis is upon purity and 'the way to holiness' in this life: Whichcote finds all necessary divinity contained in one sentence from the Epistle to Titus, II, 11–12: 'For the grace of God that bringeth salvation hath appeared to all men, teaching us that, denying ungodliness and worldly lusts, we should live soberly, righteously and godly, in this present world'. They alter, as Bunyan properly complained in his *Defence of the Doctrine of Justification* (1672), by placing a different emphasis on the idea of salvation, the traditional conception of justification by faith—and together with it the associated doctrine of predestination. The 'philosophical' basis for this approach lies in their Platonic structure of thought in which Herbert equally shares. The Christian God as Creator is easily reinterpreted in terms of the Platonic One which eternally sustains and governs the creation, but God as Redeemer may not fit so well. The doctrine of the Fall leaves Herbert's withers quite unwrung. Unlike that great Christian Platonist Sir Thomas Browne, Herbert is unable to subscribe to a literal need for redemption through a special act of grace, and this same unwillingness is evident also in the Cambridge Platonists. Their vision, like Herbert's, of a perpetual emanation of creative love from the One into the soul, a constantly operative force leading man to the divine, carried with it a tendency to dismiss too much doctrinal and intermediate machinery—a position which would seem to be the outcome in English thought of the efforts of the Florentine Neoplatonists to establish an harmonious relation and, at points, identity between fundamental Christian doctrines and the concepts of Platonism.

The religion of the stars

In a recent discussion of Herbert's religious allegiances D. P. Walker, in his book *The Ancient Theology*, has proposed a novel and interesting theory: that in Herbert's final work *De religione gentilium*, written in his last years, printed in Amsterdam in 1663 and unpublished in England until 1705, 'the ancient religion of the stars has conquered Christianity'.[15] Walker argues that Herbert's religion is in fact 'the good ancient astral religion', the religion of Hermes and the Orphic hymns, the gnostic, astrological, animistic, pantheistically inclined religion, full of sun- and star-worship, of the Platonic–Hermetic tradition. 'In at least two cases, Bruno and Campanella, we know that the ancient religion swallowed the Christianity.' Although Herbert was not a Magus, and he was without the vigorous enthusiasm and optimism of Bruno and Campanella (the *De religione gentilium* was written by a tired old man during a civil war), 'to these two cases we can add Herbert', who 'in a tentative and somewhat dessicated form' was promulgating the same religion as the two Magi and with the same eirenic intentions.[16]

That Herbert's particular aberration here should have passed undetected by his contemporaries (which could hardly be said of Bruno, burned at the stake on the Campo di Fiori in the first year of the new century, or of Campanella, familiar with the prisons of the Inquisition during a total of twenty-seven years of jail and torture and who apparently only escaped the same fate as Bruno by 'having had the presence of mind to simulate madness'—he died in 1639)[17] is to be explained, Walker suggests, by the fact that Herbert's true inclinations are not apparent in the work published in his lifetime. After 1670 Herbert could be, and was, read as a forerunner of Spinoza (Christian Kortholt's *De tribus Impostoribus magnis* of 1680, for instance, assembles Hobbes, Spinoza and Herbert as the great 'imposters' of the age), which may account for the less acceptable reputation which befell Herbert later in the century. But more important, in Walker's argument, is the fact that *De religione gentilium* was not loosed upon the public until 1663, and that in it the true nature of Herbert's religious idiosyncrasies comes fully into the light. The case is subtly argued, and the emphasis upon Herbert's Hermetic–Platonic tendencies and upon his eirenic and reunionist intentions is of crucial importance. That *De religione gentilium* is in fact such a manifesto as is claimed is more doubtful; there is for example no evidence for the subsequent recognition of the true drift of Herbert's thought from the presumably imperceptive readers of the later seventeenth century, who in fact appear to have seen in it no such advocacy of 'the good old astral religion'.

It was an inevitable and logical part of Herbert's case that he should attempt to present a factual, empirical support to his claim of the existence of 'common religious notions', and this task—an exercise in comparative religion and religious anthropology—he undertook in *De religione gentilium, errorumque apud eos causis*, to which the 1705 English translation by William Lewis adds 'The Mistakes and Failures of *Heathen Priests* and *Wise-Men*, in their Notions of the *Deity*, and Matters of *Divine Worship*, are Examin'd; With regard to their being altogether destitute of Divine Revelation'. Following this description of the work's apparent and understood intentions, the prospective reader is advised that

The following Pages, containing a Celebrated Piece of this most deservedly Renown'd Person, and having gain'd such Universal Approbation amongst the Learned; having been printed twice at *Amsterdam*, and yet is so very scarce here, that it is seldom met with, and rarely known, but only by the Curious Enquirers into and Diligent Searchers after Polite Learning . . .

are a product of a 'Master of Profound Penetration, the complete Soldier and Statesman'.[18] This certainly seems to be having it both ways: the work is both 'celebrated' and 'rarely known'; but the other option, that it is notorious, dangerous and hostile to Christianity, is nowhere offered to the curious Augustan reader.

Herbert had compiled the work *ex Vossii sententia*, that is, with the help of Gerard Vossius's *De theologia gentili et physiologia Christiana, sive de origine ac progressu idololatria* (Amsterdam, 1641), supported by Selden's *De dis Syris* (London, 1617) which was itself a source for Vossius, and informed on many points no doubt by dipping into Mersenne's *Quaestiones celeberrimae in Genesim* (1623), of which Herbert himself owned a copy.[19] Herbert intended to publish *De religione gentilium*, and entrusted the task to Vossius, who died a year after Herbert before it could be printed; it was left to Vossius's son Isaac to see it through the press eventually, some twenty years after its composition. Selden's work as an orientalist and expositor of rabbinical law left him with neither time nor inclination for religious apologetics. Vossius's intention in his *De idololatria* was much like that described in the long title of Lewis's edition of *De religione gentilium*, to review the inadequacies of the Gentile's search for God without revelation, though in practice he rambles and digresses through an historical comparison of religions. Mersenne's work, ostensibly an attack on Renaissance occultism, astrology and animism, reproduced for criticism, at great length, so much Cabalistic, Hermetic and Neoplatonic material, expounding for anyone who could not get hold of the originals a whole range of esoteric opinion including Cabalistic treatises, Ficinean astral magic and animistic cosmologies, that it provided an unrivalled source for such materials.[20] Herbert may well have learned a great deal from Mersenne's encyclopaedia, and may well too have read Mersenne's attack on Bruno in *L'Impiété des Déistes* (1624) while he was in Paris that year. 'Deists' for Mersenne are magicians and atheists—of whom Bruno, with his universal animism, his world soul, and his Hermetic–Ficinean magic, was the most dangerous, since the most religiously zealous and proselytising, representative. Bruno's universal reform aimed at returning European religion to a supposedly pre-Christian Hermetic Egyptianism, which Bruno himself in his buoyant fashion would not have regarded as anti-Christian but as acceptable within the religious framework and eventually subsuming specific Christianity. It is in his company, it is argued, that Herbert belongs. What then does Herbert reveal in *De religione gentilium*? Does it in fact provide us with a vision of the kind of religion in which Herbert would have wished to see the world united? Walker suggests that 'it does give an answer which . . . is fairly clear, though it has not been seen by other scholars': that it is 'the good old astral religion'.

A more 'orthodox' view of the object of *De religione gentilium* assumes that for 'some immovable foundations of truth resting on common consent' which will end dispute, the limits of Christian orthodoxy (itself in dispute) must be exceeded and the investigation must examine, as Herbert claims to have done, all the chief religions of the world, even the primitive belief of the heathens. Herbert's conclusion is that the five common religious notions are found in them everywhere and at all times. He attempts to get not only behind Christianity but behind the formal, organised and priestly administration of 'any Religion whatsoever'. In a classic passage he describes how he came to discover, or rather to confirm, the five articles:

When I considered, that any Religion whatsoever, when it had obtain'd in all *Ages* and *Countries*, was only promulgated, to lay a more strict obligation on Men, to do that which they were oblig'd before to do voluntarily, and that *Universal Peace* and *Concord* might be maintain'd amongst them: I began strangely to admire, that the *Priests*, for the most Part, professing the same Religion, did Animate and Excite the People to Dissentions and bitter Animosities, and make them act things quite contrary to their known and express *Duty*. This put me on the enquiry, whether there were not some Destructive and Pernicious, as well as Vain and Frivolous Opinions, mixt with Matters of Religion.

His conclusion—that all institutional religions are not only relatively true but also only relatively false—leads him to the Common Notions: 'I found those five Articles I have so often mention'd, and thought myself far more happy than Archimedes'.[21] It has often been thought that Dryden, in his *Religio laici* (1682), mimicked this proud claim in his lines

> The Deist thinks he stands on firmer ground;
> Cries *eureka*, the mighty secret's found.[22]

William Empson, though aware that 'Archimedes was tiresomely familiar in this role' and that Dryden was not necessarily thinking of Herbert in particular, takes Dryden's witty point, grumbling that 'the system of Deism claims to point out the universal sentiments of mankind, and when Herbert regards it as a clever invention he betrays its basic absurdity'.[23] To regard it as an 'invention' would indeed be absurd; to regard it as a recognition of what, amid all the distractions and red herrings, was under one's nose all the time perhaps less so. By means of dispassionate examination, Herbert seeks to argue, it is possible to isolate those elements of reason and of intuition which are the signatures of the great truths of all religious professions. No religion is entirely devoid of truth. If the barnacles and limpets planted by self-interested priesthood can be scraped away we shall uncover the rock of universal Natural Instinct beneath even the barbarisms of primitive religion, and this is because such truths pervade the universe and are imprinted by the hand of God upon the soul of every normal man: 'a rose', Herbert had written in *De veritate*, 'produces the same effect now as it did of old at Pergamum'. These truths may be summarised in the five articles: that there is a *Supreme Power*; that this *Supreme Power* must be worshipped; 'that the good ordering or disposition of the faculties of men constitute the principal or best part of divine worship'; 'that all vices and crimes should be expiated and effaced by repentance'; and finally 'that there are rewards and punishments after this life'.[24] Such a polemical aim as Herbert has in mind—the demonstration not of the inadequacies and corruptions of heathen religion (the avowed purpose of Vossius and of much Christian propaganda), but of the similarities between all religions—may well make his work look like a defence of pagan religion; even, as Walker concludes, an admiration and acceptance of it.

It becomes clear, from the very first chapter of *De religione gentilium*, that what Herbert has on his mind are the same problems that obsessed him in both *De veritate* and his *Religio laici* (1645): the institutional claim of possession of Truth and the dilemma of the contemporary layman whose eternal salvation is said to depend on acquiescence in its directions. He begins by worrying about the salvation of the pagans and their implied exclusion from all grace. To Donne's question

> shall thy fathers spirit
> Meet blinde Philosophers in heaven, whose merit
> Of strict life may be imputed faith, and heare
> Thee, whom he taught so easie wayes and neare
> To follow, damn'd?
>
> *(Satyre III)*

Herbert's answer is, unquestionably thy father's spirit will. Those who believed in and worshipped God, who confessed their crimes, and lived in the expectation of an after-life—why should they not share in 'the enormous mercy of God' (*pro ingenti Dei misericordia*)?[25] Herbert points out that we are, of course, doing the same thing to each other, within the Christian religion: 'The Divines of this last Age also pronounce as severe a Sentence against all those that are without their Pale; so that, according to their Opinion, the far greater part of Mankind must be inevitably sentenced to Eternal Punishment',[26] and he quotes a modern Calvinistic view of 'determin'd Perdition':

Now when I perceived that they resolved the Causes of Eternal Salvation and Damnation only to the Good Pleasure of God, and the death of Christ; I found that their Opinion was grounded not on Reason, but some preremptory Decrees, which nobody did pretend to know, as I could not think they were so privy to the secret Counsels of God, as to be able to establish any thing for certain.[27]

Consistent with this anti-Calvinist, Erasmian insistence on 'the immense mercy of God', Herbert's treatment of pagan religion shows an appreciation of the good religious instinct which lay behind and which preceded the 'Priests and Rabbis' with their revelations and traditions. He describes the process by which man may first have reached the first of the common notions of religion. The pagan would look to the heavens and wonder at the order of the stars and planets, at first making Gods of them. But

Religion being progressive, they began to enquire, *Whether there was any* GOD *or Deity that presided over the* Stars *themselves?* which Opinion soon obtained . . . they soon acknowledged one *Supreme* GOD, who governed all things; to whom they thought the most profound Worship and Adoration was due: Yet still they retain'd a particular Veneration for the Stars; because by their Immortal Nature, they were first led to the knowledge of the *Supreme* God.[28]

Having, through 'natural revelation' arrived at the common notions of religion, mankind lost the vision and was reduced to 'Plurality of Gods' which 'occasion'd Variety of Worship; as the natural Consequence of their Diversity; which the crafty Priests managed to their own Advantage'. These two practical themes dominate *De religione gentilium* and define its intentions: the question of salvation, and the obscurities intruded upon the religious perception by formal, competitive ecclesiastical organisation. Though the work ranges far and wide, historically and geographically, its steps never in reality stray very far from the issues of the mid seventeenth century.

It would be very surprising if, in a survey of the ancient religion of the Gentiles, Herbert did not devote the greater part of his exposition to the pagan cults of star and sunworship. Nor would it be surprising in the man to find him very sympathetic to such worship, since it would be both illogical and a disservice to his argument to claim that the expression of fundamental religious instincts in mankind was utterly perverse and erroneous. That it was perverse and erroneous in many directions Herbert freely admits and is not slow to point out. In chapter IV, 'Of the Worship of the Sun', he says that 'Those who worshipp'd the *Sun* instead of the *Supreme God* himself, did like those, who, when they come to the Court of some great Monarch, take the first person they see in a rich Habit for the King, and pay him that Respect that is due only to Majesty itself'.[29] While this may seem plain enough, it should of course be noted that it does not imply that no reverence is due to the sun. He is speaking of the 'progressive' nature of religious experience, and this is one important stage. Later, in his discussion 'Of the Supreme God' (chapter XIII), he puts the following case:

But if an *Heathen* should say, that he cannot conceive himself under such infinite obligations to any obscure or unknown Deity, that he should slight and reject those *Auspicious* and *Eternal Deities* the *Heaven* and *Stars*; and if there is any such GOD, his *Goodness* will not suffer him to count it criminal in Man to return grateful Acknowledgements to those *Superior Powers*, who are so great Benefactors to him, and pay them such Veneration as seem'd justly due to such *good* and *excellent* Causes. Nor would this in the least obstruct the *Worship* and *Adoration* of a more transcendent and eminent *Deity*, whenever he would please to appear and manifest himself, and shower down more plenty of *Benefits* upon Mankind.

To this point of view the advocate of 'the good old astral religion' would be expected to reply: and why not? But what is Herbert's comment? It is, for those who find in Herbert the star-worshipper manqué, a disappointingly orthodox answer: 'They who argue thus, do like him that should attribute the whole praise of the *Melody* to the *Instrument*, and make large *Ecomiums* on it without any regard to the *Musician*, who tuned it and made it sound so harmoniously . . .'[30]

Throughout the work Herbert (borrowing Vossius's terminology but, as Walker points out, changing its signification) distinguishes between a *cultus proprius* and a *cultus symbolicus*. Vossius had argued that sun and star-worship in pagan religion was a *cultus proprius*, that is, they believed the objects they worshipped were properly and in themselves God, or Gods; the worship was never symbolic. Herbert, as he is bound to if the Common Notions are to receive any support, takes the opposite view and regards the pagan worship, at its truest and most profoundly religious, as a symbolic cult which worships the Creator through his creatures. Herbert's purpose in the work is rather different from Vossius's, nor is it to be confused with the apologetic use frequently made of the blindness of the ancients before Christian revelation. Herbert is pointing not to their blindness but to the extent of their illumination. It is not primarily an argument *per errores philosophorum* for Christianity; disagreements among pagan philosophers are not seized on as evidence of the fruitlessness of speculation without revelation; the focus is rather on the homogeneity of fundamental religious responses. Idolatry and 'proper cults' come about, Herbert suggests, through error and through the machinations of priestcraft. Walker finds Herbert's transformation of Vossius both sinister and significant. Certainly Herbert, rather disingenuously, makes it appear that Vossius and he agree ('I am of the Opinion with the Learn'd *Vossius* that . . . the Heathens, intended nothing but a *Symbolical* worship; which terminated in the *Supreme God* . . .'),[31] but he insists that in so far as pagan worship was a *cultus proprius* 'I would here completely reject the opinion of the Gentiles', and worship of the stars in their own right he regards as 'an enormous error'. Since Herbert accepted pagan star-worship as a symbolic cult, Walker suggests that 'the good ancient religion' must therefore have been Herbert's own religion, and invites us to 'legitimately infer that he does not reject star-worship'—which may be rather like saying that since my parish priest accepts the truth of the Old Testament I may legitimately infer that my parish priest is a Jew.

It is impossible to miss the appeal of the stars and their symbolic significance in Herbert's work: it is there in the rhapsodic sections of *De veritate* on the future life, and its images occur again and again in his poetry—

> This said, in her up-lifted face,
>   Her eyes which did that beauty crown,
>   Were like two Starrs, that having faln down,
> Look up again to find their place

—and Herbert's vision of the realm of Eternal Blessedness is invariably figured in a final destiny among the stars. It is, as Rossi suggests, 'a mythology used in singing of love, of immortality, or of the beauty of the world'.[32] Its 'mythological' appeal is equally apparent in *De religione gentilium*, and it is for Herbert natural that the evidences of the religious instincts to worship and the intimations of immortality should be found in the contemplations of the heavens. He does not however stop short at symbolic star-worship. The approval of it which he gives is worth examination, since it is primary evidence for the view that he shares in the brotherhood of Bruno and Campanella to the extent Walker claims.

In 'Of the Adoration of the Fixed STARS' (chapter VIII) Herbert writes:

And indeed nothing could be more natural and agreeable, than for a *Heathen*, when he had accurately contemplated the Nature of the *Stars*, to conclude that the *fixed Stars* were the Eternal Law and Book of *God*; and the Planets his Book of *Prophecy* . . . And why may not the same *God* have exhibited to us the reasons of things present and future, by the Planets, in regard all Sublunary Motion derives its Original from Theirs?[33]

Herbert concludes that 'The Stars therefore are the Universal Law and Prophets of *God*', which wise men observe and consult 'not according to the vain and ridiculous superstitious Forms and Maxims of common, ignorant and foolish Astrologers' but 'by the observation of Events, when their Motions, Conjunctions, Oppositions and various Aspects are compar'd together'.[34] This passage is cited by Walker, with little comment, as presumably the kind of thing one would expect to find in a tentative supporter of 'the ancient religion'. Yet what is important is Herbert's rejection of astrology and magic and his sober, scientific and unexceptionable insistence that the movements of heavenly bodies influence 'sublunary motion'. In fact, towards interpretations of the nature of this dependence Herbert advances a healthy specticism: 'But whether the Divine Laws, with respect to the Beginning and End of things, are written in the *Heaven* and *Stars*, or whether they have any influence over the means, by which Food and Raiment is provided; and contain the secret Decrees concerning Eternal Rewards and Punishments, to me is altogether a Mystery'.[35] 'It would seem more probable,' he muses, 'that the Exotic Motions of all things, should depend on the different Aspects and Motions of the *Planets*' (i.e. more probable than the fixed stars), 'if it were satisfactorily prov'd.' But since it cannot be so proved, planetary influence is no more than a probability, beyond the scrutiny of 'common Reason only'. His conclusion is that

the Philosophical Opinions of the *Heathens*, concerning some Eternal Laws that were written in *Heaven* and the fix'd *Stars*, as also in the *Planets* and *Elements*; carried so much Verisimilitude in them, that a more eminently agreeable Doctrine could hardly be found by the dictate of common Reason; tho' it was next to impossible, to explain, what those Laws were: Notwithstanding it was impious to pay a Proper worship to the Heaven, Stars, and Elements.[36]

What the best of the heathens were doing, Herbert tells us, was practising symbolic star-worship and venerating the souls of dead heroes who were for them the equivalent of our saints. Corruption occurred when the false revelations, superstitious rites, rivalry, power-seeking and self-aggrandisement of the priests led the common people into idolatry, 'weaving together with wonderful artifice, True things with Probable, Possible, and False things'.

Though Herbert nowhere in his writings attempts to expound specifically Christian doctrines as a supplement of his five articles (a reluctance which he shares incidentally with Descartes), he makes frequent reference to an at least nominal Christian allegiance which is not (without unduly begging the question) to be ignored. In his chapter on 'The Most Sound Parts of the Religion of the Heathens' (XV), where we might expect a panegyric of an unsullied Platonic–Hermetic astral religion, Herbert is cautious, mindful of human error and stupidity, and finally positive in his commendation of Christianity, towards which conclusion he builds with a cumulative rhetoric:

Tho' the *Heathens* may bring such Arguments, and many more, of their Virtue, Piety and Antiquity of their Hierarchy, and that it became very Eminent and Conspicuous; tho' they produce their *Sacred Books*, full of Prophecies, which proceeded from those who were Inspired with a Divine and Prophetick Spirit, by which they prove their Communion to have been very Antient and Common: and altho' they make it appear that they used the same Means (especially as much as the Rule of Right Reason could direct) as we now do, and by that Means endeavoured to obtain a Celestial Life. It will still be impossible for them to acquit themselves of the Suspicion of *Idolatry*, or even from the Practice of it; (for they gave great occasion to the People to fall into very gross Errors, who had not a right Notion of their *Symbolical* worship) and that their Histories were not Fabulous, their Rites ridiculous, and in short, that all Virtue and Piety was not Restored and Adorned by the Christian Church.[37]

In another context (for example, that of 'orthodox' Christian apologetics) such an argument might be judged weak and even irrelevant; in the context of Herbert's brief as enquirer into fundamental religious instincts rather than Christian propagandist it assigns to the Church the recovered expression of true virtue and piety which in paganism had become overgrown with decadent superstition. To object at this point that this is not the argument of orthodox Christianity need not commit us to the conclusion that Christianity in Herbert must therefore have been swallowed by sun and star-worship. Further, our conception of what might constitute Christian 'orthodoxy' may well be stretched by Herbert's procedure. One might, for example, go back to Origen's debate with the pagan Celsus (as Herbert had done) and note again the astonishing measure of agreement between them; or, in another direction, one might pause at the arguments of the nineteenth-century German theologian Ritschl and his school on, for instance, the Incarnation or on Christianity's relation to fundamental religious instincts, some of which closely resemble Herbert's own. Unless one is prepared categorically to deny Origen the status of any kind of orthodox

Christian (as of course has been argued, proposing two different
Origens, one Christian and the other pagan), and to deny it to the
Protestant Ritschl, and possibly by implication to Whichcote et al.
as well as Herbert, the problem of relationship remains in one's lap.
Herbert challenges his interpreter to attempt to distinguish always
between tactical statements and credal statements.

For example, in an unpublished draft of his autobiography,
Herbert had explained his insistence on the five articles of religion
for various reasons, among them the fact, as it seemed to him, that
'all Misteryes, Sacraments and Revelations cheefely tende to the
Establishment of these five Articles as being at least the principall
end for which they were ordeyned':

Houlding my selfe therefore principally to these five Catholique Articles I
did neverthelesse to my uttermost embrace and believe all that the Church
in which I was borne and brought up did uniformly teach sequestring and
dismissing onely the Contraverted points to those who had either Will,
Leasure or means to study them sufficiently.[38]

The key word here is 'uniformly'. Just as Herbert's survey of pagan
religion noted that 'egregious truths' were mixed with
improbabilities and falsehoods but declined the problem of pointing
out which were which, so his statements about Christianity refrain
from defining the 'Contraverted points'. Perhaps, to a man born just
on the far side of the Reformation, they seemed obvious enough. In a
speech which is subtly alleged by Herbert to have been delivered by
a member of the House of Commons in the Parliament of 1529, in
reply to an attack by John Fisher, Bishop of Rochester, on the
House's 'want of Faith', the 'Common, Authentick, and universal
Truths' of religion find their way, via Herbert's *Life and Raigne of King
Henry VIII* (London, 1649), into the English Reformation itself. The
speaker, whom Herbert had obviously invented, is identified only as
'one who had made use of the Evangelicks Doctrine so far, as to take
a reasonable liberty to judge of the present time'. Having
enumerated the five articles, he exhorts the Commons:

Let us, therefore, establish and fix these Catholic or Universal Notions.
They will not hinder us to believe whatsoever else is faithfully taught upon
the Authority of the Church. So that, whether the Eastern, Western,
Northern, or Southern Teachers, &c. and particularly whether my Lord of
Rochester, Luther, Eccius, Zwinglius, Erasmus, Melancthon, &c. be in the
Right, We Laicks may so build upon those Catholick and Infallible grounds
of Religion, as whatsoever superstructures of Faith be rais'd, those
Foundations yet may support them.[39]

Though full of self-admiration for the elegant shape of his *religio rotunda* of the five points in the 1645 edition of *De veritate*, Herbert is in fact open to manoeuvre. He did not in practice claim that the five articles provided a complete religion, but only that they were at the heart of all true religion and were necessarily to be found there, whatever the 'superstructures of Faith'. He had not changed his mind by the time he came to write *De religione gentilium*. 'I shall not', he writes there, 'presume to assert that they are altogether sufficient: the Opinion of those who judge more tenderly and reverently concerning GOD's Judgements, seems to me the most probable, while Man does all that is in his Power . . .'[40] It may be objected that the five articles contain nothing that is specifically Christian; it may even be objected that 'the superstructure Herbert proposes [*sic*] in the *De religione gentilium* is not Christian at all' (Walker). But neither objection, though it may indicate a wary, not to say negative, attitude towards institutional Christianity, proves that Herbert cannot possibly be a Christian. He may have been a very precarious, uncertain and idiosyncratic one, but then so too were many men of his age, Milton among them, who were pressing orthodox positions and clerical claims to their limits.

In the search for evidence of Herbert's emergent advocacy of the 'ancient theology', one might also turn to the work attributed by many to Herbert, *A Dialogue between a Tutor and a Pupil*. The *Dialogue*, a late work if it is Herbert's, occurs in MS 5296 in the National Library of Wales, and is written in English. It was printed in 1768. Although Rossi firmly rejects its authenticity, several scholars have concluded that Herbert was its author, most recently Günter Gawlick who suggests that it was most probably Herbert's own work, or if not was produced by someone with access to Herbert's library and papers.[41] It would seem to be, at any rate, an unquestionably Herbertian production. The debatable nature of the text notwithstanding, it is not a work to provide any one seeking a reflection of the 'good old astral religion' with much help. It may express some anti-Christian sentiments, and may express opinions not found elsewhere in Herbert; but it certainly advances no claims for the religion of Bruno and Campanella—a fact which some may of course take as evidence for some other authorship. On the contrary, although there is strong feeling against priesthood (e.g. pp. 97–100), there is also praise of Christianity and a distinction between Gentile religion and the Christian Church: 'they ought to consider, how

much our church is preferable before theirs, in sanctity and piety . . .
I had for my part rather believe, that the spirit of truth extant in the
holy doctrine contained in the scripture, hath both preserved our
religion more intire, and diffused it further than any other cause
whatsoever' (pp. 168–9).

In *De religione gentilium* Herbert had mentioned the controversy
between Celsus and Origen, and had noted that Celsus did not fear
to object to Origen that the Gentiles were just as virtuous as the
Christians.[42] The apostles, Celsus argued, were also just as wicked
as the Gentiles, and when the Pupil in the *Dialogue* reminds the
Tutor of this, the reply comes:

I hope you remember also Origen's answer, that though they might be so
before Christ took them for his disciples, yet, after they were instructed in
his holy precepts, they became not only virtuous, but exemplary pious
persons; and truly Origen doth so handsomely answer all the objections of
Celsus, that there is no book I should sooner commend to your reading than
this, if you desire to be informed in the difference between the Christian and
heathen religion. (pp. 170–1).

Herbert possessed several of Origen's works: his copy of *De recta in
Deum fide dialogus* has numerous marginal notes in his own hand, as
also has his edition (*Contra Celsum libri viii, graece et latine nunc primum
editi a Davide Hoeschelio*, Augsburg, 1605) of Origen against Celsus,
which was precisely the edition recommended by the Tutor to his
Pupil ('I would have you get Haeschelius' edition in Greek').[43]

Uncharacteristic perhaps of Herbert's own previous attitude
towards Christianity in his published work (though it accords with
the view expressed in the draft of the autobiography) is the manner
in which, whenever the question touches on contemporary
Christianity in the *Dialogue*, or on specific doctrines, this disclaimer
appears like a refrain: 'Of which therefore I should not willingly
speak, but in the presence of some divine' (p. 84), or 'I would have
you take further information from our learned divines herein' (p.
236), etc. When the discussion eventually takes hold of the central
Christian act of the Eucharist, the Pupil complains of the total
disarray facing the laic, who, while admitting that much may be
required of us by faith alone, is not 'much edified, when . . . some
say, Christ is taken in pane, sub pane, cum pane, or circa panem; all
which opinions, are maintained, at this day, in several parts of
Christendom'. The Tutor's eirenic reply (and whether or not it is
authentically Herbert's it echoes his sentiments) is as follows:

where the text is not clear, your best ground will be the authority of the church, and the practice of the most ancient times; but then again which authority, and which church you should adhere to, will be another question; for as all of them do equally pretend to antiquity, you must read so many huge volumes, as it will not be easy to resolve that point. So that you may the better excuse yourself, if you attend to the practical parts of the catholick articles, which is, indeed, the end for which that sacrament was ordained, and not engage yourself into so many tumultuous and uncharitable disputes, as no age, nor wit of man, can extend itself so far, as to come to an equal decision of them. (pp. 250–1)

There are however two 'Contraverted points' which particularly occupy Lord Herbert, on which he does not decline to comment, and which appear clearly in all his philosophical and religious writings: the salvation of the good man, and the freedom of the will. It is here, rather than in the Hermetic–Egyptian religion of the stars, that the 'superstructure' he proposes may be found and which he wished to address to his contemporary Christian readers. It is neither a mythology nor a revival of magical, talismanic animism, but a solid and aggressively ethical Arminianism. Grotius recognised and approved it in 1623; Laud noted it in 1633; the Cambridge Platonists echoed it; and polemical deists towards the end of the century adopted and transformed it.

Sin, salvation and free will

In affirming the importance of values rather than dogma, of conduct and not creed as the true test of religion, Herbert can be seen as responding to a situation in which, in his eyes, creeds and dogmas have merely intensified the antagonism between one party and another, inducing actions which any objective mind would judge to be vicious. In his view, true moral action springs from the rational apprehension of the good and is entirely altruistic in character. That such rational apprehension is possible can of course be demonstrated by the Common Notions, and Herbert gives as an example of such an ethical notion the proposition that we should always do as we expect to have done to us. Conduct towards our fellow men can be determined by reason and the Common Notions, and its particular faculty in Herbert's system is that of 'conscience', concerning which he says he is planning 'an entire treatise':

Conscience is the common sense of the inner senses. It springs from the faculty which is conscious through which we examine not only what is good and evil, but also their different degrees, according to their value or reverse, by means of the higher authority of the Common Notions, with the aim of reaching a decision concerning what we ought to do.[44]

To speak of 'examining' good and evil, as though the human will were capable of such an examination or were somehow not a part of the very data of good and evil, or to speak of 'reaching a decision' about moral action, suggests at once that virtue is simply a question of adequate knowledge. To know the good is to do the good. And such virtue is the active realisation of man's essential nature—a view which supposes that 'mere natural men' are capable, by virtue of the light of reason or of God, of moral action independent of the injunctions of revelation or authority or even the otiose lures of future rewards. In a manner similar to Herbert's, Hooker had regarded human sin—'the singular disgrace of nature'—merely as a form of error, or ignorance, for in doing evil 'we prefer a less good before a greater, the greatness whereof is by reason investigable and may be known'.[45] To the dominant Calvinist doctrine of total depravity Herbert responds, like Hooker before him and like Whichcote, Smith or Cudworth after him, as to a slander against the Creator. He can exhibit a hearty and august self-assurance which can assume that if 'human frailty' induces us to commit 'faults', a 'serious repentance' will suffice: 'for the rest, trust to the mercy of God . . . who being our Father, and knowing well in what a weak condition we are, will, I doubt not, commiserate those transgressions we commit when they are done without desire to offend his divine Majesty'.[46] The doctrine here, though not the tongue-in-cheek tone (Herbert is perfectly serious), is perhaps reminiscent of Sterne's traveller in *A Sentimental Journey* who pauses before overturning the beautiful grisset in a Parisian shoe shop to elaborate on the indulgence of God—'for Thou hast made us and not we ourselves'. But here again Herbert's concern for the ordinary man, his basically lay attitude, comes out strongly: a man will find that, since he did not mean infinitely to offend ('I hope none are so wicked as to sin purposedly') so 'there will be just reason to believe that God will not inflict an infinite punishment'.[47] With this one might compare a dominant Augustan view (to which age Herbert seems so often to have an almost uncanny, if often deceptive, kinship), expressed in Shaftesbury's writings and formulated by Locke as 'God, who knows our frailty, pities our weakness, and requires of us no more than we are able to do, and what was and what was not in our power, will judge as a kind and merciful Father'.[48]

It could be argued of Herbert, as of others in reaction to dogmas of total depravity, that he tends to overestimate the natural power of goodness in man; such phrases as the 'giving of offence' and the almost ingenuous committing of 'faults' suggest that for Herbert sin and righteousness are almost a question of good and bad taste. It was this supreme confidence of Herbert's that led Richard Baxter, after reading *De veritate*, to counter with a persuasive addition to the list of Common Notions: 'It is as common a truth that all men are sinful and depraved almost from the first (however it came to pass), that they are indisposed to the certain duties and ends, which their nature was formed for.'[49] There is little sense in Herbert of the heavy, self-regarding recalcitrance of the 'ordinary man'; instead he merely points to the 'conscience' which will necessarily guide a man's moral actions. Yet for all his apparent bluffness he is not unaware of the problem of sin, and he rationalises it by putting forward, like John Ford or Robert Burton, a kind of psychological determinism. He speaks of a 'sickness rooted in the very marrow of our being' but refers it not to 'wickedness in general' but to some particular 'animal impulse': 'Consequently, whenever our dismal orators proceed to defile nature with their abuse, let us remember that their charges are principally directed against the viler aspects of our animal nature'.[50] Relying on the physiology of his time Herbert, with a wide and generous toleration, explains that it is illogical to accuse a lethargic man of indolence or a dropsical man of thirst. In exactly the same way, he says, 'a man goaded by the spurs of Venus or of Mars can more properly be charged with an excess of vicious humours than with wickedness'. He argues that we should behave with 'more gentleness' towards those who 'fall into sin owing to some physical, animal or almost necessary compulsion'.[51] Herbert gives the impression of not really being able to see any other way in which a man *could* be induced to sin; and he seems quite prepared to act on the conclusion, not merely by self-excuse but by the active virtue of forgiveness—'in which kind,' he says, with that disarming lack of humility, 'I am confident no man to my time hath exceeded me'.[52]

Against this kind of determinism a mind like Donne's steeped in the Christian mysteries, haunted by sin and guilt and an overpowering sense of personal involvement, responds with an imitation of its whining tone of self-justification and rejects it with a final hiss of contempt:

> Let no man therefore think to present his complexion to God for an excuse, and say, My choler with which my constitution abounded, and which I could not remedy, enclined me to wrath, and so to bloud; My Melancholy enclined me to sadnesse, and so to Desperation, as though thy sins were medicinall sins, sins to vent humours.[53]

The true reason is that 'Man hath a dram of poyson, originall-Sin, in an invisible corner . . . and he cannot choose but poyson himselfe'.[54] Herbert's buoyant rationalisation of evil in the autobiography is in the sharpest possible contrast to Donne's compelling rhetoric on the subject in the *Devotions* and in the *Sermons*. The difference is equally apparent when Herbert is writing devotional verses after the manner of Donne. He begins his sonnet 'Lord, thus I sin' with an unmistakable echo of Donne's 'Wilt thou forgive that sinne where I begunne?':

> Lord, thus I sin, repent, and sin again,
>   As if Repentance only were, in me,
> Leave for new Sin . . .

But far from the cry of 'When thou hast done, thou hast not done', Herbert begins to argue the point according to the rules of legal logic:

> and, Lord, in them [our errors] 'tis true,
> Thy Laws are just, but why dost thou distrain
> Ought else for life, save life? That is thy due:
>   The rest thou mak'st us owe, and mayst to us
> As well forgive . . .

The final, humble self-realisation of 'But oh! my sins renew, / Whil'st I do talk with my Creator thus', does not conceal the critical, rational toughness and independence, nor his fundamental suspicion of this sort of bargaining.[55] Similarly, in the poem *Echo in a Church*,[56] the confidence in the grace (or rationality) of God (or Divine Providence) is equally untroubled. The answer to the appeal 'Then quickly speak' is a resonant 'I am', the Hebrew Jaweh, the ineffable Godhead and Supreme Power—a philosophical abstraction compared with the terrifyingly intimate 'three person'd God' or 'the picture of Christ crucified' which is closer to Donne than his very self. The experimental echo device Herbert uses in this poem is itself like a symbol of the Herbertian Godhead, a reflected answer to the philosopher–poet's own demands for common sense and intellectual symmetry.

If Herbert is an exponent of 'programmatic Arminianism', as Rossi suggests, then one would expect him to be decisive in his judgements concerning free will. The ethical determinism which locates much human evil in physical dispositions over which a man does not always have sufficient control is extended to embrace the whole drift and purpose of the moral life, and centres on the question of the will's freedom. While celebrating free will as the greatest wonder of nature Herbert at the same time imposes his own kind of determinism, or internal necessity. If, as he has maintained throughout *De veritate*, the generative force of the universe directs all things to their self-preservation and hence to the preservation of the whole, our individual moral acts are bound to be, in this sense, determined. Human beings are 'free' only in relation to the means by which they achieve the end of their being, Eternal Blessedness; and this end itself is determined by God, or the Divine Providence reflecting God's infinity. 'Notice here', Herbert says, 'a fact of great interest concerning free will; clearly you are composed in such a manner that you cannot but seek happiness. To this extent you are not free.'[57] The distinction between means and the final end provides scope for truly voluntary actions whose particular directing agent is conscience. The conscience is further supplemented by the physical and spiritual effects which, in the wisdom of nature's design, are necessarily bound up with good and evil actions: 'God, who is the cause, means and final end, puts us on our guard by the recurring disgust and weariness which physical pleasure brings'.[58] Conscience induces in us a 'physical repugnance and remorse in the presence of evil' because evil is, he says, always associated with coarse and oppressive sensations; the good on the other hand produces tranquillity and happiness because it testifies to the harmony of those faculties which are analogous to God. The pleasures of the senses are, he claims, transitory and particular, giving no lasting satisfaction; since God alone is 'the eternal and universal object', and since by virtue of the 'free will or infinity that is inscribed within us' we can reach out and grasp the eternal and universal, it is only in him that true joy and goodness can be found.

The nobility of this view, and its essentially Platonic and Stoic character, is at once obvious. It leads Herbert however into a possibly naive equivalence of moral action with pleasure and immoral action with pain or antipathy. Of the pleasures of the senses he laconically remarks that 'everyone is aware how quickly we grow weary of such pursuits'. There is nothing in Herbert's most serious writing (though one is perhaps led to believe differently from the evidence of the autobiography) of, for example, Ficino's pragmatic insistence that the trouble with the senses is not that they are not pleasurable but simply that their pleasures do not last; instead there is a tone frequently reminiscent of Sir Thomas Browne's wistful desire that 'we might propagate like trees, without conjunction'—a sentiment, or sentimentality, which is also diffused over so much of Herbert's love poetry.

His conception of free will and of the conditions imposed on it by the necessity of self-preservation, seem to reach back to Bruno and Telesio in particular (Rossi finds Telesio of special importance to Herbert here), and forward to Hobbes and Spinoza. Telesio's *De rerum natura* (1587) argues that all good is connected with self-preservation, which regulates choice and conditions all individual striving; an immediate feeling of pleasure is associated with the activity by which a being preserves and maintains itself. One of the chief means to this end is knowledge: right knowledge is knowledge of the way of self-preservation, an awareness of life's harmonious processes within which we work together like the organs of an organism, and out of which arise all the social virtues and the possibility of social organisation itself.[59] Like Telesio, Herbert frequently speaks of the necessity of identifying the individual good with the common good, and insists that the value, ultimately, of all goods resides in their contribution towards our self-preservation and Eternal Blessedness. Bruno often cited Telesio with admiration, and what Bruno admired most in Telesio was his vitalism—the view that every material thing is endowed with 'feeling'. Bruno constantly speaks of the heavenly bodies as *animalia*, that is, having *anima*, an internal necessity or *raggione* compelling all growth and change and maintenance. From this notion too Herbert could obviously have found many suggestions for his own theory of 'plastic virtue'. In Bruno, as in Herbert, this necessity is an inward force, not an outward constraint; within its total influence each detailed part can behave with a measure of freedom—freedom which is however an expression of an innate urge or impulse in conformity with its own inward nature. According to Bruno, 'will concurreth with goodness, and goodness with necessity', and Bruno is led towards the same kind of anti-clerical remark that Herbert makes: 'Beware then,' he warns, 'that priest who would rank either divine freedom or our freedom as merely contingent and possible'.[60] Bruno's God is the 'universal Intellect', the 'single whole which filleth the whole', the infinite which is everywhere. Herbert similarly calls infinity 'the last sphere of the divine attributes, embracing all the rest'; and free will is 'none other than the element of infinity which is innate in us'; God himself has 'endowed us with an element of His infinity in free will'.[61] At this point Herbert draws his distinction, modifying this freedom by arguing that it is conditioned by the demands of the law of self-preservation and that 'no one can prevent himself from desiring Eternal Happiness', so that will concurs with goodness, goodness with necessity.

Pursuing a form of determinism apparently similar to Telesio's, Hobbes, later in the seventeenth century, also explains the whole volitional life in terms of the impulse towards self-preservation: egoism is the sole determining factor in human action, and the human will, for Hobbes, is merely a response to the last trigger in a mechanical process. Since mind for Hobbes is matter, not *anima*, it is subject to laws of mechanical causality; what we call acts of will, or ethical acts, are merely impulses to approach what is pleasurable and withdraw from what is painful; they are contributions to our desire for power and the self-protection it will afford. Despite superficial resemblances, the difference between Hobbes's determinism and Bruno's or Herbert's is that Hobbes's materialistic metaphysics ('the whole universe is body') and his sensualistic psychology imply that this instinct towards self-preservation is directed only towards the preservation of the sensuous existence of the individual; whereas Herbert stresses again and again that true morality consists in the satisfaction of our spiritual faculties which are analagous to God, or mind: 'it is only in Him that our hope, love and joy can lie'. This same more idealistic implication is given to the doctrine of self-maintenance in Spinoza's system, where the striving for self-preservation, while operating on a material plane, operates also and most significantly as the impulse which finds its only perfect satisfaction in 'love to God'.

In the preface to *De veritate* Herbert had stated his intention of adapting words in common use rather than coining a new terminology for himself, and two of the words he points to are 'Nature' and 'Freewill': by 'Nature', he says, 'some mean fate and others corruption', and 'Freewill' 'is interpreted by some writers in the opposite sense to mine.'[62] Herbert's approach to these terms was designed to stretch the doctrinal narrowness of the age, to provide an alternative to the one-sidedness and friction of confessional zeal, and to bring about a purely human understanding of and respect for the ethical disposition, together with modesty in personal judgments. In religion the stress falls upon moral conviction and moral action rather than upon dogma and doctrine; upon religion itself, not thought and speech about religion. This stress was by no means unique or original to Herbert. His arguments naturally suggest parallels with many moderate churchmen and lay thinkers of the earlier seventeenth century, especially men like William Chillingworth, John Hales and the Falkland circle, or that multifariously learned Erastian John Selden. Yet his views provide a basis for an early and remarkable attitude of toleration which arises primarily out of the apparently aggressive frame of mind which can argue that 'if any under the name of Seer should byd me doe a sinne or be impenitent I should not believe him though he pretended a thousand Revelations for it. On the other side, if hee byd mee bee vertuous and penitent though hee had not soe much as a piece of Revelation for it, I should give entire credit to him', for the truly religious and moral response is elicited not by authority and custom but only by 'the Goodnes of ye doctrine it selfe'.[63] It is that kind of integrity which is reflected clearly in the Cambridge Platonists, of whom Whichcote, for example, argues that religion itself is always the same, and that (*pace* Rossi) 'the state of religion lies in a good mind and a good life, all else is about religion' and warns that 'men must not put the instrumental part of religion for the state of religion'.

Herbert's assertions concerning the relationship between sin and ignorance and the autonomy of the individual will within the limits of Divine Providence need to be seen within the context of the gloom of Calvinist predestination. Herbert attempts to stretch the frame of reference of concepts like 'freedom' or 'nature', and he does so in such a way that the whole question seems turned inside out. Indeed, it is possible to accuse Herbert, as it is to accuse Spinoza, of substituting one form of determinism for another. Doubtless Herbert would have been aware of this possible charge, and would probably have answered it by pointing out that it was better to propose a determinism which led to our completion in Eternal Blessedness than one which led (unless we were fortunately one of the elect) to our eternal damnation.

Above all, Herbert finds it impossible to accept the orthodox doctrine of 'original sin', particularly as it was propounded in Calvinist and radical Protestant theology. It seems to him an affront to God to believe that 'in Adam all sinned': '. . . this Principle of Evil cannot be derived from *Adam*; for all our sins and Trangressions are our own meer voluntary Acts; and no Mortal was so necessarily determin'd to do *Evil*, but by the *Divine Goodness*, he could both see and avoid it'.[64] We should, he urges, 'make some Enquiry, whether the Fall of Adam were the Original Source and Cause of all this Evil; or whether it were the Serpent which Symbolically is the Devil'.[65] Herbert's difficulties with the problem of evil have led many readers to the conclusion that he exhibits the most facile kind of optimism and that his Common Notion that we should repent of our sins has little religious significance in it. On this point Rossi is emphatic. 'What Herbert did not see (and this is the real defect of his religious position, and the reason for its subsequent development in the direction of deism) is that religion is not simply conduct of life, that faith goes beyond morality'.[66] Rossi points out that throughout his life Herbert remained sure of the indulgence of God and of a heaven made to his measure. Although admitting that Herbert knew how to pray and that in some sense he was a mystic, Rossi thinks his religious consciousness was defective; 'above all, he lacked that sense of evil which is the true basis of every experience of faith'.[67] There is a strong case for such a view of Herbert but it is not the whole story. Rossi frankly admits his own prejudices in a footnote to his discussion of deism: 'It is needless to confess that the light in which I present deism is determined by my aversion to every confusion of philosophy and theology, to every religious rationalism, to every immanentism, as well as by my aversion to Pelagianism in all its forms'.[68] It is a bias discernible in other aspects of Rossi's treatment of Herbert's work and personality. It is worth bringing to the foreground, for instance, Herbert's early and extraordinary 'satire', *The State Progress of Ill* (written in August 1608 at 'Merlow in France'), which is a vision of ubiquitous evil and corruption:

> Though *Ill*
> Great'ned in his long course, and swelling still,
> Be now like to a Deluge, yet, as *Nile*,
> 'Tis doubtful in his original; this while

> We may thus much on either part presume,
> That what so universal are, must come
> From causes great and far.[69]

The whole state of man is poisoned with multiplying sins:

> While in this monstrous birth they only dy
> Whom we confess, those live which we deny.

Although

> The World, as in the Ark of *Noah*, rests,
> Compos'd as then, few Men, and many Beasts,

evil is regarded—and it is not an unsubtle view—as having 'some part of Godhead', 'as Mercy, that Store / For Souls grown Bankrupt, their first stock of Grace' logically participates in its existence. Similarly in the work of his last years, *De religione gentilium*, Herbert notes that 'All Christian Divines unanimously have Recourse thither [to the doctrine of the Fall] for the redemption of Mankind'. But what, he asks, *is* Evil in fact? His answer shares in that same gesture of sober and paradoxical Christian optimism which could inscribe the legend over the entrance to Dante's Hell:

> *Justizia mosse il mio alto Fattore;*
> *La somma sapienza, e il primo amore.*

For that cannot be justly call'd *Evil*, which is made use of by the just, tho' secret Judgement of God, for the Punishment of *Sin*; nor can the Will of *Man*, tho' never so propense to *Sin*, be call'd simply *Evil*; for tho' the most vile Actions may be the Consequence, and proceed from thence, yet the Principle was not ill in it self; because by God's Assistance, it may be determin'd to either side.[70]

It is evident that however bumptiously confident Herbert may sometimes appear, he has glimpsed, and recorded, a more deeply religious response than he is often credited with.

In his frequent reproofs of Calvinism, particularly in its ethical aspect, Herbert reveals his own vision of the workings of Providence:

Those who hurl blasphemies against Nature or universal Providence, declaring that it is wholly wicked and corrupt, are guilty of impiety, considering that they are only permitted to abuse it by its beneficence. They maintain that they thereby extol Grace. I reply that if this Grace is universal it is a part of Common Providence. If on the other hand they hold it to be particular, they have failed to find any cure for evil. They abandon universal Grace in order to commend their particular Grace. They entangle it with so many dispensations, secret decrees, and doctrines of predestination, that unless salvation could be sought from the eternal benevolent Will, it would be useless to demand it by faith, prayer, or by any power at our disposal which invokes Grace or special Providence,

and he warns, as Hooker had warned, 'Let them take care that they do not destroy both ways of Grace in attempting to justify special Grace; with the result that the whole secret of salvation would be consigned neither to Nature nor to Grace, but to a kind of Stoic fate.'[71]

Recoiling from the determinism implied in theologies of generic corruption Herbert argues, in *De religione gentilium*, that 'all our sins and Transgressions are our own meer voluntary Acts'; we are not 'necessarily determin'd to do *Evil*'. The difficulties of this position with regard to interpretations of the Atonement are not altogether avoided by Herbert, and he appears to do his best to side-step discussion of the Atonement wherever possible. William Empson, in retreat from Milton's God and on the track of new materials, wonders what prevents a revolutionary seventeenth-century deist like Charles Blount from saying, as Shelley did, 'The more we reverence the Son who endured, the more we must execrate the Father who was satisfied by his pain'. Empson claims that 'It does get said, by Lord Herbert of Cherbury, but in a very mumbling way, and in Latin, and in Amsterdam, and after he was dead'. The answer to our (natural) question why it was not said more often probably lies, Empson tells us, 'in a fear that to say it would excite actively vengeful indignation'.[72] The passage to which he refers is the following remark in *De religione gentilium* where Herbert asks how Adam's sin could

perpetuate so horrid and tremendous a *Crime*, for which his innocent *Posterity*, that could not be concerned in it, should be doom'd to eternal *Punishments*; and after so many Ages, nothing could appease and reconcile *GOD* but more than Human Sacrifice. Let the learned *Divines* explain and confirm these difficult Doctrines, so that they may be clearly understood, and evidently prov'd to the Capacities of the Laity[73]

('If', Empson interprets, 'they can contrive to think of anything decent to say'). The point of Empson's evident approval of Herbert, despite Herbert's mumbling, is to go on to argue that Dryden's *Religio laici* carries an interesting answer to this query by reviving the Patripassian heresy of the third century and asserting that the Father suffered and was tortured along with the Son, and so everything is all right. Herbert's own drift is of course rather different. What he is resisting here is a rigid doctrine of the

Atonement which places in irreconcilable juxtaposition God's attributes of love and mercy. It is the dogma of eternal punishment which appals him and the interpretation offered of the God who is supposed to have ordained it, and in particular the implied consequences for all those, whether pagan or modern European, who fall outside the variously and ecclesiastically defined orbits of God's grace.

Herbert's general context here is a running argument against predestinationists, for whom will is nothing but a superfluous evil springing from the corrupt elements of nature. In his vigorous denial of such corruption Herbert celebrates free will as that 'unparalleled wonder of nature' by means of which alone our moral acts are made meaningful: 'Determined actions are not our own actions at all . . . Only voluntary actions belong to us.'[74] His question about Adam's sin, God's appeasement, and individual voluntary action, is a gibe at the cornerstone of the Calvinist structure of theology, the impregnably secret and inscrutable bargain apparently struck between the Father and the Son concerning the election or non-election of those fortunate enough to have the benefit of a Calvinist minister, and in which free will has no part to play. The issue is not man's sin and redemption, but a particular highly structured and immovable ecclesiastical interpretation of the mechanics of sin and redemption. A similar sort of thing does of course get said by others besides Lord Herbert, though perhaps without the particular destructive or Patripassian edge Empson is looking for. For instance—and apart from Origen and other patristic 'heretics' on the Atonement—Richard Hooker, newly appointed as Master of the Temple in 1585, confirmed the darkest suspicions of the Calvinist opposition in his sermon *Of Justification* by proposing the possible salvation of both our popish ancestors and present papists and had warned his hearers to 'beware lest we make too many ways of denying Christ', commending them to 'a merciful God ready to make the best of that little which we hold well', no 'captious sophister which gathereth the worst out of everything wherein we err'. The robust common sense of Fielding's Parson Adams takes the matter much further (as his position in the cooler Anglican air of the eighteenth century allows him) and he attacks the doctrine of the Atonement preached by the leader of the Calvinist Methodists, George Whitefield, and offers the Herbertian opinion 'that a virtuous and good Turk, or Heathen, are more acceptable in the sight of their Creator than a vicious or wicked Christian, though his Faith was as perfectly Orthodox as St Paul himself'.[75] A recent study of Fielding's novel has, incidentally, brought Parson Adams posthumously to trial for this, found him guilty of Pelagianism, and condemned him as a heretic. 'This Pelagian doctrine', it is claimed, 'corresponded to the deism, for example, of Lord Herbert of Cherbury, who had refused to believe that a benevolent God would condemn those ignorant of scriptural revelation.'[76] In a straight attack on sloppy or mechanical interpretations of the Atonement, the eighteenth-century divine William Law had pointed out, in a parody of Calvinism, 'what a paltry logic' it was 'to say, God is righteousness and justice as well as love, and therefore His love cannot help or forgive the sinner until His justice or righteous wrath has satisfaction! Every word here is in full ignorance of the things spoken of'.[77] Herbert would have agreed with him.

The virtuous pagan

Just as questions about the Atonement are as old as Christianity itself, so too are related questions about the salvation of the heathen. What, simply, was or is the fate of those who die ignorant of Scriptural revelation? Phillip Harth, in his study of Dryden, writes with some justice that 'There seems to be a fairly widespread belief among literary historians that any disposition among Anglicans of the seventeenth and eighteenth centuries to include the heathen within the terms of salvation is a certain sign of deism, Pelagianism, or Arminianism (described as a popular 'heresy' of the time)'.[78] The facts, as Harth points out, are quite otherwise. There was no 'orthodox' position in the seventeenth century, and to imagine that the seventeenth-century Christian invariably and cheerfully acquiesced in the damnation of the pagan, or even necessarily of those outside his own particular Church, is far from the truth, and it is to men of a more liberal disposition that Herbert adds his voice and lends his support. There were of course difficulties, and Catholic and Protestant had different answers. The Protestant dogma of justification by faith alone and of special, individual saving grace left the pagan in a parlous condition; yet even among the reformers a place was made for them by some. Zwingli expressly defended the use of non-Christian authorities on the grounds that they form part of the true, universal gospel 'when they give utterance to that which the holy, pure, eternal and infallible soul experiences'. Even the heathens may be elected to eternal life: Moses, Plato, St Paul, and Seneca are placed side by side as inspired authorities. Zwingli was exceptional. The general logic of the Protestant view had to conclude that the pagans were without merit and their damnation was certain. Erasmus's well-known 'Saint Socrates, pray for me' was an expression of his own sense of a practical Christianity which, he believed, was contained no less in the writings of the ancient philosophers than in the documents of Christianity: 'Their philosophy lies rather in the affections than in syllogisms; it is a life more than a debate, an inspiration rather than a discipline, a transformation rather than a reasoning. What else, pray, is the philosophy of Christ?'[79]

The Catholic was generally able, in fact, to take a less rigorous view; the popular scholastic maxim, *Facienti quod in se est, Deus non denegat gratiam* ('God does not refuse grace to one who does what he can')—a tag which Herbert places at the opening of *De religione gentilium*—allowed a measure of liberality not only to the Christian who found himself in difficulties but also to the virtuous man before Christ. But, as Harth has shown, there was no simple division between Catholic and Protestant on the issue, and as the seventeenth century progressed some Catholics began to take up more Protestant positions (for example, the heretical Jansenists adopted a limited atonement and the sinfulness of good works without faith, assigning the heathen to predestined damnation in a manner almost indistinguishable from Calvinism), and some Protestants moved to a more Catholic stance—Arminius and his followers spoke of the universality of atonement and the efficacy of good works in a voice that was not always easy to distinguish from Catholic opinion. Arminius's encounter with the rigours of Calvinism had led him, as it led Herbert, to attempt to modify the reformers' condemnations of Catholic errors and to find some middle position. What in Arminius, Grotius or Herbert was a minority view at the beginning of the seventeenth century was to become, by the later seventeenth and early eighteenth centuries, the majority view shared by bishops, clergy and laity of the national church of Locke and Newton, Joseph Butler and Gilbert Burnet.

Among the most vocal agents of this change in theological sensibility were the Latitudinarians and the Cambridge Platonists, who put up unremitting opposition to the Calvinist doctrines on justification, reprobation, and atonement. The puritan Richard Baxter, writing in 1665, spoke of 'A second sort of Conformist . . . those called *Latitudinarians*, who were mostly *Cambridge*-men, *Platonists* or *Cartesians*, and many of them *Arminians*, with some additions, having more charitable Thoughts than others of the Salvation of Heathens and Infidels'.[80] On this issue Baxter shared the same sentiments as the Latitudinarians. Dryden's *Religio laici* (1682), answering the Deist's objection to traditional Christianity that

> what Provision could from *thence* accrue
> To *Indian* Souls, and Worlds discover'd New?

blandly replies that the Deist has got it all wrong. Although Dryden has no sympathy with the epistemology of innate ideas of the Cartesians and the Cambridge Platonists, he argues, like them, that Christianity is by no means committed to condemning the greater part of mankind to perdition, and that the necessity of revelation does not exclude the heathen, past or present, from salvation.

Moreover, the efforts of many a Renaissance humanist, whether Catholic or Protestant, had for generations moved towards a reconciliation of ancient wisdom and Christian revelation. The question arose whether the wisest human voices and the divine voice might not be pointing in the same direction and to the same end. The baptising of pagans was a characteristic activity especially of Renaissance Neoplatonist thinkers: Pico della Mirandola's *Heptaplus*, a monument of Renaissance syncretism, attempted to put together the Bible, Plato, Aristotle, Hermes Trismegistus and the Cabala into a coherent Christianised whole. Scholarly humanists like Erasmus were continually at pains to make Christian theology compatible with humanistic reason; Hooker constructed his synthesis of the Laws of God and the Law of Reason in an effort to reconcile the apparent contradictions of nature and grace, reason and revelation, the human and the divine; Milton made an epic virtually out of this conflict, justifying, from one aspect of *Paradise Lost*'s many layered meanings, the fall of Adam and Eve in terms of the consequent creation of a full humanity. The attempted reconciliation is an activity which we see everywhere in the Renaissance and its results, becoming clearer and clearer as the seventeenth century proceeds, may be seen on the one hand as the gradual rational straightening out of religion, making the paradoxes and mysteries of the Christian faith acceptable to the lay philosophic mind until corporate religion, in the later seventeenth and early eighteenth centuries, looks suspiciously like little more than good solid sense, natural, rational, full of enlightened optimism and general sociability. Another of its results, on the other hand, may be seen as the promotion of individual religious independence, even isolationism, the religious minority of one, the irreducible reconciliation in the individual of reason and a personal sense of revelation—I think, therefore I am, therefore I believe this, that, or the other, and no institutional authority on earth can coerce me. This latter path is one that Milton's independent mind was to follow, and it is too the position Herbert found himself in, though his apparently individual response was buttressed by the claim that what he advocated was in fact a sharing in the fundamental and universal features of religious experience since the beginning of mankind's search for God. The paradox is that the two manifestations of the change in religious sensibility should be apparent in one man, the Herbert who looks both like a robust Augustan optimist, a prototype Earl of Shaftesbury, and also like a disillusioned and Church-less Milton.

Dryden's answer to the Deist, both in *Religio Laici* and in the preface to the poem, puts forward some points of view which, if Lord Herbert is supposed to represent the Deist (whether explicitly by Dryden—which Harth has shown not to be the case—or whether by historical implication), are curiously consistent with Herbert's own point of view, with the exception that Dryden does not lay any emphasis on innate ideas of God as part of his defence of the Christian religion. In the preface to *Religio laici* Dryden explains how originally monotheistic mankind (thanks to the revelation by God to Adam) had gradually been corrupted into polytheism. Herbert had of course attributed this corruption to the machinations of the priestly orders. The idea that the primitive and original revelation was lost and corrupted was a fairly common one. The Anglican apologist Richard Burthogge, himself one of the earliest commentators on Herbert (his *Organum Vetus et Novum, or A Discourse of Reason and Truth*, 1678, contains an early discussion of Herbert's theory of truth), wondered why the religion of the Gentiles, 'so *diversified* in it self' should have so many resemblances to Christianity. 'It is because,' he says, *that* all men came from one, and *that* not only *Adam*, but *Noah* did instruct his children in the Mysteries of the True Religion, and in the Rites of it, and these again *Reported* to theirs, and so onward. But we may easily believe it to have happened in this Tradition, as it doth in all others, that there was in almost every *New* delivery and Transmission . . . some *departure* and Recess from the *Former*.[81]

Burthogge, Sir Charles Wolseley (in his *The Reasonableness of Scripture-Belief*, 1672, the most likely source for the ideas in the first part of Dryden's *Religio laici*), and Dryden himself, all suggest that there is another explanation than that of natural reason for pagan religious ideas, and that primitive revelation may just as well account for them as human reason. Better in fact—for Dryden goes on to argue that the assumed cause (human reason) is insufficient to produce the observed effect (i.e. the five Catholic Articles). How, he asks in his poem, 'can the *less* the *Greater* comprehend? / Or *finite Reason* reach *Infinity*?' Herbert would of course have found the question a perfectly proper one. In the preface to *Religio laici* Dryden argues that God cannot be demonstrated to us by natural reason, but only by some kind of revelation, whether specifically Christian or pre-Christian:

That there is some thing above us, some Principle of *motion*, our Reason can apprehend, though it cannot discover what it is, by its own Vertue. And indeed 'tis very improbable, that we, who by the strength of our faculties cannot enter into the knowledge of any *Beeing*, not so much as of our own, should be able to find out by them, that Supream Nature, which we cannot otherwise define, than by saying it is Infinite; as if Infinitie were definable, or Infinity a subject for our narrow understanding.

All of this Herbert would have found entirely acceptable and in accord with his own view of a Natural Instinct above reason as the agent of both primitive and of modern revelation. Herbert's five Catholic Articles were presented as examples of Common Notions which, like all such, do not depend for their discovery or recognition on sense experience, logical enquiry, or demonstration. They are the product of Natural Instinct, and are innate faculties recognised by intuition and universally resident in men of normal healthy minds. When Dryden tells the Deist ' 'Tis *Revelation* what thou think'st *Discourse*', one can imagine Herbert quite happily joining Dryden in re-affirming his own view that man's original and natural knowledge of God *is* the product of revelation (in the sense of Natural Instinct of divine origin) and not of *discursus*. Where Dryden differs—and, as we saw in the case of Locke, it is one tradition of Christian rationalism criticising another—is that he insists that man's *natural* knowledge of God is in fact limited to demonstration, and at no point does he concede that mankind may possess innate or instinctive knowledge. He refers instead, drawing on the famous five inductive proofs elaborated by Aquinas (*Summa theologica* I, 2, 3), to arguments from efficient causation, motion, and particularly from design—a favourite argument of both Christian and deistic apologists at this stage of the debate, prominent in both Dryden and Locke, and one to which Herbert, the so-called 'deist', referred (as far as I can discover) only once or twice, as in *De religione gentilium* where he compares, in a routine fashion, a watch, 'the product of Art and Labour' with 'the vast Machine of this World'[82], and where that phrase, resonant later, is in Herbert innocent of any 'deistic' implication.

Notes to Chapter VI

1 Ben Jonson, *Poems*, ed. B. H. Newdigate, Oxford, 1936, p. 38.

2 Aubrey, *Brief Lives*, ed. A. Powell, London, 1949, pp. 39f.

3 See e.g. Margaret Bottrall, *Every Man a Phoenix*, London, 1958, p. 65; W. K. Jordan, *loc. cit.* II, p. 438.

4 *D.V.*, p. 229; Carré, p. 311.

5 Quoted in A. G. Dickens, *The English Reformation*, Fontana Books, 1969, p. 116.

6 Baxter, *More Reasons for the Christian Religion, and No Reason Against It*, London, 1672, especially p. 43; p. 77; p. 110.

7 *D.V.*, p. 209; Carré, p. 290.

8 Whichcote, *Moral and Religious Aphorism*, ed. S. Salter, London, 1753, No. 220.

9 Whichcote, aphorism 957.

10 Whichcote, aphorism 500.

11 C. A. Patrides, *The Cambridge Platonists*, London, 1969, p. 331.

12 E.g. *D.V.*, p. 7; *Religio laici*, 1645, *passim*.

13 Whichcote, aphorism 499.

14 Whichcote, aphorism 712.

15 D. P. Walker, *The Ancient Theology*, London, 1972, chap. 5, pp. 164–93.

16 Walker, pp. 175–6.

17 See Frances Yates, *Giordano Bruno and the Hermetic Tradition*, London, 1964, chap. XX.

18 *De religione gentilium*, Amsterdam, 1663. Facsimile reprint ed. Günter Gawlick, Stuttgart, 1967. English translation by William Lewis, *The Antient Religion of the Gentiles*, London, 1705 (hereafter *DRG*). Lewis, p. xiii.

19 See Rossi, III, pp. 108f. For Herbert's own library, see Fordyce and Knox.

20 See Walker, pp. 189–91, and Frances Yates, *Giordano Bruno*, pp. 433f.

21 *DRG*, p. 218; Lewis, pp. 366–7.

22 Philip Harth, in his *Contexts of Dryden's Thought*, Chicago, Ill., 1968, convincingly argues that Dryden knew very little of Herbert and that the source of the first part of *Religio laici* is to be found in Sir Charles Wolseley's *The Reasonableness of Scripture-Belief*, 1672.

23 William Empson, 'A deist tract by Dryden', *Essays in Criticism*, 25, (1975), lp. 74–100.

24 Herbert's fullest account is in *D.V.*, pp. 208–25; Carré, pp. 289–307.

25 *DRG*, p. 3; Lewis, p. 1.

26 *DRG*, p. 1; Lewis, pp. 1–2.

27 *DRG*, p. 3; Lewis, p. 5.

28 *DRG*, p. 6; Lewis, p. 11.

29 *DRG*, p. 20; Lewis, p. 33.

30 *DRG*, pp. 162–3; Lewis, p. 262.

31 *DRG*, p. 27; Lewis, p. 44.

32 Rossi, I, p. 295.

33 *DRG*, p. 49; Lewis, p. 79.

34 *DRG*, pp. 49–50; Lewis, pp. 79–80.

35 *DRG*, p. 221; Lewis, p. 371.

36 *DRG*, p. 230, Lewis, p. 387.

37 *DRG*, pp. 216–17; Lewis, p. 364.

38 R. I. Aaron, 'The Autobiography of Edward, first Lord Herbert of Cherbury: the original manuscript material', *Modern Language Review*, XXXVI, 1941, pp. 184–94.

39 *Life and Raigne of King Henry VIII*, second ed., 1672, p. 324.

40 *DRG*, p. 217; Lewis, pp. 364–5.

41 See Rossi, III, pp. 530–3; Gawlick, facsimile ed. Stuttgart, 1971, p. xiv. For support of Herbert's authorship see R. I. Aaron, 'A possible early draft of Hobbes's *De corpore*', *Mind*, 54 (1945), pp. 342–56, and Harold R. Hutcheson, *Lord Herbert of Cherbury's De Religione Laici*, New Haven, Conn., 1944, introduction.

42 *DRG*, p. 185; Lewis, p. 299.

43 See Fordyce and Knox.

44 *D.V.*, p. 104; Carré, p. 184.

45 Hooker, *Ecclesiastical Polity*, I,vii,7.

46 Lee, *Autobiography*, 1886, pp. 60–1.

47 Lee, p. 61.

48 Locke, *Essay Concerning Human Understanding*, 1690, II, 21, 54.

49 Baxter, *More Reasons for the Christian Religion*, 1672, p. 123.

50 *D.V.*, p. 101; Carré, p. 181.

51 *D.V.*, p. 100; Carré, p. 180.

52 Lee, p. 62.

53 *The Sermons of John Donne*, ed. G. R. Potter and E. M. Simpson, Berkeley and Los Angeles, 1957, III, p. 286.

54 Donne, *ibid.*, I (1953), p. 293.

55 *The Poems of Lord Herbert of Cherbury*, ed. G. C. Moore Smith, Oxford, 1923, p. 2.

56 *Poems*, pp. 47–8.

57 *D.V.*, p. 64; Carré, p. 143.

58 *D.V.*, p. 65; Carré, p. 144.

59 Telesio, *De rerum natura*, Naples, 1587, ix.

60 Bruno, *De immenso*, I.xii, in *Opere latine*, Naples and Florence, 1879–91, I.i, pp. 246–7.

61 *D.V.*, pp. 82–3; Carré, pp. 162–3.

62 *D.V.*, p. a4r; Carré, p. 73.

63 *Religio laici*, unpublished MS in National Library of Wales, ed. Herbert G. Wright, *Modern Language Review*, 28 (1933), pp. 295–307.

64 *DRG*, Lewis, p. 266.

65 *DRG*, Lewis, p. 44.

66 Rossi, I, p. 519. So also the anonymous author of *Religio clerici* (1681), complaining of deist infestation: deists are 'willing to suspect that all Religion is but the general *Laws of Nature*, and (at the best) they reduce Christianity it self to the first stage from whence it long ago set out, *viz. Common Morality*' (*Religio clerici*, London, 1681, sigs. A4v–A5).

67 Rossi, I, p. 558.

68 Rossi, I, p. 506 n.

69 *Poems*, ed. Moore Smith, p. 9.

70 *DRG*, Lewis, pp. 44–5.

71 *D.V.*, pp. 57–8; Carré, pp. 136–7.

72 William Empson, 'A deist tract by Dryden', *Essays in Criticism*, 25 (1975), pp. 74–100.

73 *DRG*, Lewis, p. 266.

74 *D.V.*, p. 84; Carré, p. 164.

75 Fielding, *Joseph Andrews*, bk. I, chap. xvii.

76 See Martin Battestin, *The Moral Basis of Fielding's Art: A Study of Joseph Andrews*, Weslyan University Press, Middletown, Conn., 1959, pp. 95–7; p. 21. Quoted in Philip Harth, *Contexts of Dryden's Thought*, Chicago, Ill., 1968, pp. 148–9.

77 *Selected Mystical Writings of William Law*, ed. Stephen Hobhouse, second ed.

78 Harth, *Contexts of Dryden's Thought*, p. 149; see also Louis Capéran, *Le Problème du salut des infidèles: essai historique*, second ed., Toulouse, 1934. Originally published 1912.

79 Quoted in *Erasmus*, Preserved Smith, New York, 1923, pp. 52–7.

80 *Reliquiae Baxterianae*, London, 1696, p. 386.

81 Richard Burthogge, *Causa Dei*, London, 1675, p. 339. Quoted in Harth, p. 121.

82 *DRG*, Lewis, p. 257.

VII
TOLERATION

How many wounds have been given, and credits slain, for the poor victory of
an opinion . . .

Sir Thomas Browne

The theory of persecution

In sixteenth-century Reformation dispute, those who proposed a
toleration were generally and officially regarded as either indulging
an extravagance at odds with the facts of life, or bluntly and
definitively as heretics. The Reformers themselves were in no sense
tolerant: Luther in 1530 sanctioned the death penalty for
Anabaptists, and Calvin urged the execution of Michael Servetus
while Melanchthon stood by applauding. The justification for such
action rested in that very dogma Herbert so stoutly contested: the
conviction that outside of a particular Church there was no salvation
and that heresy damned souls eternally.

As Shaw portrayed in *St Joan*, persecution could assume the
highest of therapeutic ideals. To the Catholic the purpose of
persecution and the curbing of religious liberty was to save souls.
The Calvinist Theodore Beza put his finger on something more
sinister when he denounced toleration as a most diabolical doctrine
because it simply meant that everyone should be left to go to hell in
his own way. In either case, however, the theoretical alternative to
persecution was to permit souls to suffer eternal damnation. The
Catholic claim was in its own terms logical; but the Protestant,
himself a Catholic 'heretic', was bound to ask *what* particular good
persecution achieved? If he were a Lutheran or especially a Calvinist
he could never say that its purpose was to save souls, for the saving of
souls was determined by God in his secret purposes of
predestination. This doctrine could cause embarrassment in two
directions: if man's salvation depends wholly on God's
predetermined edict, then both evangelism and constraint may be

futile. But though God's decrees could not be altered, Beza's remark suggests, his honour could be vindicated, and those going to hell by election should at least take the approved route. The liberal reply to this was that persecution is here equally ineffective since God is quite able to look after himself; nor can his honour be vindicated by burning and execution, for he takes no delight in burnt offerings. At this uncertainty of theory in the Protestant premise the liberal attack was levelled, prising apart the chinks and involving an attack on the whole conception of God as expressed in the doctrine of predestination. Over against the Calvinist deity is set the God of Erasmus, 'slow to anger and plenteous in mercy' (on both Catholic and Protestant thought Erasmus's tract on *The Immense Mercy of God* was of considerable influence). In this strategy of undermining Calvinist theology Herbert plays his part. He shares also in different degrees in the other chief modes of attacking the theory of persecution that can be discerned in this period: the Erastian approach, as exemplified chiefly in the French 'Politiques'; the 'syncretic' way of the Neoplatonists and Hermetists; and the approach to the problem through detached epistemological enquiry into the nature of truth and certainty.[1]

Herbert's interest in the question of religious persecution was undoubtedly aroused in part by the contemporary English situation. Though men like Giordano Bruno, Jacob Acontius or Isaac Casaubon, refugees from religious compulsion, regarded England as, comparatively speaking, a haven, the country was not without its own recent history of persecution, zealously documented in John Foxe's *Actes and Monuments* (1559 and 1563), nor without present dispensation. To take only the most extreme examples, Francis Ket had been burned at Norwich in 1591; and in 1612, at James's personal intervention, the heretic Bartholomew Legate was burned at Smithfield for Arian views; while the last person (as it turned out) to be executed in England for heresy was Edward Wightman, at Lichfield in 1612, again at the King's urging. The public outcry which these executions provoked led Thomas Fuller, the church historian, to comment bitterly that the King 'politicly preferred that Heretics hereafter . . . should silently and privately waste themselves away in prison than to grace them and amuze others with the solemnity of a public Execution'.[2]

Equally certainly Herbert's first visit to France in 1608 could hardly have failed to influence his views on persecution and the part played in its promotion by the priesthood, whether Catholic or Huguenot. The account of this period in the autobiography gives, as usual, precious little information about its author's intellectual development. Two clues, however, are important. The first is conjectural. Herbert mentions 'that incomparable scholar Isaac Casaubon, by whose learned conversation I much benefited myself',[3] and it is possible that these learned conversations were more formal than Herbert indicates, and that Herbert and the young Henri Montmorency (the heir of the Duke who was Herbert's host at Merlou) both studied for a time under Casaubon.[4] Herbert met Casaubon towards the end of 1608 when that great scholar's position was particularly difficult. All parties were contending for the prestige of his favour but Casaubon, since he could not profess an unreserved sympathy with either side, took a neutral position and refused to be drawn in. His writings, boldly independent, scholarly and humanistic, were conspicuous for their spirit of toleration and absence of heresy-hunting. Herbert would doubtless have been impressed and roused to interest in ideal religious problems by Casaubon's example, even if the teacher's influence did not directly form Herbert's particular ideas.

The second clue lies in the character and opinions of Herbert's host at Merlou and Chantilly, none other than Henri Montmorency-Damville, Governor of Languedoc, Constable of France, and leader of the French 'Politiques', whom Herbert affectionately calls 'that brave old General'. The history of the 'Politiques' is intimately connected with the activities of one family, the Montmorencys: Constable Anne Montmorency, who died in the Battle of St Denis in 1567; his sons, François, Duke of Montmorency and Governor of Paris, who died in 1579 to be succeeded by Henri; Charles, Lord of Méru, colonel-general of the Swiss mercenaries; and Guillaume, Lord of Thoré. Around this kernel of the Montmorencys and the Cossé-Brissacs their allies, and supported by Michel de l'Hôpital, the clan of the 'Politiques' was formed in 1561, composed of lawyers, diplomats, army men, even churchmen such as Jean du Bellay and Charles de Marillac, and numbering among their sympathisers men like Rabelais, Montaigne, La Boétie, Mornay and Hugo Grotius.[5] The attitude of the 'Politiques', and what bound them together, may be quickly summarised: better, they believed, toleration than desolation. The religious wars in France had ravaged the country; Spanish and Italian mercenaries in the pay of the Catholics or

English and German mercenaries in the pay of the Huguenots had trampled the kingdom, and growing religious dissension threatened the stability of the State. The 'Politiques', many of them liberal Catholic noblemen though a number too were Protestants, determined that the unity and security of the State were of greater importance than the victory of a single religion. They supported the monarchy as a centralising force, and vigorously argued that a toleration was a necessity in France if she were to maintain her existence as a consolidated State. Naturally, they were attacked as men who 'preferred the repose of the kingdom to the salvation of their souls'; towards the dangers both of the Catholic League's interpretation of the Catholic religion as an international religion and the Calvinist Huguenot's inclination to favour the political rights of the nobility, they responded with practical, civil arguments, advocating toleration as the only means of survival and the only hope of national strength. It is difficult to believe that Sir Edward Herbert came away from Montmorency-Damville's company at Merlou without finding both his faculties stirred and his notions of knightly chivalry greatly expanded. Not that there is any strongly Erastian or 'Politique' element in Herbert's own attitude towards toleration; his own response is ethical rather than political. Yet he is unlikely to have been left unmoved by what he learned of religious affairs in France on his first visit to Merlou.

The urgent plea for toleration made itself felt not only on a national but on an international level. The more stable and powerful a national State, the more pressing was the problem of each State's relation to its neighbour. Catholic Spain and Italy ranged themselves against Protestant Germany and England, and skirmishes were being fought all over Europe—with Herbert himself colourfully campaigning in the Netherlands against Spanish aggression. His knowledge of religious dispute was more than theoretical, and he was experienced in both the military and the diplomatic arenas. It is particularly interesting that the man who put forward a solid basis for international law which would sustain the collapse of Catholicism as a universal Church and universal empire, would replace both the Protestant-disputed canon law and the internationally unworkable Roman law, and offer an alternative to the controverted and vague authority of the Bible, was the man who warmly praised Herbert's *De veritate* and encouraged its publication, Hugo Grotius. Grotius's great work, *De jure belli ac pacis*

(1625),[6] sought to establish a theory of natural law no longer
identified with the law of Moses in the Pentateuch but derived from
secular, 'natural' observations grounded (like Locke's theory of
knowledge at the end of the century) in experience and nature,
immune to religious division, and accessible to the understanding of
the natural man. Grotius's position is the outcome, in legal theory,
of the nominalist division between faith and reason: his 'natural law'
is, as a response to that division, the exact parallel of the 'natural
religion' of Herbert of Cherbury. The main point here is that in the
De jure we find Grotius reducing religion to four (compared with
Herbert's five) fundamental and universal beliefs upon which the
church might reunite; and the possibility of such reunion depends
on a 'naturalised' concept of law. Where Melanchthon had said that
the execution of heretics is authorised by the code of Deuteronomy
and the *Codex Justinianus*, or the Catholic Inquisition had relied on
the latter and on the canon law of the Church, Grotius declares that
variety of religious belief is the law of nature, by which he means the
actual, visible order of society which, in Europe in 1625, exhibits
religious diversity. Underlying this variety, however, are a number of
fundamental beliefs held in common: his own four points, or
alternatively Herbert's five articles. From this position the step
towards toleration is a simple and logical one. In the interests of
international order, as in the national concerns of the 'Politiques',
toleration once more emerges as of more importance than the
dominance of any one religious group. And in both of these
movements Herbert had close association through his intimacy with
their two outstanding apologists.

The vision of concord

The significance of the relationship between Herbert's metaphysics
and his religious theories comes into sharpest focus in the grounds of
his desire to promote a toleration; the strongly Neoplatonic and
Hermetic elements in his metaphysics, far from being a lengthy and
learned preamble bearing little relation to the simple 'deistic'
principles which he enunciates towards the end of *De veritate*, and
which he repeats again and again thereafter, are connected
intimately with those principles and are the expression—the first in
England, unless one includes that other remarkable Welshman of

the fifteenth century, Reginald Pecock, whose *Repressor of overmuch blaming of the Clergy* (*c.* 1450) exalted reason and natural law above revelation as the independent foundation of morality and reached, in its extreme opposition to the Lollards, a position of advanced rationalism which is of great interest[7]—of a persistent line in European thought that may be traced back through Patrizi, Ficino and Cusanus to Tertullian and the early Fathers. That such a ubiquitous and recurrent response to religious belief and organisation can meaningfully and exclusively be called 'deism' seems extremely doubtful; Mario Rossi acutely pointed out that 'deism is not a philosophical doctrine, nor a scientific discovery: it is a human tendency'[8]—a view whose wisdom is chiefly that it should prevent us from pinning the vague and indecisive label of 'deist' (the descriptive significance of which is, after all, primarily historical in a specific sense) upon every manifestation of this constant 'human tendency', and from finding in every such manifestation a necessary anticipation or reflection of the deism which came to flower so vigorously in the early eighteenth century. I want here to trace briefly something of the connection between Neoplatonic and Hermetic thought and the growth of religious toleration—for the two seem related in a particularly interesting way—and to relate the toleration that emerges to what is generally called 'deism'.

Deistic principles may be found, as Arthur Lovejoy once suggested, even in Tertullian, on one side of whose thought there are affinities with the modern deists, particularly in his insistence that fundamental moral and religious truths are known universally and without special revelation, and in his plea for the rights of individual freedom in religious matters—a plea however which Lovejoy finds common throughout history 'among religions and other minority groups seeking to obtain liberty for themselves, and rare among the same groups after they have attained a position enabling them to deny it to others':[9] a cynically realistic remark which nevertheless leaves Herbert and other liberal reunionists quite untouched. It is in Cardinal Nicholas of Cusa (1401–64), also known as Cusanus, that the roots of a metaphysical basis for a religious toleration seem to lie. Cusanus's metaphysics begin as a criticism of Aristotelian methods of reasoning: since Aristotelian and scholastic reason is a discursive power which compares and relates, Cusanus argues, its province is the finite and the relative; it is therefore unable to grasp the unity of the infinite. In order to grasp the Infinite Being who transcends all distinctions, multiplicities and contradictions, the power we must employ is that of the whole intellect, through whose insight or intuition we can perceive unity where reason alone can perceive only diversity and division. From this Cusanus moves on to the assertion of the ultimate identity of contraries and the coincidence of opposites. This same conception, which occurs repeatedly in his works, is applied in his *De pace fidei* to the problem of differences of belief. Cusanus relates the vision of a 'certain man in Constantinople' who prayed to God that persecution because of differences in religious ceremonies should be moderated. In the vision, spokesmen of many different peoples appear in turn, and at last the reconciliation of all contraries is achieved through 'a concord of the mode [*rationis*] of all religions'.[10]

The argument of *De pace fidei* rests also on Cusanus's conception of knowledge. All knowledge that we may or can possess is relative, always aiming at greater truth; our relative knowledge is, with respect to absolute knowledge of infinity, in the nature of conjecture. Since none of our conjectures can completely apprehend the divine or exhaust its meaning, it may also be said that each conjecture, if it springs from a true religious conviction, shares in some sense in the divine. In his own discussion of the conditions of perception Herbert similarly limits the possibilities of knowledge, for, he says, 'no sensible man will ever deny, not only that the marvels of the heavens, but also the inmost details of the world below, fall beyond the ordinary forms of apprehension'.[11] Or again, in his discussion of probability, he states that 'the field of probability is extremely wide, while the area of truth' (in the sense of complete and absolute knowledge) 'is very restricted'.[12] Consequently a good deal of our knowledge will be in the nature of conjecture and hypothesis. Herbert argues that

it is not only the smallest things which escape the perception of our senses, but any transcendental object surpasses human perception. It follows that we can only faintly imagine the infinite and eternal order after the analogy of the finite and temporal [*ideo infinitum, aeternum imperfecte & non nisi sub ratione finite, & temporis adumbrantur*].

The faculty employed here is 'our divine understanding' which 'comprehends objects and reaches even beyond them'.[13] Such 'conjecture' or 'adumbration' Cusanus had defined as 'a positive assertion in place of truth, having some part in truth'. Single truth, according to Cusanus, is shown to us only in difference; but since there is infinite inter-relationship, an identity of all diversity, there can be no difference which does not attain to and share in the unity of all truth.[14] Herbert's theory of truth is, as we have seen, dependent on the view that 'all instances of truth will be relations', each instance definable in terms of its distinctive *differentiae*; at the same time however he maintains that 'the principles of all the differences in the world are inscribed in man'.[15] Hence he can claim that by virtue of that part of our minds which corresponds to God (that is, man's unique qualities of religion and faith) 'we are not only transported to loftier realms but are enabled to bring these down to our level. They serve to unite distant spheres; and accordingly their dwelling is in man, who is himself posed between the higher and lower realms'.[16] If there is an apparent inconsistency in Herbert's thought here it is because he is drawing on the Neoplatonic theory of the identity of opposites, according to which the finite and the infinite can be run together without ultimate contradiction and whose unifying microcosm is man himself and his whole intellect. The divine faculties of the intellect, with their 'illimitable power of religion and faith' can unify all discord and 'there is nothing . . . they cannot bring into harmony'.[17] As Ralph Cudworth was to put it, proposing a similar vision of the unity of truth within our particular and fragmented apprehensions, 'Truths are not multiplied by the Diversity of Minds that apprehend them; because they are all but Ectypal Participations of one and the same Original or Archetypal Mind and Truth'.[18] The application of such an epistemology to religious belief affirms that variety and freedom in moral and religious life must be accepted because each truth, though distinguishable only by difference, has a part in the unity of the infinite. There can be no dogmatic assertion, no establishment of one binding and universally valid and exclusive body of doctrine (beyond the common religious notions), and above all no persecution in pursuit of such an end can be justified.

So too Marsilio Ficino, leader of the Florentine Academy, pursues the search for unity and harmony, following the direction of Cusanus. Ficino's *De christiana religione* centres upon the axiom *una est religio in ritum varietate*, 'Religion is one amid a variety of ceremonies'.[19] It is a unity ruled by the principle of harmony rather than mere uniformity. A motto Ficino used as a chapter heading in the work epitomises the liberal Platonic viewpoint:

Omnis religio boni habet nonnihil, modo ad Deum ipsum creatorem omnium dirigatur, Christiana syncera est.

Every religion has something good in it; so long as it is directed towards God the Creator of all things, it is a true Christian religion.[20]

From the Florentine Academy also came Pico's famous *Oration on the Dignity of Man* (1486), a preface which Pico wrote to introduce a public debate in Rome of his nine hundred theses, but which the Church, finding some of the theses heretical, refused to allow to take place. In the second part of the *Oration* Pico celebrates the unity of truth, culling from various philosophical traditions to extract 'universal Truth': a method which is justified, Pico argues, because rival philosophical systems, far from possessing a common share of error possess rather a common share of truth, or (to represent Pico more accurately) a common share of statements which are true. It has been suggested that Pico's intention here was to give a broader basis to his master Ficino's doctrine of natural religion and to his own attempt to reconcile Platonic philosophy and Christian theology.[21] This characteristic concern of Christian Platonism with the achievement of a universal religion rather than the building of any single 'true' visible Church resides in the conviction, re-emphasised in Herbert's 'natural theology', that differences in external signs or in the specific formulae used to express dogma do not represent threats to the community of believers; on the contrary, difference and diversity reinforces the unity of true faith by gathering the strength of truth from many sources.

The application of Neoplatonic theories of harmony to religious questions is nowhere more apparent than in the work of two strangely eccentric yet powerful and prophetic thinkers, the notorious Giordano Bruno and the little known but fascinating Guillaume Postel (1510–81), an immensely learned philologist, traveller, missionary enthusiast and publicist who threw off a shower of ideas.[22] Postel seems to have quite remarkable affinities with Lord Herbert, both in his character—impulsive, indefatigably optimistic, in a philosophical sense, and always concerned with results rather than theories (he was an active lobbyist at the Council of Trent)—and in his writings, in which one finds almost all the germinal ideas of Herbert's thought, propounded with great zeal and with a purpose as wide and as evangelical in its desire to resolve dispute and end persecution.

Like Herbert, Postel conceives the universe as a vast system of correspondences in which the general is mirrored everywhere in the particular; a universe dominated by the idea of unity and giving rise to methods of argument which are essentially analogical and deductive in their principles. His interest in cabalistic literature—he knew Hebrew and translated important cabalist sources—is especially significant, for in such literature is presented a comprehensive and integrated view of the universe founded upon analogy. The attraction of the cabalist writings for Postel lay, so Postel's modern commentator W. J. Bouwsma suggests, in their effectiveness as a means of combating the break-up caused by the metaphysical scepticism of the prevailing schools[23]: precisely the reason for which Herbert was attracted to Paracelsian analogy and Hermetic ideas of unity. Postel therefore shows a vigorous opposition to the dualism between faith and reason of both the Averroists and the nominalists, for, apart from the question of the consequences of their views, Postel found their epistemological theory antipathetic to his sense of order and the necessary unity of things. And like Herbert too, Postel displays the typically Alexandrian attitude towards knowledge as the key to salvation, finding the root of evil to be ignorance, for which, surely, God will not everlastingly condemn us: 'for what parent would condemn his son for ignorance?'[24] If sins are merely errors, then men should show a Christian compassion and toleration, for we are commanded to help, not to destroy, the weak in faith.[25]

Postel regarded as the most important of his writings the long *De orbis terrae concordia libri quatuor* (Basle, 1544) in which he intended to teach the Christian doctrines by 'philosophical reasons', as the title page states. His complete universalism asserts that because God has created everything good, all men have equal access to his grace, through the power of reason, the common possession of all. Once men have agreed, as rational beings, upon a few fundamental principles of religious truth, a concord of all parties could be achieved. More than once Postel listed his 'demonstrable propositions' about religious truth (there are sixty-seven propositions in the *De orbis concordia*), reached by magnifying similarities of belief among the peoples of the world and minimising differences, and basing such agreement on the principles of natural or philosophical reason: for 'the law common to all peoples can be sought in the wells of philosophy'.[26] The essential religious truths were, he believed, contained within the variety of the world's religions, only waiting to be detached from the accretions of detail which kept mankind apart.

As for the Church, Postel subordinates the *ecclesia generalis* to the *ecclesia specialis* in a formal sense, yet believes that the 'general Church' is endowed with a large measure of general grace and revelation. He was convinced that nature and grace co-operate to obliterate the distinctions between Churches, basing this conviction on an assertion that is now familiar from Herbert's writings:

> For since God, the best of all beings, wishes that all men everywhere and without exception, should be saved, since He loves them all and hates nothing He has made, He would not have given the grace of the Holy Spirit to the whole world in vain, if no one could be saved but him who has been initiated into the narrow worship of the external church.[27]

In his confidence in reason and in his universalist sentiments Postel naturally approximates to 'rational religion' and the deism of the Enlightenment; but his thought is closer to, and paralleling as it were, that of the Florentine Neoplatonists, and closer still to the Cusanus of the *De pace fidei*.[28] The needs of religious unity and the hatred of persecution are the driving force behind Postel's thought. Men, Postel writes to Melanchthon, are rational, and are susceptible only to the arguments of 'reason, not of authority, which anyone twists according to his will';[29] true religion forbids the forcing of conscience and should generate the compassion of the apostles rather than the self-righteous use of sword and fire. In his search for the great reconciliation of all religions Postel finds a justification for his enterprise in an analogical, unifying metaphysics and in theories of correspondence.

The influence of the Cabala and the manner in which its analogical doctrines naturally supported, or led to, a movement towards 'natural religion' is clearly evident in Bruno. In his *Spaccio della bestia trionfante*—a glorification of the magical religion of the Egyptians—Bruno describes how the Egyptians' worship ascended through the multiplicity of things to the unity of the One beyond all things, 'so that in the end, the whole Deity is reduced to one fountain, as all light to the first and of itself lucid principle; and the images which are in diverse and numerous mirrors, as in so many particular subjects, all centre in one formal and ideal principle, the fountain of them',[30] and in which description Cusanus's 'coincidence of opposites' is at once apparent. When Bruno, as a young man, made his first visit to Paris in 1581, he taught for a time at the Collège de France under the patronage of Henry III; at the Collège the chair of Greek had previously been occupied by Louis le Roy (d. 1577), a Platonist scholar who had championed religious toleration chiefly on the grounds of the 'coincidence of opposites'. In his most famous work, *Douze livres de la vicissitudes ou variété des choses de l'univers* (a work which in Robert Ashley's English translation of 1594 became an Elizabethan bestseller), le Roy gives a philosophical survey of history interpreted according to the thesis that 'everywhere contraries balance one another'; and in an earlier work dedicated to the King, *Exhortation en françois pour vivre en concorde* (Paris, 1570), he applied the formula to the differences of religions and philosophies and advocated a toleration based on unity within diversity. It may be that during Bruno's stay at the Collège le Roy was still discussed and that his views influenced Bruno's own thoughts on toleration. At any rate, Coleridge, with his often remarkable insight, perceived in Bruno's astrological and esoteric complexities the seeds of true religion and truly Christian behaviour. Coleridge had come across Addison's remark on Bruno's *Bestia triofante* in the *Spectator* (V. 389, 1712), where a notice of the sale of a copy of the work provoked the comment, 'the author is a professed atheist'; Coleridge leaps to Bruno's defence, and his observations are worth quoting in full:

By the bye, Addison in the *Spectator* has grossly misrepresented the design and tendency of Bruno's *Bestia trionfante*; the object of which was to show of all the theologies and theogonies which have been conceived for the mere purpose of solving problems in the material universe, that as they originate in the fancy, so they all end in delusion, and act to the hindrance or prevention of sound knowledge and actual discovery. But the principal and more important truth taught in this allegory, is, that in the concerns of morality, all previous knowledge of the will of heaven, which is not revealed to man through his conscience; that all commands, which do not consist in the unconditional obedience of the will to the pure reason, without tampering with consequences (which are in God's power, and not in ours); in short, that all motives of hope and fear from invisible powers, which are not immediately derived from, and absolutely coincident with, the reverence due to the supreme reason of the universe, are all alike dangerous superstitions. The worship founded on them, whether offered by the Catholic to St Francis or by the poor African to his Fetish, differ in form only, not in substance. Herein Bruno speaks not only as a philosopher but as an enlightened Christian; the evangelists and apostles everywhere representing their moral precepts, not as doctrines then first revealed, but as truths implanted in the hearts of men, which their vices only could have obscured.[31]

It was not only in obviously unorthodox and independent thinkers like Bruno that the gesture towards Hermetism and Neoplatonism, made in the interests of religious toleration, was to be found. That other Elizabethan bestseller, Philipe Mornay's *De la vérité de la religion chrétienne* (Antwerp, 1581), turns to the Hermetic philosophy to raise men above the agonising conflicts and use of force in religious dispute. Mornay synthesises, as Ficino and Bruno had done, Hermetism and the Cabala—a synthesis which in Mornay's hands is not at all 'magical' or 'mysterious' but essentially philosophical and theological. Mornay in fact emphatically rejects magic as misguided and vain.[32] Mornay's work was translated by Sir Philip Sidney and Arthur Golding as *A Woorke concerning the trewnesse of the Christian Religion*.[33] Before the completion of his part of the translation Sidney died in 1586, fighting in the cause of the South Netherlands—as Herbert later fought in the Netherlands campaign. The chief purpose of the work is to prove that God exists, and that there is only one God. Herbert doubtless found it a very useful source book, for it sets out to establish several of his common religious notions in advance and chiefly on Platonic and Hermetic authority and upon the evidence of 'Universall Consent':

Let a man ronne from East to West, and from South to North: let him ransacke all ages one after another: and wheresoever he findeth any men, there shall he find also a kind of Religion and serving of God, with Prayers and Sacrifices. The diversity whereof is very great: but yet they have alwayes consented all in this poynt, That there is a GOD.[34]

As support to the proposition 'That the Wisdome of the World hath acknowledged one onely God' a dense series of citations and authoritative reference follows to prove God's singularity, beginning significantly with '*Mercurius Trismegistus* . . . the founder of them all . . . who teacheth everywhere, That there is but one God: That one is the roote of all things, and that without that one, nothing hath bene of all things that are . . . the Father of the world, the Creator, the Beginning . . . the worker of all powers, the power of all works'.[35] Throughout the work reference is constantly made to Trismegistus, either by direct quotation or by marginal glosses, supported by a solid phalanx of Platonists and Pythagoreans. The 'Peripateticks' receive short shrift, for Aristotelians 'have no voyce here, because they stand all in commenting upon Aristotle'.[36]

The Hermetic tenets of the One and the All and of man the abridgement of the universe figure prominently. God 'in our bodies hath framed a Counterfet of the world, and in our Soules hath engraven an image of himself'.[37] After reciting numerous proofs of God derived from the opposition-within-harmony of the elements and the universal harmony of the whole cosmos, Mornay declares: 'What shall I say more? or rather what remaineth not for mee to say? I say with the auncient Trismegist, Lord, shall I looke upon thee in the things that are here beneath, or in the things that are above? Thou madest all things, and whole nature is nothing els but an image of thee.'[38]

Mornay's collection of quotation and example is not merely a 'proof' of the trueness of Christianity. By its appeal to doctrines held universally by all men at all times it sets out to demonstrate the basic unity within diversity of 'opinion'. The informing spirit of this enquiry is the religious philosophy of Hermetism. This philosophy was reflected too, Frances Yates suggests, in Sir Thomas More's description of 'the religion practised by the wisest of the Utopians, which prepared them to receive Christianity'; 'the converted Utopians are ... perhaps Christian Hermetists'.[39] It is worth emphasising that Isaac Casaubon's scholarly paper on the *Hermetica*, written in 1614, alleged that the Hermetic writings were in fact Christian forgeries, showing what a firm hold the Christian interpretation of them had taken.

As a final example, one might cite Patrizi's *Nova de universis philosophia* (1591), with its fascinating dedication to Pope Gregory XVI.[40] Patrizi says that a philosopher nowadays is thought to be an atheist because the only philosophy studied is that of Aristotle, who denies the omnipotence and providence of God. Why, he asks, are those parts of Aristotle's works which are hostile to God so extensively studied? He proposes a truer philosophy by which we might return to God: the philosophy of Hermes. And he hopes that the Pope and his successors will adopt this religious philosophy and cause it to be taught everywhere, together with Plato's dialogues, Plotinus, Proclus, and the early Fathers. But the schoolmen are dangerous because they are too Aristotelian. Patrizi's effort was ultimately of no avail—he was summoned to Rome in 1592 by Pope Clement VIII to teach Platonic philosophy in the university, but the Inquisition got wind of heresy, were hard to satisfy, and the book *Nova de universis philosophia* was finally condemned.[41] The significant point is that the pious philosophy of Hermes was used in a Counter Reformation context and advocated as a peaceful way for Jesuits to attract Protestants without the traditional racking and burning.

In Lord Herbert's own writings we come up against the constant problem (a problem, that is, if we are attempting to track down his specific sources) that he gives no references and acknowledges no authorities. The only work in which references appear to any extent is the *De religione gentilium*. Platonists and Neoplatonists, except for Plato himself, do not play a great part in that work as overt authorities. Herbert quotes several times though from the Orphic Hymns, and at one point he refers to Hermes 'in the speech of the Mind' where 'Goodness, Beauty, Happiness and Wisdom are the Essence of God', and confides that 'Hermes has very sublime thoughts concerning God, calling him, The Preserver of Beings'—a title which Herbert would naturally have found worthy of repetition.[42] He cites fairly extensively from Ficino's commentaries on Plato, quotes Patrizi's edition of Zoroaster (that is, the *Oracula Chaldaica*) and frequently cites Patrizi's other works. With characteristic obliqueness he suggests that he could if he wished 'be very copious', 'but so many excellent Authors have gone before, especially Platonists, that I should only repeat what has already been said'.[43] In the course of surveying religious history Herbert refers to the time of the Emperor Julian, the 'apostate' who endeavoured to revive Hellenism in A.D. 361 and to assert the continuity of the Platonic tradition, and points out that 'Almost all the Platonick and Stoick Philosophers in those days strove to reduce all Religion to Virtue and Piety, towards God, and Men; as it is to be seen in their Works, where proper Remedies are applied against the Epidemical Distempers of the Times'[44] Clearly Herbert saw himself as a Neo-Stoic or Neo-Platonic in this very exact sense, as a man whose mission it was to apply 'proper Remedies' to the confusions of his own age.

Nor was Herbert alone in this ambition. In the last few years of the sixteenth century the French thinker Jean Bodin was writing his *Colloquium heptaplomores*, a dialogue in six books between seven interlocutors, each of whom speaks for a different faith: a Roman Catholic, a Lutheran, a Zwinglian, a Mohammedan, a Jew, a philosopher who appears to represent a religion of nature, and a sceptic or indifferentist who is content to observe any form of religion. The title of the work was perhaps an imitation of Pico's commentary on Genesis, the *Heptaplus*. Exactly which of the speakers represents Bodin's own point of view is not clear, and has been matter for dispute; a possible conclusion is that Bodin himself, the artist conducting the debate, embodies his own meaning in the form itself. Probably written in the early 1590s, the work was never printed. George H. Sabine has summarised Bodin's religious stance in a manner which may, with little modification, be applied equally to Herbert:

What mood of pessimism or fear of consequences prevented Bodin from attempting the publication of the *Heptaplomeres* we do not know, but throughout the work we can read his fear of religious innovations, his sense of the danger of controversy, his growing feeling that religious disputes are futile, and his firm conviction that differences of belief can and must be tolerated. His point is not at all that religion is unimportant. On the contrary it is the cement of society. Its vast importance is just what makes tampering dangerous. But real religion is neither doctrine nor ritual but a pure heart turned towards God, and this no sect, nor even all Christianity, can monopolise. To recognise this universal element in all religion, to retain your own belief while sympathizing with the belief of others, is the only remedy which Bodin can see for the endless moral and civic difficulties which religious warfare has created for his generation.[45]

Among his English contemporaries, Herbert's thought may be compared with that of the 'puritan' Robert Greville, Lord Brooke, whose *The Nature of Truth* (1640) reveals, as Herbert does, a strongly Neoplatonic conception of the unity of truth within diversity. Our search for truth, Greville says, is an effort to recombine the scattered fragments into the unified form of the whole.[46] He consequently takes a universalist view of religious differences and, in his anti-Laudian *Discourse* in particular, he rejects as criminal the philosophy of coercion as practised by the Churches.[47] There is, moreover, an obvious relation between Christian Platonism and the attitudes in particular of Sir Thomas Browne, Lord Falkland and his fellow moderates, Milton, and the Cambridge Platonists and Latitudinarians: men more concerned with what is universal in faith than with a faith dependent upon precise agreement on all points of dogma and practice. Here is Browne, dismayed at any claim of exclusive salvation and the ready and easy consignment to damnation of those who wander from the officially defined way:

nor must a few differences more remarkable in the eyes of men than perhaps in the judgement of God, excommunicate from heaven one another, much lesse those Christians who are in a manner all Martyrs, maintaining their faith in the noble way of persecution, and serving God in the fire, whereas we honour him but in the Sunshine.[48]

And here too, in the earlier years of the century, is Robert Burton's melancholic eye observing 'this hatred, malice, faction and desire of revenge' which 'invented first all those racks, and wheels, strappadoes, brazen bulls, feral engines, prisions, inquisitions, severe laws to macerate and torment one another'. With a hopefulness which he does not perhaps quite believe in (Burton found himself supporting Beza and Calvin against Castellio on religious liberty), he exclaims:

How happy might we be, and end our time with blessed days and sweet content, if we could contain our selves, and, as we ought to do, put up injuries, learn humility, meekness, patience, forget and forgive, as in God's word we are enjoined, compose such small controversies amongst ourselves, moderate our passions in this kind, and think better of others, as Paul would have us, than of our selves: be of like affection one towards another, and not avenge our selves, but have peace with all men.[49]

William Chillingworth's *The Religion of Protestants* (1638) also aims at removing the barriers separating sect from sect and confession from confession, not by quoting St Paul and generally encouraging people to 'forget and forgive', but by formally stressing the saving truth they all possess. Chillingworth speaks too of the uncharity of damning men by narrow laws of men's making that were never ordained by God and ought never to be promoted by constraint. Joseph Glanvill exposes the Vanity of Dogmatising. Milton extols variety and diversity as evidence of spiritual health and the victory of truth; he praises that Church in which the individual is 'both priest and congregation within his own conscience'—reflecting that individual emphasis so basic to Herbert's thought and equally to the Latitudinarian ideal of toleration. Such 'proper Remedies' to the sectarian confusions of the seventeenth century were, as Herbert saw it in 1624, in great need of application, for it appeared to him, as to others, that the warring parties had discarded them in favour of a hardened efficiency in combat.

The epistemology of toleration

But if Herbert, like Cusanus, Patrizi or Lord Brooke, found a basis for the urging of religious toleration in the Hermetic and Neoplatonic philosophy, he also found a strong appeal in the arguments which emanated from the Renaissance humanists, in the

line of Coluccio Salutati, Lorenzo Valla, Sebastian Castellio and
Jacob Acontius—men who wanted to unite the human and the
divine by making Christianity not necessarily conformable with
Platonism but at least acceptable to humanistic reason. To be
acceptable it had to be simplified, which meant, if not a reduction of
'all Religion to Virtue and Piety', an abandonment of the central
dogmatic complex of original sin and divine atonement and the
establishment of commonly agreed fundamentals upon which
reasonable men might be able to accommodate one another. There
was therefore inherent in their strategy of toleration the offering of a
theory of knowledge and a critique of the nature of certainty.

One of the most formidable advocates of toleration in the
sixteenth century was Jacob Acontius, an extraordinary man who
became a Protestant when almost sixty and fled from Italy to
Switzerland, to arrive there in 1557 within five years of the execution
of Michael Servetus. From Switzerland he came to England, was
well known at Elizabeth's court, applied for and was granted letters
of naturalisation in 1561, and spent part of his large talent in
devising a remarkable scheme for draining and reclaiming the Fens.
Acontius vigorously condemned all temporal punishment and
persecution of heretics. In his treatise *De methodo* (1558) he applied a
logical intelligence to the problem of persecution, offering a 'legal'
defence of toleration on the basis of 'the absence of sufficient guilt on
the part of the heretic to warrant prosecution'.[50] In the later work,
Satanae strategemata, written in England and dedicated to Queen
Elizabeth,[51] he presented a psychological theory of persecution in
which Satan is seen to be continually exploiting men's weakness and
egoism; the greatest hindrances to clear sight and true judgement
are pride, passion, prejudice and arrogance, which are only
aggravated by vainglory on the part of the one who is trying to
persuade or prosecute. Humility and absolute devotion to truth,
Acontius suggests, are the prerequisites of evangelism, not the sword
and the stake. Acontius criticised—like Postel, Castellio and
others—the dogma of exclusive salvation, and sought to reduce the
Christian doctrines to the smallest possible number. As a typical
humanist, he based his plea for complete religious freedom on 'the
inherent capacity of the ordinary layman to understand the
essentials of religion' and upon a conviction that 'men love truth and
hate error by their very nature'; the rights of private judgement must
always be defended, and 'in the last analysis people must determine

religious truth for themselves'.[52] Beneath the argument there lies that Herbertian, and Miltonic, confidence in the ability of truth to command its own assent in the long run.

Acontius was a friend of both Lelio Socinus and of his nephew Faustus Socinus (1539–1604), and there is a definite connection between Acontius's urgings and the Socinian teachings; the Socinians too sought to reduce the essential doctrines to a few easily comprehended principles of the New Testament upon which agreement might easily be reached. The impulse behind this desire was, as in Acontius and later in Herbert, the disgust and indeed despair with which so many men were confronted in the recurrent wars of religion. The Socinian programme was founded on the principles of 'the light of reason', and is certainly one of the many and various sources which contributed to eighteenth-century deism. One of the most persistent opponents of the Socinians was Francis Cheynell, whose work on *The Rise, Growth and Danger of Socinianisme* was published in 1643. It is as much an attack on 'natural religion' as upon Socinianism itself, and upon all religion which rejects 'the weightiest Articles of the Christian faith, because Reason cannot discover them to be true by her own light'. It is in fact a rejection also of the tradition we have been following, for Cheynell throws up his hands and exclaims with high-pitched irony: 'Let us then Canonize the Heathen for Saints, and put Hermes, Phocylides, Pythagoras, Socrates, Plato, Plotinus, Cicero, Zorcaster, Iamblichus, Epictetus, Simplicius into our Rubrike', and he adds, apparently for good measure but it betrays his lack of perception, 'let not Aristotle, Alexander, or Averroes be left out'.[53] It is therefore no surprise to find that to Cheynell is attributed the first formal denunciation of Acontius's classic plea for toleration: Cheynell condemned the 'pestilent heresy' of the *Satanae* to the Westminster Assembly in 1648, and got himself appointed to head a committee to investigate further. The committee later recommended that the book be interdicted and its author declared, ironically, a heretic.[54]

Herbert's *De veritate* stands almost equidistantly between two writers on toleration, Castellio and Locke, who are of special significance because they offer, together with the plea for religious liberty, a formal epistemological basis. Roland Bainton pointed to the importance of such a combination when, in his fine series of essays on Castellio, he suggested that 'so far as I know, Castellio and Locke are the only two persons in the history of the struggle for religious liberty who wrote treatises both on the problem of liberty and on the problem of knowledge and brought the two into relation with each other'.[55] Herbert's own treatise may equally be seen as incorporating discussions of both problems in one.

Castellio's plea for the reduction of necessary dogma (and with that reduction a weakening of the platform of persecution) is reinforced by a moderated and tactical scepticism which examines belief in terms of the nature of human knowledge and points to the prevalence in religious matter of things which, because they are neither wholly certain nor wholly uncertain, cannot be maintained by coercion. It is not however a Pyrrhonian scepticism, for Castellio appeals to Reason 'the daughter of God', the inward principle of rationality common to all men, one of the tests of which is universality. Like Herbert, Castellio points to common notions as indicative of God's universal gift of reason, and he claims of our basic religious instincts that 'these rules are inscribed, as it were, by the finger of God in the hearts of all, and can no more be erased than the other common notions of men'; or again, 'the existence of God may be discerned by reason, for all nations following reason—unless they were savage and akin to brutes—have agreed on this'.[56] The practical consequences of this kind of rationalism for religious liberty was that the mind can be convinced only by evidence and reason, not the sword of the magistrate, and that persecution in the interest of dogmas which cannot be positively known is criminally inappropriate.

Castellio's influence is hard to determine; indeed it is doubtful whether he exerted any direct influence at all. But through natural successors like Acontius (who, though probably familiar with his work, made no acknowledgement) the position Castellio had taken was indirectly continued and, eventually and in different circumstances, implemented. To Castellio's rationalist defence of religious liberty and Acontius's urgings, Herbert adds his own contribution of the eirenic of the Commons Notions and the assertion of the universality of religious truth. It has been suggested that Locke, during his exile in Holland, became acquainted with Castellio's work, confirmed in Locke's correspondence with Philip Limborch in Amsterdam.[57] The similarities and the differences between their ideas, and the comparison of both with Herbert, is especially interesting. Where Locke and Castellio propose an epistemology in which the source of knowledge is sense experience and revelation corrected by reason (loosely, the Aristotelian, Ciceronian tradition), Herbert characteristically uses his 'reason' in apparently antithetical ways which allows, like Aristotelian and scholastic method, the empirical derivation of general ideas from the data of sensation, and which employs also reason in its Platonic and Augustinian sense as that rational consciousness which grasps ultimate truths through intuition and faith. In neither Castellio nor Locke, however, is a pure empiricism maintained, otherwise reason could never surmount the data of sense. Castellio posits common notions, and Locke (in this more sophisticated but perhaps less coherent) denies innate ideas and puts forward instead intuitive modes of apprehension which can be seen as amounting to wellnigh the same thing. Both men relate the problem of knowledge to the problem of liberty, but with a difference of emphasis that suggests the difference in religious climate created by nearly a hundred years of propaganda on behalf of toleration. In Castellio's day men persecuted on behalf of 'truth'; in Locke's day in England on behalf of good order. Lord Herbert's own experience included both motivations, from the earlier passionate friction of ideal religious questions to the confused religio-political skirmishing of the English Civil War. Theological bitterness and intensity of religious feeling was steadily subsiding throughout the Restoration period; the power of Calvinism had declined and neither the Anglican Church nor the nonconformist Churches and sects made any pretence any longer of being custodians of exclusive truth. Locke, formally designating religion to that mode of knowing which he calls probability, whose evidence is the conformity of the belief in question with previous experience, knowledge and sensation, and the testimony of other persons (the first and 'highest degree of probability' being 'when the general consent of all men, in all ages, as far as it can be known, concurs with a man's constant and never failing experience in like cases'[58]), uses this epistemological basis for the ethical principle of toleration. In his *Third Letter for Toleration* (1690) he argues that in matters which are only probable—and he refers particularly to religion—and since another person's views may be as 'correct' as one's own, or perhaps even more so, it would seem the better course of action for men to respect each other's views. As a response to religious problems it is a far cry from both the rancour and the idealism of sixteenth- and early seventeenth-century controversy and leads, with little modification, to that comfortable attitude of Addison's friend Sir Roger, who 'told them, with the air of a man who would not give his judgement rashly, that much might be said on both sides'.[59]

As a natural link between Herbert and Locke on the epistemology of belief, William Chillingworth illustrates the manner in which a 'reasonable' religion encouraged a toleration of other 'reasonable' men's religious opinions, at least within the broad dispensation of Protestantism. Chillingworth's *The Religion of Protestants* (1638) was occasioned by the claim of the Catholic Edward Knott that Protestantism, so long as it refuses to admit the spiritual jurisdiction of the infallible Church of Rome, is damned.[60] In the course of his polemic Chillingworth expounds, though in a rather sketchy and unsystematic way, what is involved in the judgement of human certainty, and distinguishes between the truth of a proposition and the certainty one has that it is true. In terms of the Church, he argues that she may be infallibly certain of her rule yet not infallibly certain that the rule has been adhered to: 'she may be certain of the truth of some particular decrees, and yet not certain that she shall never decree but what is true'.[61] He argues too of the Scriptures that though they constitute the perfect rule of faith, when the rule is used to judge the truth of a proposed doctrine there is no assurance that the rule has been correctly applied, any more than we can be certain that our metaphysical or mathematical deductions from certain and true axioms are also certain or true. Chillingworth suggests in fact that very weakness in the human mind's capacity for applying rules correctly which David Hume pointed to in his *Treatise of Human Nature* (1739–40). From the distinctions he makes and the problems they raise Chillingworth goes on to determine how much certainty is possible, and to distinguish between the respective certainty of knowledge, belief and opinion. The main point here, however, is that Chillingworth is proposing first of all that one may not always infallibly know of a principle which is true that it is so, and secondly that error may well occur in its application. With regard to the claims of an infallible Church and the damnation of those without it his epistemology brings its own cautionary word; and with regard to the theory of the persecution of heretics it bears obvious resemblances to the epistemological arguments of Castellio which affirm that we simply do not know enough to persecute. Chillingworth develops further Castellio's prototypal idea of a 'reasonable' religion and regards—as Herbert in one of his aspects had done and as Locke was even more rigorously to do—religious truth as propositional, the evidence of which is the same as for non-religious truth. In making the certainty of commonsense, or of common experience, together with the modified and diminished status of revelation, the basis for religious belief, the traditional arguments for persecution simply wither and die for lack of nourishment.

Chillingworth's particular sort of ecclesiastical scepticism and his emphasis on the experience of reason and common sense was inevitably interpreted by some as atheism or at best Socinianism. That same Francis Cheynell who declared Acontius a heretic was to be found persecuting Chillingworth—goading him, while Chillingworth was on his deathbed, definitively to consign Turks, Papists and Socinians either to heaven or to hell. Disheartened by Chillingworth's refusal to comply, Cheynell denounced the heresy of *The Religion of Protestants* at its author's funeral, after throwing a copy of the book into the grave.[62]

Yet Chillingworth's work, and that of Acontius and Herbert and of all who pleaded for freedom and moderation, was not without its fruits. The Act of Toleration, passed in 1689, was the beginning, at least in England, of the triumph of an idea. Just before its passing we find the pungent judgement of Gilbert Burnet, in his Preface to *A Relation of the Death of the Primitive Persecutors* (1687), on the history of the Christian Church: 'such a Body, I say, if we may take our Saviours Character for a Rule, looks more like the Followers of that fallen Spirit, than the body of which the Lamb of God is the Head'.[63] And we recognise the voice of Cusanus and Bruno, Castellio, Acontius, Bodin and Herbert in a passage such as this:

a man may prevaricate, but still he thinks as he thinks, and cannot think otherwise, because he would have himself do so: But if a man is not the master of his own mind, much less is any other man the Master of it. No man has that Superiority over any other mans reason, as to expect, that it should always accommodate itself to his: and the severest exercise of Tyranny must still leave the thoughts at liberty.[64]

Before such a statement as Burnet's, too many men had been tried and burned according to the lights of what Herbert called 'particularised' Christianity, some of whom remain with us as testimony to the cause to which a man like Herbert added, however indirectly, a not insignificant contribution: Michael Servetus, whose scientific work betrayed an unorthodox (though accurate) theory of the pulmonary circulation of the blood and whose theology, foreshadowing Unitarian thought, modified Christ's Godhead, was found guilty of heresy and died at the stake in Geneva, on 27 October 1553, by edict of the Calvinist Inquisition;[65] on the Catholic side, Francesco Pucci, frequently in dispute with the Calvinists about predestination, published in Holland in 1592 his *De Christi Servatoris efficacitate*, dedicated to Pope Clement VIII, in which he expounded a universal redemption embracing even the pagans—a doctrine as heretical to the Holy Roman Office as it was to the Calvinists. Pucci was condemned for heresy, executed in the Tor di Nona, and afterwards burned on the Campo di Fiori in Rome in 1597. On the same Campo di Fiori, in the first year of the new century, Giordano Bruno (so stoutly to be defended by Coleridge) was also burned at the stake.[66] As Montaigne had once said, 'there is no enmity so excellent as the Christian'.

It was the eighteenth-century historian John Leland who described Herbert's design as the overturning of 'all revealed, or, as he calls it, particular religion', and the establishment of 'that natural and universal religion, the clearness and perfection of which he so much extols, in its room'[67]—highlighting a conflict between the 'particular' and the 'universal' which had produced in practice such agonising results. The 'universal' religion with which Herbert wished to replace 'particular' religion found its philosophical basis in Hermetism and Neoplatonism and its emotional impetus in the humanist criticisms of the accepted Christian synthesis. We have already seen how Herbert passes over the basic Christian mysteries of Incarnation and Atonement because he cannot believe in hereditary corruption any more than he can believe in a God who, unlike man his image, cannot forgive and forget. Both of these forces contributed to Herbert's inevitable destination in 'natural religion' as the only justifiable one, based on the ubiquitous Fatherhood of God, and on the perfectibility of man.

How accurately Herbert's position can be described as 'deistic' will be discussed in my final remarks; but certainly the 'philosophy of nature' in terms of which his conclusions are formulated and underpinned is manifestly and vastly different from the 'philosophy of nature' of eighteenth-century deism, however inexorably Herbert's writings may have contributed to its emergence. It is something of a paradox that Lord Herbert, by using the arguments and axioms of religious Hermetism and Platonism and by enunciating the metaphysical unity of God and man and the material universe, should in part be responsible for the radically dualistic conception of a deism for which the words 'in God we live, and move, and have our being' are destitute of all real significance. Indeed, the *coincidentia oppositorum* seems proved yet again as the extreme of Neoplatonic pantheism meets and joins the extreme of Newtonian deism. And yet this would perhaps seem to be the inevitable and necessary consequence of removing the profound metaphysical paradoxes which lie at the core of Christianity and which are the ground of spiritual experience and the life of the soul. In the effort to make religion 'acceptable' to the lay philosophical mind, and with the goal of universal tolerance, if not concord, achieved, religion itself is turned into little more than solid good sense, ripe for the inconclusive and elephantine simplicities of Charles Blount, John Toland and the rest.

Notes to chapter VII

1 For general works on toleration in this period, see especially W. K. Jordan, *The Development of Religious Toleration in England*, 4 vols, London and Cambridge, Mass., 1932–40, and Joseph Lecler S.J., *Histoire de la tolerance au siècle de la réforme*, 2 vols, Paris, 1955, trans. as *Toleration and the Reformation* by T. L. Westow, 2 vols, London, 1960. Other studies are those of Thomas Lyon, *The Theory of Religious Liberty in England, 1603–1639*, Cambridge, 1937; M. Searle Bates, *Religious Liberty, An Inquiry*, New York, 1935; and the valuable collection of essays in *Persecution and Liberty, Essays in Honor of George Lincoln Burr*, New York, 1931.

2 See Thomas Fuller, *The Church-History of Britain* (1655), ed. J. S. Brewer, Oxford, 1845, V, p. 419, and T. B. Howell, *State Trials*, II, pp. 731–5.

3 Lee, *Autobiography*, 1886, pp. 104–05.

4 See Hutcheson, *De Religione Laici*, introduction, New Haven, Conn., 1944, pp. 15–16.

5 See Lecler, *Toleration and the Reformation*, II, pp. 83–8; A. de Ruble, 'Francois de Montmorency, gouverneur de Paris et de l'Ile de France', in *Memoires de la Société de l'Histoire de Paris et de l'Ile de France*, VI, 1879, pp. 200–89; F. C. Palm, *Politics and Religion in Sixteenth-century France: A Study of the Career of Henry of Montmorency-Damville, Uncrowned King of the South*, Boston, Mass., 1927.

6 Trans. as *The Rights of War and Peace* by A. C. Campbell, London, 1901.

7 Pecock''s *Repressor* was edited by Babington, London, 1860.

8 Rossi, *Alle fonti del deismo*, Florence, 1942, p. 9.

9 A. O. Lovejoy, '*Nature* as norm in Tertullian', in *Essays in the History of Ideas*, New York, 1955. On Tertullian's attitude to freedom of conscience,

see P. de Monceaux, *Histoire littéraire de l'Afrique chrétienne*, I, Paris, 1902, pp. 237–45.

10 Cusanus, *De pace fidei*, in *Opera omnia*, Basle, 1565, pp. 860–79.

11 *D.V.*, p. 14; Carré, p. 90.

12 *D.V.*, p. 239; Carré, p. 321. It may be noticed that at the beginning of *D.V.*, under the proposition 'This truth is everywhere', Herbert had stated that 'the area of truth . . . is vast, and approaches so nearly the quality of infinity that it may be said to surpass existence itself' (*D.V.*, p. 8; Carré, pp. 83–4). It should be said in Herbert's defence that he is there pointing out the paradox that fictions and falsehoods can *truly* be described as such.

13 *D.V.*, p. 14; Carré, p. 91.

14 Cusanus, *De coniecturis*, lib. I, cap. xiii, in *Opera omnia*, pp. 88f. Cf. also *De venatione sapientia*, cap. xxxvi, *Opera*, p. 327, and many other passages.

15 *D.V.*, p. 89; Carré, p. 169.

16 *D.V.*, p. 175; Carré, pp. 256–7.

17 *D.V.*, p. 175; Carré, p. 257.

18 Cudworth, *True Intellectual System*, London, 1678, p. 737.

19 Ficino,, *De christiana religione*, in *Opera*, 2 vols, Basle, 1576, I, pp. 1–77, especially chap. 4.

20 Ficino, *loc. cit.*, I, 4, chap. 4.

21 See P. O. Kristeller's introduction to the *Oration*, in *The Renaissance Philosophy of Man*, Chicago, 1948, pp. 218–20. On Pico generally see Eugenio Garin, *Giovanni Pico della Mirandola, vita e dottrina*, Florence, 1937.

22 For the account that follows of Postel I am indebted to William J. Bouwsma's study, *Concordia Mundi: The Career and Thought of Guillaume Postel*, Cambridge, Mass., 1957, Harvard Historical Monographs, 33.

23 W. J. Bouwsma, 'Postel and the significance of Renaissance Cabalism', *Journal of the History of Ideas*, 15 (1954), pp. 218–32.

24 Postel, *De nativitate mediatoris ultima*, Basle, 1547, pp. 150–1. See Bouwsma, *Concordia mundi*, p. 118.

25 Postel's argument appears in the *Apologia pro Serveto*, ed. J. L. von Mosheim, Helmstaedt, 1748, p. 475. Bouwsma, *Concordia mundi*, p. 127.

26 Postel, *De orbis concordia*, pp. 266–70; Bouwsma, *Concordia mundi*, pp. 102–3.

27 Postel, *Absconditorum a constitutione mundi clavis*, Basle, 1547, pp. 33–4; Bouwsma, *Concordia mundi*, p. 173. Cf. also Postel, *De orbis concordia*, I.vii–viii.

28 For discussion of Postel's tendencies to natural religion Bouwsma refers to Léon Blanchet, *Campanella*, Paris, 1920, pp. 428–40, and to Francesco Oligiati, *L'anima dell' umanesimo e del rinascimento*, Milan, 1924, pp. 778–80.

29 Letter to Melanchthon, in *Postelliana*, ed. J. Kvačala, Juriev, 1915, p. 34. Bouwsma, *Concordia mundi* p. 126.

30 Bruno, *Spaccio della bestia trionfante*, 1584, dial. III, *Dialoghi italiani*, Florence, 1957, pp. 781–3. The passage cited here is in the eighteenth-century translation attributed to W. Morehead.

31 Coleridge, *Omniana or Horae Otiosores*, 2 vols, London, 1812, I, pp. 240–5.

32 Mornay, *De la vérité*, pp. 633f.

33 *A Woorke*, etc., London, 1587, 'Begunne to be translated into English by Sir Philip Sidney Knight, and at his request finished by Arthur Golding'. In

Sir Philip Sidney, ed. A. Feuillerat, Cambridge, 1923, III, pp. 249f.

34 Feuillerat, p. 272.

35 Feuillerat, p. 292. Mornay refers in the margin to *Pymander*, II, III, IV, V, VI, IX, XI, XIII (i.e. in the *Corpus hermeticum*), and to the *Asclepius*.

36 Feuillerat, p. 365.

37 Feuillerat, p. 264.

38 Feuillerat, p. 272. No marginal gloss.

39 F. A. Yates, *Giordano Bruno and the Hermetic Tradition*, London, 1964, p. 186.

40 Patrizi, *Nova de universis philosophia*, Ferrara, 1591, 2nd ed., Venice, 1593. A translation of the dedication is in W. Scott's edition of the *Hermetica*, Oxford, 1923–4, I, pp. 39f.

41 See F. A. Yates, *loc. cit.*, p. 183; Luigi Firpo, 'Filosofia italiana e controrifirma', *Rivista di Filosofia*, XLI (1950), pp. 150–73.

41 *DRG*, Lewis, pp. 89–90.

43 *DRG*, Lewis, p. 269.

44 *DRG*, Lewis, p. 386.

45 George H. Sabine, 'The *Colloquium heptaplomores* of Jean Bodin', in *Persecution and Liberty*, New York, 1931, p. 289.

46 Lord Brooke, *The Nature of Truth*, London, 1640, chaps. VI–VIII.

47 Lord Brooke, *Discourse opening the nature of that episcopacie which is exercised in England*, London, 1641, p. 33.

48 Browne, *Religio medici*, I, 56.

49 Burton, *Anatomy of Melancholy*, 1621, part I, sect. ii, mem. iii, subs. viii.

50 Acontius, *De methodo, hoc est, de recta investigandarum tradendanumque scientiarum ratione*, Basle, 1558. See W. K. Jordan, *The Development of Religious Toleration* in England, I, p. 318.

51 Acontius, *Satanae stratagemata*, Basle, 1565, and many reprints. *Satan's Stratagems*, trans. W. T. Curtis, introd. by C. D. O'Malley, in 'Occasional papers: English series No. 5', parts I and II, Sutro Branch of California State Library, San Francisco, April–May 1940.

52 W. K. Jordan's paraphrase, *loc. cit.*, I, pp. 358–9.

53 The passage is quoted in full in George T. Buckley's *Atheism in the English Renaissance*, Chicago, Ill., 1932, p. 59.

54 See Jordan, I, p. 364 n.

55 R. H. Bainton, 'Sebastian Castellio and the British–American tradition', in his *Studies on the Reformation*, London, 1964, p. 183.

56 Castellio, *De arte dubitandi et confitendi, ignorandi et sciendi*, written 1563; Latin text ed. D. Cantimori and E. Fiest, in *Reale Accademia d'Italia, Studi e Documenti*, VII, Rome, 1937, p. 352; p. 383. See R. H. Bainton, 'New documents on early Protestant rationalism', in *Studies on the Reformation*, chap. II; and E. Fiest, 'Castellio's *De arte dubitandi* and the problem of religious liberty', in the collection *Autour de Michel Servet et de Sébastien Castellion*, Haarlem, 1953, pp. 244–58.

57 R. H. Bainton, 'Sebastian Castellio and the British–American tradition', *loc. cit.*, p. 182.

58 Locke, *Essay Concerning Human Understanding*, London, 1690, IV, 16, 6.

59 Addison, *The Spectator*, No. 122.

60 Chillingworth, *The Religion of Protestants, a Safe Way to Salvation*, Oxford, 1638; Edward Knott, *Mercy and Truth, or Charity Maintained by Catholiques*, St Omer, 1634.

61 *The Works of William Chillingworth*, Philadelphia, 1844, p. 204.

62 See Cheynell's pamphlet, *Chillingworthi Novissima; or the Sickenesse, Heresy, Death and Buriall of William Chillingworth*, London, 1644.

63 Burnet, *A Relation* etc., by Lactantius, 'Englished by Gilbert Burnet D.D. to which he hath made a large Preface concerning Persecution', Amsterdam, 1687, p. 25.

64 Burnet, *ibid.*, p. 16.

65 Servetus's trial is recorded in *Registres de la Compagnie des Pasteurs de Genève au Temps de Calvin, II (1553–1564)*, ed. J-F. Bergier, *Travaux d'Humanisme et Renaissance*, LV, Geneva, 1962.

66 See Luigi Firpo, 'Processo e morte di Francesco Pucci', *Rivista di Filosofia*, XL, 1949; for the record of Bruno's trial, see D. W. Singer, *Giordano Bruno: His Life and Thought*, New York, 1950.

67 John Leland, *A View of the Principal Deistical Writers*, London, 1754, p. 11.

VIII
DEISTS AND DEISM

If our religious tenets ever want a further elucidation, we shall not call on atheists to explain them.

Edmund Burke

One of the difficulties in describing Herbert's religious position is that categories like 'deist', 'rationalist', 'theist', or 'naturalist' seem to fit him only where they touch, and the reason is that Herbert was himself instrumental in giving to such words the content we now ascribe to them. Some commentators, both seventeenth-century and modern, may frankly give up the unequal struggle against the plethora of labels and 'isms' bandied about in the seventeenth century to define religious adversaries, and allow the term 'deist' to mean simply 'a follower of Lord Herbert', or 'one who subscribed to the position on religion expressed by Lord Herbert'.[1] The problem with this kind of definition of deism is of course that it cannot accommodate the *differences* between the 'position on religion' expressed by Herbert and the positions of either earlier and contemporary 'deists' or of his later subscribers. There is, for example, little for the 'sceptical deist' of the Enlightenment to warm to (beyond the phrase 'matters impertinent to salvation') in Herbert's (entirely characteristic) discussion of the Reformation necessity for a 'Catholick and visible Doctrine' and his commendation of the early Reformers for attempting to replace papal authority with doctrines that reached to 'Antiquity in all times' and 'Universality in all places', praising men who did not 'think themselves bound to study the Intricacies and Sophisms of Authors in matters impertinent to salvation; but were content with a Single Faith in God, the Comfort of a good Life, and Hope of a better upon true Repentance; taking the rest for the most part upon the Faith of the Church.'[2] Whatever the ultimate influence of his work, there is little in the tone of these passages from *Henry VIII*, or from similar expressions elsewhere of the relation of particular

Churches to his conception of an *ecclesia generalis*, that warrant the
identification of Herbert's motives and goals with those of later
'deists', however directly or indirectly he may have contributed to
their emergence.

  For the popular and inherited description of Herbert as 'the father
of English Deism' we are indebted to John Leland, in his *A View of
the Principal Deistical Writers* (1745), in which Herbert is the subject of
letters I and II. Leland, looking back over a century of controversy,
sees Herbert as the progenitor of the deistical writers and the author
of English rational theology. His perspective is however an English
one, and he has little to say about those continental relations and
currents of thought in which Herbert himself—as an international
Renaissance *uomo universale*, a European Latinist, diplomat and
energetic publicist—so actively participated. Leland, always an
acute critic, takes special care not to attribute to Herbert all the
errors and excesses which subsequent deists of a different colour
have propagated. He describes Herbert's intentions justly and
without obvious prejudice, notes his eirenic ambitions, and includes
an interesting postscript in which 'A Remarkable Incident relating
to Lord Herbert' is considered—the account, that is, of Herbert's
sign from heaven which is recorded in the autobiography and which
was quoted to Leland by an anonymous letter-writer who had
obviously come across it in MS (the text of the autobiography was
not printed until 1764). The correspondent defends Herbert stoutly:
'He was nevertheless a Deist of more honour, and of greater candour
and decency, as he was of far greater parts and learning, than many
that have appeared under that denomination since'. Leland
substantially agrees.

  The reaction of the Presbyterian Thomas Halyburton was
altogether more violent. In his polemical *Natural Religion Insufficient*
(1714) he turns to Herbert as the author of lies: 'The learn'd Lord
Herbert was the First who did cultivate this Notion, and lick'd
Deism, and brought it to something of a Form'. Halyburton roundly
satirises deism as 'a fine, Modish, Reasonable Religion, meet for a
Gentleman, a Man of Wit and Reason', and refuses to recognise any
distinction betwen 'deist' and 'atheist': 'the empty Cavills of the
execrable Herd of blasphemous Athiests, or Deists, as they would be
called, amount to a very small, and contemptible account'. He
points repeatedly to Herbert and never tires of observing that there
is nothing in the contemporary deists which was not to be found first

of all in Herbert. He largely ignores Herbert's philosophy and responds only to the 'peculiar Notions'; he does not, as Herbert himself would have insisted he should, refer back to the metaphysics of *De veritate* in order to appreciate the point of the religious ideas, but shows a not altogether surprising reluctance to expend 'greater Application than perhaps the Matter is worth'. Like so many readers of Herbert, he jibs at Herbert's style ('our Author's Way of Writing made it somewhat difficult to find his Argument') and claims that 'we are bid search a Needle amongst a Heap of Hay'—'which', he adds knowingly, 'looks exceeding suspicious like'.[3] The general summary of deism as 'Paganism-à-la-Mode', immediately identifiable in Halyburton's mind with a profligate court and an irreligious Restoration stage, indicates an important aspect of 'deist' manifestations and accounts in part for the tone of moral outrage which Halyburton brings to bear on a man so determinedly upright and honourable as Lord Herbert.

We may well wonder what schisms and arguments, what political, ecclesiastical and cultural pressures and upheavals contributed to Herbert's easy assimilation into the Enlightenment, and what misunderstandings, falsifications or modifications were involved in his apparent destiny among the revolutionary iconoclasts of the early eighteenth century. Any attempt at a 'history of deism' is notoriously difficult, partly because the term is itself so confused in its usage, both by the men most intimately involved in such controversies and by more modern historians of ideas; and partly because some of the most philosophically significant aspects of a 'deistic' point of view are to be found embedded in Christian theology from Tertullian and the early Fathers, through Neoplatonist theologians over many centuries, to Renaissance syncretists and tolerationalists, and shared in the seventeenth century by such a motley assortment as rationalist philosophers and mathematicians, Erastian monarchists, international legalists, radical Puritan republicans, and political and ecclesiastical anarchists. The caveat here must be Mario Rossi's observation that in an important sense 'deism is not a philosophical doctrine or a scientific discovery: it is a human tendency'. The word itself seems to have arisen first among men who wished, by its use, to avoid the charge of atheism. In the mid sixteenth century the Swiss reformer Viret, a colleague of Calvin at Geneva, said that he had heard of a band calling themselves 'deists', 'a quite new word, which they wish to oppose to atheist'. He was apparently describing a group of controversialists who held that God may be known by the light of nature apart from revelation, and Viret went on to remark (a little cynically one might feel) that these deists 'mock all religion, notwithstanding that they accommodate themselves, as far as outward appearance is concerned, to the religion of those with whom they have to live, or whom they wish to please, or whom they fear'.[4] It is interesting too to note that the energetic reunionist Guillaume Postel was also regarded by his Protestant enemies as the founder of 'a sect of those who through mockery of God call themselves deists'.[5] What may have been true of those wary and timorous early deists Viret described was not true of more convinced and serious thinkers nor of course was it true of Herbert, who consistently turned an independent and even eccentric face to the world about him.

From its earliest use, the term included two elements: a body of philosophical or theological opinion concerned with the nature of reason, revelation and belief; and a political, social or moral stance usually involving suggestions of political deviousness, ecclesiastical indifference, and most controversial of all, of epicureanism, libertinism and general moral laxness. The two elements often seem to run in parallel or become confused with each other, so that the libertine posture of many a 'deistic' representative can rest on no serious religious response whatever, and men wrestling with the fundamentals of belief or the nature of ecclesiastical allegiance can immediately be consigned to the ranks of lascivious moral anarchists.

Herbert's more immediate contemporaries obviously felt the need for some kind of classification of opponents and their characteristics, so that the unwary might hope to pick their way through the chaos of post-Reformation schismatics and avoid atheistical errors. Such a list was furnished by Gisbert Voetius, a professor at Utrecht whose lectures on atheism were delivered before the university in the summer of 1639 and printed in his *Disputationes selectae* (Utrecht, 1648–60). Voetius distinguishes between 'proper atheists' who sow seeds of doubt by over-subtle argument, and 'participating atheists' who try to blot out the human consciousness of God. Atheists are generally divided into 'practical' and 'speculative' varieties, further subdivided into those who practise a wrong religion (heathen); those who fail to observe proper ceremonies (indifferentists); those who attend worship for the sake of policy (Machiavellists and Politiques); those who are merely careless sensualists; and those, among them Epicureans, libertines, and 'deists', who consider religion useless. 'Speculative' atheists may be of either the mild or the dangerous kind. The former 'refuse to believe in immortality or the resurrection of the body', and the latter sort do not believe in Providence, scorn the Bible, distrust the natural light, and doubt some or all of the divine attributes.[6] What is of particular interest here is that deists are classified as 'practical athiests' who belong in the company of libertines and Epicureans. Lists very similar to Voetius's can be found in Thomas Edwards's celebrated *Gangraena*, 'Or a Catalogue and Discovery of many of the Errors, Heresies, Blasphemies, and pernicious Practices of the Sectaries of this Time'. The Presbyterian Edwards lists one hundred and eighty sects, among them anti-scripturists, Skeptics and Questionists, and libertines or deists, and yet is able to declare, in the face of this manifest challenge, that 'a Toleration is the grand design of the Devil, his masterpiece and chief engine'.[7] In the latter part of the century Voetius's terms of practical and speculative atheists find their way too into Dr Sherlock's *Practical Discourse of Religious Assemblies* (1681).

Herbert's own contacts with early continental deism may be deduced both from the personalities he met, or clashed with, in France, or whose university lectures he attended, and also from the works he collected for his own library. A large proportion of his books was naturally on religious or ecclesiastical matters, and the fair proportion of recent works of a controversial or provocative nature (rather than, for instance, devotional works or works of biblical exegesis) would indicate Herbert's own enquiring and provocative mind, and particularly (in addition to his obsessive concern with immortality) his interest in the two issues of free will and predestination, and of the relation of ancient religions to Christian faith. Some random examples might suggest Herbert's penchant: besides works by Bruno, Campanella (including his *De praedestinatione et reprobatione*, Paris, 1636), Arminius (*Opera theologica*, Leyden, 1629), Grotius, and Bernard Ochinus on free will and predestination, he owned copies of the writings of Francisco Vicomercato (1500-70) who, in 'deistical' fashion, separated faith from reason, substituted Nature for Providence, and turned the world over to the operation of natural laws; Nicolas Vedelius's

Rationale theologicum, sue de necessitate et vero usu principiorum rationis et philosophiae in controversiis theologicis (Geneva, 1628); Henry Bullinger's *Antiquissima fides et vera religio* (Zurich, 1544); or an unidentified work entitled *De ecclesiastica et politica potestate*—besides the monumental works on comparative religion by Mersenne, Vossius and Selden.

'Deistic' ideas were implicit in the teachings of Averroist Aristotelians of the schools of Venice and Padua, as they were, potentially or actually, in the sceptical and relativist stance of Montaigne, Charron and Bodin. The reunionist strategies and the 'natural religion' of men like Ficino, Pico, Postel, Castellio, Acontius, Grotius and others foreshadowed 'deistic' principles, as indeed did the thought of that moderate and enlightened Christian Erasmus, whose pronouncements and general attitude could lead inexorably to the more radical theology of his Protestant countrymen, Coornhert, Oldenbarneveldt and Grotius—in fact to a universal theism closely resembling (in so far as it can be defined in isolation from such complex movements of ideas) 'deism'. With the gradual extension of freedom of thought and expression, such deistic ideas could acquire a wider and more open circulation, particularly in sophisticated court and university circles, and inevitably gathering up with them more exhibitionist or adventurous attitudes. No one might publish Bodin's *Heptaplomores*, or the anonymous sixteenth-century treatise on deism, *Origo et fundamenta religionis. Christianae*, in which deistic statements of the relation between God and natural human reason and between primitive religion and Christianity are clearly presented,[8] but they were undoubtedly circulated, along with more flamboyant and notorious productions such as the legendary *De tribus impostoribus*, said to have originated in the cosmopolitan court of Frederick II, in which the founders of the three religions, Jesus, Mohammed and Moses, are held up as impostors.[9] It is of course highly probable that Herbert, during his travels in Europe and during his long residence at the court in Paris, had taken part in discussions with 'deistic' spokesmen and was aware of a deistic tradition of thought of which he knew himself not to be the first exponent and towards many aspects of which he may have felt himself to be totally opposed, not least the 'deistic' denial of immortality and of God's involvement with the world of man.

Among the most energetic of the revolutionary 'deistic' thinkers we may number the notorious Lucillo Vanini (1585–1619), the

'Eagle of the Atheists', who disseminated a doctrine of an absentee God, exhibiting a kind of Averroism which 'removed' God from the world; not God but Nature had created man, and man is thrown back, in Stoic fashion, on ethical self-sufficiency and natural reason. Vanini tended to deny the immortality of the soul, though he remained hesitant on the point. Caesarius Cremonini (1550–1631), whose lectures Herbert attended at Padua, followed much the same lines as Vanini, denying God's involvement in the world, affirming clearly that the human soul was mortal, and allowing Christ no tenable place in his doctrines. Indeed, for both Cremonini and Vanini, Christ and Moses were no more than impostors who had tricked mankind. What the young Herbert made of all this we can only surmise; what is not surmise is that such doctrines made no appearance in Herbert's subsequent religious philosophy, however stimulating he may have found Cremonini's attitude towards ecclesiastical discipline and towards revealed religion. Christ as Impostor formed the theme of a group of poems written by Théophile de Viau (1590–1626), with whose career Herbert also had some connection and whom he may well have met in Paris. The burden of Théophile's message is a kind of parody of Montaigne's sceptical epicureanism, though without Montaigne's fideistic conclusions: indulge your own nature and your own passions, enjoy yourself on earth, for God is far above the tribulations of a world where Nature not God is the governor. Théophile exhibited the libertine ingredient in deism, and his own moral adventurousness and that of his band of disciples caused a scandal at the court of Louis XIII. Théophile's ideas were popularised in the *Quatraine du Déiste* (1622).[10] Both Vanini and Théophile visited England. Vanini preached in the London Italian churches, but left England after a short time to join his group of disciples in Languedoc. Théophile came to England in an embassy sent by Louis XIII, and his reputation preceded him. James I refused to see him, but the Duke of Buckingham was less fastidious and fulfilled the function of patron while Théophile was in England. When Théophile, back in France, was briefly imprisoned by Louis for scandalous behaviour, Buckingham interceded on his behalf, the poet having earlier presented the Duke with some verses.[11] Théophile's patronage in the French court was equally impressive, for in Paris this role was taken first of all by Louis's favourite the Duke of Luynes (with whom Herbert, it may be recalled, had violently quarrelled and grew to

detest) and later by the son of Herbert's host at Merlou, the younger
Duke of Montmorency, active among the French 'Politiques'. It is
evident that a form of deism, even as represented in Théophile's
'libertinage', found some support in court circles as well as in
universities like Padua, invariably flourishing among men of high
birth or of great learning who regarded themselves as an aristocratic
coterie whose teachings simpler folk could never appreciate. It was
certainly not conceived of as in any sense a general layman's
religion, nor as a basis for coming to terms with the claims of
particular Churches.

The writings of these continental atheist-deists were not widely
known, certainly not in England. Despite their visits to England,
Vanini found no translator, though excerpts existed in MS (Donne
owned a copy of his works); Théophile's poems did not find a
translator either, though it seems that at least two of Cremonini's
lectures circulated in MS, whilst a copy of his writings had a place in
Herbert's library. Any excitement that this kind of deism may have
generated seems to have been more concerned with its libertine
aspects than with a serious consideration of religious principle, and
what support it gained probably derived from its usefulness as a
sophisticated fly-whisk to beat down what was seen as religious
hypocrisy or fanaticism. As far as it had a doctrinal character, it
revealed Moses and Christ as impostors, tended to deny the
immortality of the soul, and regarded the concept of religion merely
as a utilitarian device for keeping the common people in check.

Specific criticisms of the doctrinal character of Herbert's own
religious views came from a number of hands, few of them addressed
to Herbert in his own lifetime. The most obvious and predictable
criticisms of Herbert's five common religious notions (his 'deistic'
Articles of Religion), were that they are not innate, that they are not
universal, and that they are certainly not sufficient. The first
criticism could rest, as we have seen earlier, on a misunderstanding
of Herbert's theory of knowledge: the ideas are not innate, only the
modes of thought that will elicit them—though in practice the result
might be seen, with some justice, as coming to the same thing.
Montaigne for one would have doubted their universality; and John
Leland makes the opposite point that a thing's not being universal
does not therefore make it untrue: 'He ought not therefore to make a
thing's being controverted to be a proof of its uncertainty, and that
men can come to no satisfaction about it.' And Leland adds the

comment—somewhat ironically in the light of Herbert's avowed motives—that this procedure is 'a principle which he and other Deists often insist upon, but which manifestly leads to universal scepticism'.[12] To support the final criticism of insufficiency a whole throng of voices were at last raised, directed not necessarily at Herbert specifically, but at all who made such claims of 'natural revelation', and their fulminations echoed far into the eighteenth century. Herbert himself had never claimed that the articles were sufficient, or that by themselves they constituted a complete religion; he simply intended to demonstrate, in a context of religious truth-claims and counter-claims, that such beliefs form the core of all religious experience and other beliefs advanced as necessary to salvation must either comply with the same stringently rational and universal standards he himself had employed in laying down these common notions, or be left entirely to the individual conscience—a procedure which was of course neither so unusual nor so original to Herbert as one is sometimes led to think.

The most serious objection from 'orthodox' Christianity focused on Herbert's rationalist and strategic omission of the cardinal doctrine of the Incarnation. One of the first comments in English came from Richard Baxter, and he presents us with a characteristic early criticism of Herbert's views. The second part of Baxter's tract *More Reasons for the Christian Religion, and No Reason Against It* (printed in 1672) was entitled 'Some ANIMADVERSIONS on a Tractate *De Veritate*, written by the Noble and Learned Edward Herbert, Baron of Chirbury', and was dedicated to Sir Henry Herbert, Lord Herbert's brother. It is interesting for the gently satirical comparison Baxter draws between Edward and his other brother George, the author of *The Temple* and saintly priest of Bemerton:

I am so far from writing against the whole Book, that I take most of his Rules and Notions *de Veritate*, to be of singular use. And had so great a wit had but the Internal Conditions due to such an Intellectual apprehension, as his and your holy and excellent Brother had; no doubt but our supernatural Revelations and Verities, would have appeared evident to him, and possesst his soul with so sweet a gust and fervent ascendent holy LOVE, as breatheth in Mr G. Herbert's Poems, and as would have made them as clear to him in their kind, as some of his *Notitiae Communes*.[13]

Baxter gets to the nub of the problem after a few preliminary remarks about Herbert's philosophy generally. His central objection, which by implication separates Edward from George

Herbert, is that there is no mention of 'the eternal logos, wisdome or word of God Incarnate': 'you', Baxter accuses, 'lay the main stress on this, that All men may be saved by true faith in God and true Repentance without believing in a Crucified Christ'.[14] In a less guarded aside Baxter gives an opinion of *De veritate* as 'but learned froth and vanity', but he nowhere refers to Herbert as a deist.

With the further publication of *Religio laici* and the later *De religione gentilium* (which made its rather uncertain and muted entry into a religious climate rather different from that of its genesis), Herbert gradually became known as someone more than merely 'learned', and he was accordingly abhorred or welcomed as the only begetter of the revolutionary deists who appeared to be springing up on all sides. To some of his accusers 'atheist' and 'deist' were more or less interchangeable terms; to others there was some distinction to be drawn, but in neither case could Herbert possibly be regarded as having offered the Christian churches any service. To yet others, Herbert's reputation as a deist, whether true or merely imputed, provided the prestige of learning and position which they felt would enhance their own religious speculations. Those who claimed his support, like his professed 'disciple' Charles Blount (who also managed to claim at various stages of his career the conflicting benefit of Montaigne and Hobbes), often read him with a mind predisposed to find in him what they were looking for. Blount, in his own *Religio laici* (1683) (which he appears to have written up from both Herbert's *Religio laici* and possibly the Herbertian MS of the *Dialogue of a Tutor and his Pupil*),[15] claims with characteristic enthusiasm and fulsomeness that

The Articles which I propose, are Five in number; and the same which the great Oracle and Commander of his Time, for Wit, Learning, and Courage, *tam Marti quam Mercurio*, the Lord Herbert, Baron of Cherbury, delivered; and which (I am confident) are so Catholique or Universal, that all the Religions that ever were, are, or (I believe) ever shall be, did, do, and will embrace them.[16]

Generally speaking however Herbert's writings seem in fact to have been little read in England during the twenty-five years or so following his death; his 1645 'collected works' of *De veritate*, *Religio laici* and *De causis errorum* was reprinted only once, in 1656, and the posthumous *De religione gentilium* was not published in England at all in the seventeenth century, being printed twice in Amsterdam in 1663 and 1665. Only a few enthusiasts or professional plunderers like Blount appear to have read his works with any degree of attention, though he attracted rather more notice on the continent. In two works in particular he was pilloried as an atheist of the most dangerous kind, being elevated as one of the three 'Erz-Betrieger' or great impostors of the age. Christian Kortholt the Elder attacked Herbert in his own version of the trinity of impostors, *De tribus impostoribus magnis* (Cologne, 1680), together with Hobbes and Spinoza; Michael Berns assembled the same trio in his *Althar der Atheisten, der Heyden, und der Christen* (Hamburg, 1692). The combination of Herbert and Hobbes gives some indication of the extent to which Herbert was either misunderstood or not read, and the extent to which deistic and Hobbesian motives could be run together in the later seventeenth century. Criticisms of specific Herbertian doctrines also came from Johann Musäus, whose *Examen Cherburianismi* (Jena, 1675; Wittenberg, 1708) attacked the theory of the sufficiency of natural light, as did Peter Musäus's *Contra Edoardum Herbertum* (Keil, 1667), Christopher Franke's *Dissertatio de religione naturali contra Naturalistas et Remonstrantes, maxime Eduard Herbertum* ... (Kiel, 1666), George Seerup's *De legis Mosaicae divina origine et auctoritate diatribe, adversus E. Herbertum, Baronem de Cherbury* (Copenhagen, 1678), Gerhard Titius's *Disputatio theologica* ... *opposito libro De Religione Gentilium* (Helmstedt, 1667), and Ezechiel von Spanheim's *Animadversiones ad Eduardi Herberti de Cherbury* (Leipzig, 1745).

There were other commentators, with a greater appearance of impartiality, who either took a more indulgent view or had read Herbert more comprehensively. The first modern history of atheism, Jenkins Thomas Philipps's *Dissertatio historico-philosophico de atheismo sive historia atheismi* (London, 1716), relates all the traditional anecdotes about the Renaissance Italian atheists, condemns Hobbes for an atheist, but refrains from condemning Herbert of Cherbury. The *Theses theologicae de atheismo et superstitione* (1716) of Johan Buddeus, professor of theology at Jena, also reprints the conventional list of atheists, and votes blackly against Aretino, Cremonini, Bruno, Pomponazzi, Rabelais, Cardano, Vanini and Campanella; the sceptics Montaigne, Charron and Descartes escape the ultimate censure; Sir Thomas Browne was simply an indifferentist, while Herbert of Cherbury was no atheist, merely a deist. Buddeus praises Socrates as an enemy of superstition, thinks Plato very close to Christianity, and has a soft spot for Platonists generally. His *Theses*, directed especially against Spinoza, pillory Spinoza as Satan's pope and Hobbes his nuncio to Englishmen. But Buddeus is not prepared to complete the trio with Herbert; instead he claims that in unhappy England they now endure John Toland who 'surpasses in impiety all other atheists of all time'.[17] The judicious *Historia universalis atheismi* (Hildesheim, 1725) by J. F. Reimann (who was a friend of Leibniz) also seeks to weed out the falsely from the justly accused, and Reimann discusses the cases of Cardano, Charron and Montaigne and considers them either falsely or unfairly indicted. He refers to England as 'that home of sects and schisms' where the obvious atheists Hobbes, Charles Blount, Anthony Collins and John Toland flourish. But while condemning Herbert of Cherbury's 'disciples' and agreeing that men have said Herbert was a deist, Reimann is less prepared to take it on trust and even asks the question whether Herbert was not in fact a Christian.[18]

In such times of religious and ecclesiastical flux as these historians seek to document, it is hardly surprising that a card-index system of judgements breaks down, for the age began to feel its lack of a criterion of dismissal as acutely as it felt its lack of a criterion of truth. 'Deism' may be equivalent to 'atheism', and like atheism it may be used as an indiscriminate term of abuse for libertines, freethinkers or intransigent opponents alike. Other terms too were applied to those thought of as holding 'deistical' positions, the most common of them being 'antiscripturist' and 'theist', the latter term being used almost as frequently as 'deist' until at least the end of the century. Just as men open to charges of deism tended to be individualists who, eschewing tradition, avoided acknowledgement even of each other, preferring generally to speak as representatives of the intelligent, reflecting layman and appealing where necessary to the voice of the age (usually, as it finally turned out, as embodied in Locke), so definitions of their imputed activities tend to be variable and even contradictory. A characteristic comment, for example, that the sufficiency of reason in matters of religion and a rejection of any revelation which goes beyond the limits of reason constitute the marks of 'the Theists of our Age', could only be applied to Herbert by ignoring a great deal of what he actually says. Or again, one of the earliest answers to 'deism', William Assheton's *Admonition to a Deist* (1685), is addressed to someone who, while not denying God, denies the eternity of hell's torments and doubts that there is an afterlife or any reward or punishment in another world. Ralph

Cudworth's note on 'deism' describes only the Hobbesian doctrine that 'we are generally inclined to religion by the prejudices of education'.[19] Others, like Joseph Glanvill or the Cambridge Platonist George Rust, in his *Discourse of the Use of Reason in Matters of Religion* (London, 1683; Rust himself died in 1670), can diagnose in enthusiastic dissenting sects just that misunderstanding of the use of reason in religion that so many so-called 'deists' (like Herbert, and like too many a later Latitudinarian and Anglican divine) were seeking to correct. Rust in fact appeals to Herbert himself for support, and introduces Herbert's theory of Natural Instinct and its product the Common Notions to underline his own point about the way in which reason serves as a source of religious knowledge.[20] When Rust's friend Henry Hallywell edited the MS for printing (a few months, incidentally, after the appearance of Dryden's *Religio laici*, in which the 'Deist' assumed a somewhat clearer role), he saw fit to add a sub-title on his own account: 'Shewing, That Christianity Contains Nothing Repugnant to Right Reason; against Enthusiasts and Deists'. When a 'deist' is invoked to support (and in such a fundamental way) arguments against 'deists', we may feel driven to consult Herbert's Zetetics for help.

It has been argued that what prepared the English scene for the arrival and eventual triumph of liberalism, or of modes of religious thought of a 'deistic' chartacter, was the current of ideas already implicit in much radical Puritan and republican thought, and emanating not from continental coteries or massively learned works of rational theology but from within the Christian Churches of the Reformation itself.[21] Accounts of the background of English deism have usually concentrated on the philosophic, scientific or latitudinarian aspects of its growth, but it is as well to note the resemblance, both in its basic logic and in its ecclesiastical outworkings, between the rational or natural theologian's search for universally agreed points of religious experience and radical Puritan concern with 'fundamentals', for both could equally be regarded by an 'established' or traditionalist Church as dangerous threats to stability and security. Inner light, conscience, or right reason may not be very different in their operations; and arguments which assert the absolute supremacy of personal illumination can be assimilated easily with arguments from reason and its self-evident character. Philosophical debate in the abstract about criteria of truth or about authority and belief could be transformed, by the mid seventeenth century, into the most immediately pressing issue on the lips of all who were involved in the competing truth-claims and authority-claims of the ascendant sects. Besides the larger groupings of Presbyterians, Anglicans, Independents or Baptists, the Socinians, Levellers, Unitarians, Diggers and others were all competing for 'truth', ready to accuse others of imposture, and ready too to hold the 'priesthood' of others in contempt, generating in many, whether through passion or through disillusionement, an anticlericalism which differed scarcely a whit from the anticlericalism of 'deistic' or of Hobbesian propagandists.

Frequently, men of radical religious views were also political rationalists, for to many contemporaries religious 'heresy' and republicanism in politics went hand in hand. For example, among Leveller religious views, those of the literate and eirenic William Walwyn returned, like Hooker before him, to a reinstatement of reason as the faculty which justifies a belief in Scripture as a revelation. Richard Overton emphasised the primacy of reason in religious debate (though it led him to deny, like a number of 'deists', the soul's immortality). An extreme and colourful example of the association between radical Puritan views and 'deism' may be found in the libertine Ranter minister, Thomas Webbe, who contrived to call Christ an impostor, deny God's presence in the world, and applaud the necessity for indulging one's passions and appetites. The recognition which comes through from the moderate centre is that religion must indeed be simplified, cleansed, reformed; that sectarian strife is shameful; that fundamental Christianity is being betrayed on every hand. The Leveller Gerrard Winstanley's Herbertian conclusion was that self-interest prompted cults and sects, and that men ought to worship God in spirit and truth, with simple prayers and good works.

It is in fact quite possible to view the course of 'deism' and the course of radical Puritanism and republicanism as parallel movements with similar ambitions and similarities of method. Certainly, many an early eighteenth-century pamphleteer and satirist found the connection between republicanism and deism an established fact: a pamphlet by Ned Ward in 1703 identifies deism with a secret "Calveshead Clubb" which met to celebrate the anniversary of the beheading of Charles I; Abel Evans's *The Apparition* (1710) has some verses associating the republican Milton with Hobbes, Blount, Vanini, Spinoza and Matthew Tindal as a

deist; others could point to the deist Blount's borrowings from
Milton and Hobbes, or to John Toland's edition of Milton (1698);
and commentators like John Edwards and Jonathan Swift could
plausibly trace the origins of English deism not to Herbert of
Cherbury at all but to the republicanism of the 1640s. The Leveller
1649 draft of *An Agreement of the People* reads, in retrospect perhaps,
astonishingly like later deist proposals. It is worth noting how many
eighteenth-century republicans were also deists: Trenchard,
Molesworth, Gordon, Toland, Tindal, Baron, Paine; while
Unitarians, such as Price and Priestley, were also republicans.[22] It
would seem that many of the ideas usually associated with the deism
of the Enlightenment were very much in the Interregnum air, simply
waiting to be labelled 'deist' by critical historians like William
Stephens (*An Account of the Growth of Deism in England*, 1696), John
Leland and Thomas Halyburton. For such writers the association of
Herbert with later deism appeared natural and inevitable,
notwithstanding the inconvenience that he died before the
republicanism of 'the Puritan revolution' gained its temporary
victory and could not easily be identified with its ideals. In so far as
Herbert appeared to diminish the status of individual Churches,
minimised Christ, rehearsed a programme of fundamental religious
beliefs, and appeared to have reservations about the miraculous and
the supernatural (and what room for manoeuvre Herbert left on that
issue was appropriated quickly enough), he could, it appears,
confidently be called a deist, despite the fact that he signally failed to
'remove' God from Nature and history, failed to cancel out the Last
Judgement, failed to deny the soul's immortality, and failed to assert
republican precepts. The important fact to emphasise here must be
that in this confusion of currents of thought and the movements of
social, political and religious change, attention must be directed not
simply to apparently common ideas associated retrospectively with
deism, but to the motives and circumstances of those promoting
such ideas and of those accepting or rejecting them. There are in fact
many things in Herbert's cast of mind which distance him
irreconcilably from the title of 'deist' as it is generally and loosely
understood.

Confusions and disagreements about Herbert's theological
relationships are by no means the prerogative of the Restoration, but
are evident everywhere. J. M. Robertson, for instance, appeared to
make the same mistake as Christian Kortholt in regarding Herbert

and Hobbes as philosophic brothers; Robertson so emphasised the
'free-thinking' aspect of Herbert's writings as to ignore almost
entirely the other elements, so that his general view is the extremely
odd one of Herbert as the natural link between the philosophic
sceptic Pierre Charron and the materialist–atheist Thomas
Hobbes.[23] Uncertainty is again reflected in Sir Sidney Lee's aside (in
his article on Herbert in the *Dictionary of National Biography*) that
Herbert probably has more in common with the Cambridge
Platonists than the deists, and reflected back in Harold Hutcheson's
conclusion that, despite the differences between Herbert and the
deists, there is 'little resemblance' with the Cambridge Platonists
beyond 'a general dislike of intolerance and petty dogmatism'. [24]
Charles Lyttle probed deeper and considered Herbert in antithesis
to the deists as an 'ethical theist' and the advocate of a true religion
above their materialistic conceptions.[25] Rossi's conclusion, after a
thorough appraisal, asserts that in a deist like Matthew Tindal,
whose *Christianity as Old as Creation: or, the Gospel, a Republication of the
Religion of Nature* (1730) was known as 'the Deist's Bible', 'the
naturalistic, innatistic and finally mystical point of view of Herbert
is abandoned', and that 'the deism of Tindal is utterly remote from
Herbert'.[26]

Herbert is primarily concerned with the problems of sectarian
persecution, the claims of individual Churches to possession of an
exclusive route to salvation, and the abuse of the religious instinct by
'authority'—concerns which are intimately related to the problems
of his immediate age and surroundings. But with the marked
increase in toleration after the Restoration the motive for 'deism'
had shifted significantly. The traditional enemy, the Church, was, as
Dryden observed as early as 1682 in the Preface to *Religio laici*, itself
suspect of infection with deism. The bombardments of a Toland or a
Thomas Woolston or an Anthony Collins become superfluous, for
the battle was already won. The path indicated by Lord Herbert
may be seen as broadening out into the rationalistic religion that
was to dominate English religious thought throughout the next
century, rather than narrowing into the by-ways of scoffers of
miracles or of ecclesiastical anarchists. The point is well illustrated
by Bishop Joseph Butler, who roundly attacked Tindal's *Christianity
as Old as Creation* though Butler himself, like Locke, was not in the
least exceptional in firmly emphasising the reasonableness of
Christianity. He gives a telling and sombre picture of the motives of

'deism' as they appeared to the orthodox, and it is a comment which could scarcely be made to incorporate Herbert of Cherbury:

> It is come, I know not how, to be taken for granted, by many persons, that Christianity is not so much as a subject of enquiry; but that it is now at length discovered to be fictitious. And accordingly they treat it as if, in the present age, this were an agreed point among all people of discernment, and nothing remained but to set it up as a principal subject of mirth and ridicule, as it were by way of reprisals, for its having so long interrupted the pleasures of the world.[27]

What is in Herbert a positive and constructive response to religious organisation ends in Bolingbroke in complete negation. In his posthumously published letters to Pope, Lord Bolingbroke makes some 'deistical' points which may bear some resemblance to issues raised by Herbert: that ecclesiastical tradition had been from the first ages for the most part founded on fraud, ignorance, superstition and 'enthusiasm'; and Christianity as it is usually conceived was the invention of men either very weak, very mad, or very knavish. The conclusion that 'it requires, therefore, no regard nor any inward conformity to it', and the sceptical and disingenuously self-demeaning shrug of the shoulders to justify such an assertion ('Man is a creature placed in the lowest form of intelligent beings' and only 'downright madness' would attempt to unveil the mysteries of divine wisdom), are of course utterly alien to the spirit of Herbert's inquiry. John Ogilvie, surveying the progress of deism, regards 'the present age' (he is writing in 1783) as one of 'total inanity' and notes some of deism's paradoxes: 'Among their first leaders, Lord Herbert is often the advocate of Christianity; and even Hobbes is not always explicit in his declarations against it'. But subsequent contestants sought to overthrow the Christian dispensation by various means, until 'with the names of Shaftesbury and Bolingbroke' the doctrine of future existence is expunged and all the moral perfections of the Deity annihilated. Ogilvie shrewdly and ironically remarks on the progress of Herbert's *notitiae communes*, which are

> in truth so far from being universal characteristics, that some of them are reprobated by his immediate successors in the same department. His doctrine of immortality, impressed upon every mind, comes out to be 'like children's tales, the amusement of the mere vulgar'. (Shaftesbury, *Character. Miscel.* 3. ch. 2.) His idea of punishment is inconsistent with our notion of the goodness of the Deity. (Shaftesbury, *Let. on Enthus.*) His maxim, that pardon will be the effect of repentance, is wholly irreconcileable with the more enlarged plans of his successors.[28]

It would begin to appear that Herbert gave rise to, or was thought of as having initiated, a movement which he would have detested. Bertrand Russell once observed that frequently 'the stages in the evolution of ideas have had almost the quality of the Hegelian dialectic: doctrines have developed, by steps that each seem natural, into their opposites'.[29] Clearly there was in Herbert's exploratory intelligence an element which anticipated the urbane dismissiveness of eighteenth-century deism—an element which, extended by circumstance and emotion to an intellectual extreme, could provide a Charles Blount with all the assistance he needed. And yet in Herbert himself this advanced rationalism was tempered by a sense of worship, actively exercised; a passionate religious instinct which could see the superfluity of proliferating Churches and professions; and, despite his warnings about revelations, by such a sense of the numinous that this extraordinary 'deist' has even been described as an animistic sun and star worshipper. Herbert's general relation to Christianity and more orthodox thought may be clarified a little by the reflection that, from the point of view of historical Christianity, both Protestant and Catholic, the 'orthodox' faith of the rationalistic Christianity of the Enlightenment to which Herbert contributed was itself dangerously close to heresy. Even without the benefit of deist activists, it tended to deny Christianity a monopoly of the truth, it consigned much that was crucial in the great Christian paradoxes to the status of superstitious mysteries, it diminished the force of the idea of a personal God, diminished the relevance of Christ's redemptive work in this world, and appeared uncomfortable about admitting any supernatural above the natural. Yet Herbert's involvement with it may be seen as an inevitable outcome of his earlier strategies against the excesses and dangers of his own age.

Where Neoplatonist Christians like Henry More and Ralph Cudworth confront both the problems posed by the Cartesian dualism of substances (Descartes's two realities of *res extensa* and *res cogitans* which implied the metaphysical separation of God and nature), and the problems posed by Hobbesian materialism and mechanistic determinism, so Herbert had earlier confronted the similar threats to an organic theism proposed in Montaigne's radical doubt and relativism and in Calvin's theological and ethical determinism. Herbert, like the Cambridge Platonists under similar pressure, goes back to those things that had held together the medieval and Renaissance synthesis of reason and religion, God and the natural world, drawing upon a Renaissance Hermetism and Platonism which sees no separation between God and the world but rather finds in them a total, organic and analogically related whole. On such metaphysical assumptions, and only on such, can Herbertian Common Notions be established. John Toland betrayed more than he suspected when he declared 'I banish all hypothesis from my philosophy'; and Matthew Tindal, perhaps the most important apologist of deism, was unable to list any common notions, nowhere precisely defined any positive articles of his creed, and above all was unable to establish his 'universal consent' upon any metaphysical basis.

If the rationalism of Descartes could threaten a dualism of God and the world, and thus contribute philosophically to deism's status, so too could the philosophy of empiricism. As a theological view deism, while drawing sustenance from rationalism, also marches hand in hand with empiricism. The English empiricists, from Bacon to Locke, were primarily concerned with drawing proper inferences from the observed facts of experience, with the result that first causes and metaphysical prepossessions generally came to be isolated from the more interesting and accessible second causes. Violence was threatened to the traditional view of God as transcendent and yet immanent, as distinct from the world and yet intimately and mysteriously concerned in all the workings of creation. A 'deistic' dualism was anticipated by Raleigh when, in an often quoted passage, he referred to Nature as 'nothing else but the strength and faculty which God hath infused into every creature, having no other self-ability than a clock, after it is wound by a man's hand', and suggested the exact jargon of later deists.[30] Robert Burton accused the contemporary empiricists of irreligion (by which he meant 'natural religion') because the empiricists insist that 'in spiritual things God must demonstrate all to sense, leave a pawn with them, or else seeke some other creditor. They will acknowledge Nature or Fortune, yet not God'.[31] It might of course be argued that Herbert's theory of 'plastic nature' posits such a deistic delegated autonomy, a world rendered describable in terms of apparent proximate causes; but that would be to misconstrue the point of the theory which was (as with Cudworth and More's insistence on it) to combat the materialists and empiricists for whom proximate causes were the *only* causes, entirely separable from God's immediate activities.

Locke, for example, presents a theory of knowledge dependent on sense experience and ratiocination; and although Locke can hardly be called a deist (despite Toland's entirely accurate boast that Locke was his inspiration), it is experience and ratiocination which form the ground of the deistical synthesis. When the Restoration deist or Christian apologist appeal again and again to the teleological argument they do so because it is based upon what, in an age of Newtonian physics, had come to be regarded as the only proper objects of knowledge—that is, mechanistic second causes—and because it can be 'demonstrated' by the light of empirical reason alone. As Bishop Berkeley observed, regretting this contraction of the world and the loss of a sense of the numinous, the effect of this new knowledge could be ambiguous: 'This consistent, uniform working, which so evidently displays the goodness and wisdom of that governing Spirit whose will constitutes the laws of Nature, is so far from leading our thoughts to him, that it rather sends them a-wandering after second causes'.[32]

In the religious apologetics of Restoration England, there is a stream of writings attacking or defending specific positions or Churches within the Christian community; and there is another stream of Christian apologetics addressed to the question of the reasonableness of the Christian religion, in which a supposed non-believer is subjected to a series of arguments and demonstrations. Towards the end of the century and for many years after this proposed non-believer requiring reasonable proofs was a sceptical deist. It is a little ironic that much earlier Christian apologetics on behalf of reason and common notions offered by men like Grotius or Philipe Mornay should be thought of as eventually leading, via Lord Herbert, to the sort of deism being attacked, with precisely similar arguments, by Restoration divines. It would seem that once the suggestions being made by Grotius or Mornay or Herbert became generally acceptable, the whole question was vastly altered. A new and different impulse can be discerned in the writings of Augustan deists and culminating in Bolingbroke which diverged further and further from the purposes and beliefs of Herbert. Herbert's stance is rooted in particular historical conditions of the earlier seventeenth century which did not embarrass Augustan minds, and to associate Herbert too uncritically with subsequent deists, or even to regard him as the best of a bad lot, is to look down the wrong end of the historical telescope. Herbert's arguments grow from the radical scepticism of Montaigne, the religious absolutism of Calvin, the turbulent history of the Reformation and the Counter-Reformation, and finally the beginning of the unique and catastrophic Civil War from which so much of the eighteenth century receives its bent and in which Lord Herbert ended his days, writing on his tomb that he was the author of the book named *De veritate* as a reminder, it could almost seem, of his unheeded vision of concord.

In reality Herbert is, for all his independence and apparent pragmatism, 'a true child of the Renaissance'.[33] He is a seeker after truth according to his lights, resisting the wordplay of authoritarian quibblers and reasserting the stature and dignity of man: man who, he says in true Renaissance fashion, 'is borne towards everything that the understanding comprehends or faith can grasp', man who 'raises his head, in other words, his intellectual faculties, above the clouds and freely contemplating all things, paces at large the courts of heaven and earth'.[34] In a prayer which he seems to have been in the habit of using Herbert praises God the Creator in terms which echo the spirit of Pico's *Oration on the Dignity of Man*, giving thanks because 'I was brought into this world, a living, free and reasonable creature, not senseless or bruitish, but capable of seeinge and understanding Thy wondrous works herein'.[35] This is the starting point of all his investigations, and its basis lies essentially in the Neoplatonic, Stoic and humanist world from which Herbert drew his deepest inspiration and by which his sensibility was formed. Its expression in philosophy is the concept of man the mediator and the theory of analogy; its expression in religious knowledge is an insistence on 'natural instinct' and intuition, by means of which alone we can speak of God. Such an emphasis is everywhere in Herbert, despite the elaborate and sophistic dressing of *De veritate*, and it is an emphasis which recurs later in the seventeenth century as a conscious resuscitation of Renaissance Platonism in the face of an advancing materialism.

It is in Coleridge that we find perhaps the most accurate 'placing' of Herbert in the seventeenth-century context—Herbert's Janus-like stance that looks at the same time backwards and forwards. In his discussion of John Smith's *Select Discourses*, Coleridge criticises the Cambridge Platonists for their want of 'a pre-inquisition into the mind, as part organ, part constituent, of all knowledge, an examination of the scales, weights, and measures themselves, abstracted from their objects'. Herbert specifically claimed the initiation of such an examination, and it is noteworthy that

Coleridge singles out Lord Herbert as one who had attempted it
(though it is also true that his criticism of the Cambridge Platonists
is not well founded, for Cudworth in fact carries such a
preinquisition further than any critic of empiricism had done up to
the time of Kant). In their search for a 'transcendental aesthetic,
logic and noetic' which would revive true religion the Cambridge
men were, Coleridge says, forced into Platonism, or Plotinism, 'by
the catachrestic language and skeleton half-truths of the systematic
divines of the Synod of Dort on the one hand, and by the sickly
broodings of the Pietists and Solomon's-Song preachers on the
other'. And he perceptively adds that 'Lord Herbert was at the
entrance of, nay, already some paces within, the shaft and adit of the
mine'.[36]

Notes to Chapter VIII

1 E.g. Phillip Harth, *Contexts of Dryden's Thought*. Chicago, Ill, 1968, pp. 77–8.
Cf. also G. R. Cragg, *Reason and Authority in the Eighteenth Century*, Cambridge,
1964, pp. 65–7.

2 *The Life and Raigne of King Henry VIII*, London, 1649, p. 71.

3 Halyburton, *Natural Religion Insufficient*, Edinburgh, 1714, p. 219; p. 23; p.
17. The full title of Halyburton's work reads: 'Natural Religion Insufficient;
and Reveal'd Necessary to Man's Happiness in his present State, or a
Rational Inquiry into the Principles of the modern Deists: Wherein is
largely discovered their utter Insufficiency to answer the great Ends of
Religion, and the Weakness of their Pleadings for the Sufficiency of Nature's
light to eternal Happiness; and particularly the Writings of the learn'd Lord
Herbert, the great Patron of Deism . . . in so far as they assert Nature's
Light able to conduct us to future Blessedness, are consider'd, and fully
answer'd.'

4 Viret, 'Epistre aux fidèles', *Instruction Chrestienne*, II. Quoted in Pierre
Bayle, *Dictionaire historique et critique*, Rotterdam, 1697, new ed., Paris, 1820,
14, p. 418, col. 2; p. 419, col. 1.

5 See *Histoire ecclésiastique des églises réformées au royaume de France*, Antwerp,
1580; ed. G. Baum and E. Cunitz, Paris, 1883

.6 *Disputationes*, part I, '*Dissertatio de atheismo*'. See Don Cameron Allen,
Doubt's Boundless Sea: Skepticism and Faith in the Renaissance, Baltimore, Md.,
1964, pp. 8f.

7 Edwards, *Gangraena*, second ed. 1646, pp. 152–3.

8 *Origo et fundamenta religionis Christianae*, first published in MS in *Zeitschrift
für die historische Theologie*, Leipzig, 1836, VI, pp. 180–259. See Louis I.
Bredvold, 'Deism before Lord Herbert', *Papers of the Michigan Academy of
Science, Arts and Letters*, 1924, IV, i, pp. 431–42.

9 A reprint of an early printed copy, dated 1598, is to be found in *De tribus impostoribus*, ed. G. Brunet, Paris, 1861, and in Philomneste Junior's *Le Traité des trois imposteurs*, Paris, 1867

10 The work may be read in *Voltaire Mourant*, Frederic Lachèvre, Paris, 1908, pp. 99–136.

11 See *Oeuvres Complètes de Théophile*, Paris, 1856, I, pp. 166–9

12 Leland, *A View*, *loc. cit.*, p. 11.

13 Baxter, *More Reasons*, London, 1672, p. A3.

14 *More Reasons*, p. 110.

15 See Blount's *Religio laici*, London, 1683, sig. A8v; Harth, *Contexts*, pp. 89–90.

16 Blount, *Religio laici*, pp. 48–9.

17 Buddeus, *Theses*, Jena, 1716. Trans. as *Traité de l'athéisme et de la superstitition* by L. Philon, Amsterdam, 1740, *Traité*, pp. 51–3. See D. C. Allen, *loc. cit.*, p. 17.

18 Reimann, *Historia*, Hildesheim, 1725, pp. 439f.

19 Cudworth, unpublished commonplace book, BM Add. MSS 4984; quoted in Harth, *loc, cit.*, p. 76 n 35.

20 Rust, *Discourse*, London, 1683, pp. 31–2.

21 See e.g. Gerald C. Brauer, 'Puritan mysticism and the development of liberalism', *Church History*, 19, Sept. 1950; George L. Mosse, 'Puritan radicalism and the enlightenment', *Church History*, 29, Dec. 1960; Roger L. Emerson, 'Heresy, the social order, and English deism', *Church History*, 37, 1968.

22 See R. L. Emerson, *loc. cit*; on Milton's imputed deism see Joseph Frank, 'John Milton's movement towards deism', *Journal of British Studies*, I, 1961, pp. 38–51.

23 J. M. Robertson, *A History of Free Thought*, fourth rev. ed., London, 1936, II, pp. 611–14.

24 H. R. Hutcheson, Introduction to *De Religione Laici*, New Haven, Conn., 1944, p. 8l.

25 C. Lyttle, 'Lord Herbert of Cherbury, apostle of ethical theism', *Church History*, 5, 1935, pp. 247–67. Lyttle's corrective view is perhaps spoiled by over-enthusiastic mannerisms which tend to persuade rather than demonstrate.

26 Rossi, III, pp. 328–9.

27 Butler, *Analogy of Religion*, London, 1736, 'Advertisement'.

28 Ogilvie, *An Inquiry into the Causes of the Infidelity and Scepticism of the Times*, London, 1783, p. 56; pp. 179–80.

29 *History of Western Philosophy*, rev.ed., London, 1961, p. 618.

30 Raleigh, *History of the World*, London,1614, I,i,10.

31 Burton, *Anatomy of Melancholy*, Oxford, 1621, III, 440.

32 Berkeley, *The Principles of Human Knowledge*, 1710, sect. 32; in *Works*, ed. Luce and Jessop, London, 1948–57, II, p. 54.

33 The phrase is Heinrich Scholz's, in his 'Die Religionsphilosophie des Herbert von Cherbury', *Studien zur Geschichte des neueren Protestantismus*, Giessen, 1914, V, p. 1.

34 *D.V.*, p. 245; Carré, p. 328.

35 The prayer appears in *Epistolary Curiosities*, ed. Rebecca Warner, London, 1818, as No. 66 of the appendix, pp. 187–9. The editor gives no indication of the source or authenticity of the prayer beyond her note at the conclusion: 'N.B. From the original, in the handwriting of Edward Lord Cherbury'. It is however entirely characteristic and emphasises themes central to *De veritate*, especially the insistence on the innate idea of 'eternal bliss'.

36 Notes from *The Literary Remains of Samuel Taylor Coleridge*, ed. Henry Nelson Coleridge, 4 vols., London, 1836–9, III, pp. 415–19; reprinted in *Coleridge on the Seventeenth Century*, ed. Roberta F. Brinkley, Duke University Press, 1955, p. 366.

Select bibliography

This is a short list for reference and further reading. Extensive bibliographies may be consulted in Rossi, Hutcheson and Gawlick (q.v.).

The works of Edward Herbert

De veritate, prout distinguitur a revelatione, a verisimili, a possibili, et a falso. Hoc opus condidit ED. Herbert. Miles ord. bal. et leg. sui regis M. Britanniae in Gallia. Et universo humano generi dicavit. Paris, 1624.

De veritate, etc. 2nd edn. London, 1633.

De la vérité, en tant qu'elle est distincte de la revelation, du vraysemblable. du possible et du faux (anonymous translation from the Latin). Paris, 1639.

De Veritate etc. . . . *cui operi additi sunt duo alii tractatus: primus, de causis errorum: alter, de religione laici; una cum appendice ad sacerdotes de religione laici, et quibusdam Poematibus. Editio tertia.* London, 1645.

De veritate etc. Facsimile of the London 1645 edition, ed. with introduction and bibliography by Günter Gawlick. Stuttgart–Bad Cannstatt, 1966.

De veritate, translated with introduction, by Meyrick H. Carré. University of Bristol, 1937.

De religione laici, ed. and trans. by Harold R. Hutcheson. Yale Studies in English, vol. 98. New Haven, Conn., 1944.

De religione gentilium. Amsterdam, 1663. Trans. William Lewis, *The Ancient Religion of the Gentiles.* London, 1705.

De religione gentilium, Facsimile of the Amsterdam 1663 edition, ed. with introduction by Günter Gawlick. Stuttgart–Bad Cannstatt, 1967.

The Life and Raigne of King Henry the Eighth. London, 1649.

Occasional Verses of Edward, Lord Herbert, Baron of Cherbury and Castle-Island. Deceased in August, 1648. London, 1665.

The Poems, English and Latin, of Edward Lord Herbert of Cherbury, ed. G. C. Moore Smith. Oxford, 1923.

The Autobiography, Dedication and Advertisement by Horace Walpole. Strawberry Hill, 1764.

The Autobiography of Lord Herbert of Cherbury: With Introduction, Notes, Appendices, and a Continuation of the Life, ed. Sidney Lee. London, 1886. 2nd edn. revised, London, 1906.

The Life of Edward, First Lord Herbert of Cherbury, Written by Himself, ed. with introduction by J. M. Shuttleworth. Oxford, 1976.

A Dialogue between a Tutor and His Pupil, facsimile of London, 1768 edition, ed. by Günter Gawlick. Stuttgart–Bad Cannstatt, 1971.

Religio laici, English MS 5295E in the National Library of Wales Herbert Collection, Aberystwyth, Printed by Herbert G. Wright, *Modern Language Review*, 28, 1933, pp. 295–307.

A selection of modern comments on Herbert

Blunden, Edmund, *Votive Tablets*. London, 1931.

Bottrall, Margaret, *Every Man a Phoenix: Studies in Seventeenth-Century Autobiography*. London, 1958.

Bush, Douglas, *English Literature in the Earlier Seventeenth Century, 1600–1660*, 2nd edn. revised. Oxford, 1962.

Cruttwell, Patrick, *The Shakespearean Moment and its Place in the Poetry of the Seventeenth Century*. London, 1954; repr. New York, 1960.

Delany, Paul, *British Autobiography in the Seventeenth Century*. London, 1969.

Ellrodt, Robert, *Les Poètes métaphysiques anglais*, 2 vols. Paris, 1959–60.

Güttler, Carl, *Eduard Lord Herbert von Cherbury, Ein Kritischer Beitrag zur Geschichte des Psychologismus und der Religionsphilosophie*. Munich, 1897.

Hutcheson, Harold, *Lord Herbert of Cherbury's De Religione Laici. With a Critical Discussion of his life and philosophy etc.* New Haven, Conn., 1944.

Jordan, Wilbur K., *The Development of Religious Toleration in England*, 4 vols. London and Cambridge, Mass., 1932–40.

Popkin, R. H., *History of Scepticism from Erasmus to Descartes*. Assen, 1960.

Rémusat, Charles de Lord Herbert de Cherbury, *sa vie et ses oeuvres, ou les origines de la philosophie de sens commun et de la théologie naturelle en Angleterre*. Paris, 1874.

Rossi, Mario M., *Alle fonti del deismo e del materialismo moderno*. Florence, 1942.

— *La Vita, le Opere, i Tempi di Edoardo Herbert di Chirbury*. 3 vols. Florence, 1947.

Scholz, Heinrich, *Die Religionsphilosophie des Herbert von Cherbury*, in *Studien zur Geschichte des neueren Protestantismus*, V. Giessen, 1914.

Smart, Ninian, *Historical Selections in the Philosophy of Religion*, ed. J. McIntyre and I. T. Ramsey. London, 1962.

Sorley, W. R., *A History of English Philosophy*. Cambridge, 1920.

Walker, D. P., *The Ancient Theology*, London, 1972.

Periodical articles

Aaron, R. I., 'The autobiography of Edward, First Lord Herbert of Cherbury: the original manuscript material', *Modern Language Review*, 36, 1941, pp. 184–94.

Carlini, A., 'Herbert di Cherbury e la scuola di Cambridge', *Rendiconti della Reale Accademia dei Lincei*, 5.A, vol 26, pp. 273–357. Rome, 1917.

Fordyce, C. J. and Knox, T. M., 'The books bequeathed to Jesus College Library, Oxford, by Lord Herbert of Cherbury', *Proceedings and Papers of the Oxford Bibliographical Society*, 5, 1936–9, Part II.

Lyttle, Charles, 'Lord Herbert of Cherbury: apostle of ethical theism', *Church History*, 5, 1935, pp. 247–67.

Merchant, W. Moelwyn, 'Lord Herbert of Cherbury and seventeenth-century historical writing', *Transactions of the Honourable Society of Cymmrodorion*, 1956, pp. 47–63.

Sorley, W. R., 'The philosophy of Herbert of Cherbury', *Mind*, 3, 1894, pp. 491–5408.

Steinbeck, Wolfram, 'Das Problem der Wahrheit und die Philosophie Herberts von Cherbury', *Blätter für deutsche Philosophie*, 7, 1934, pp. 467–78.

Stephen, Leslie, 'Lord Herbert of Cherbury', *The National Review*, 35, 1900, pp. 661–73.

Willey, Basil, 'Lord Herbert of Cherbury: a spiritual Quixote of the seventeenth century'. *Essays and Studies*, 27, 1941, pp. 22–9.

INDEX